SHOOTING THE SCALP-LOCK

MIKE FINK

KING OF MISSISSIPPI KEELBOATMEN

BY
WALTER BLAIR
AND
FRANKLIN J. MEINE

GREENWOOD PRESS, PUBLISHERS
WESTPORT, CONNECTICUT

CONTENTS

INTRODUCTION

In the final years of the eighteenth century and during the nineteenth century the American nation marched from the Atlantic to the Pacific, and the spanning of a continent was a glorious adventure the like of which cannot be found in all history. The conquest bred a group of valiant men, molders of the nation's destiny during lives which were strange and wonderful. To this group belonged Mike Fink, ranger, boatman, and trapper, whose adventures had as their background the shifting frontiers of half a century.

There were giants in those days, mighty men who, because of their craft and their strength, became heroes of the stalwart movers and settlers of the old West and the old South. Their deeds were celebrated in story telling sessions which shortened hours of drifting down the rivers, which relaxed tense gatherings by wilderness campfires, or which whiled away long winter evenings by hearths in log cabins.

For always when the day's tramp over stubborn trails was ended or when the men had come in from the forests or the fields, the weatherbeaten pioneers yarned about the great leaders of a migrating people— the mightiest Indian fighters, the toughest hunters and trappers, the blazers of trails. Every successive frontier had its idols—heroes in the drama of conquest. In Pennsylvania, Captain Sam Brady hacked off countless scalps; he it was who knocked down three Indians with one shot. In Ohio, Simon Kenton was the most celebrated enemy of the redskins. Eight times he ran the gauntlet, three times he was tied to the stake for burning, only to escape at the last moment. The Wetzel family—father and five sons, were potent hunters and Indian fighters in West Virginia—and the most famous was Lewis Wetzel, whose life business was annihilating redmen.

The frontier drifted westward, and new heroes arose. Gamecock of the Tennessee canebrakes, Davy Crockett shot his hundreds of wild critters and Indians, played his fiddle, danced jigs, told iridescent yarns, and went to Washington to conquer politics, elected by adoring buckskin pioneers. Later, with Sam Houston, Davy became a god in Texas. On the Missouri frontier whose gateway was St. Louis, Hugh Glass, trapper, was long remembered by tellers of tales. Little Kit Carson, who studded the stock of his rifle with shiny brass tacks—one for each Indian or white he killed—and Jim Bridger, discoverer of the petrified forest in which birds, animals and even the law of gravitation were petrified, were mountain men, plainsmen and pathfinders. Wild Bill Hickok on the cattle frontier and Paul Bunyan on the lumbering frontier—these were heroes.

These giants were garbed colorfully in the splendor

of actual adventures, but the tongues of exuberant
frontiersmen at times added somewhat to their glories.
Folk invention passed the mundane boundaries of mere
fact and made the sagas of these characters much more
interesting than are dry biographies compiled by scru-
pulous historians.   And the result was that in the end
the homely narratives re-created the men and the times
with more vividness and more flavor than most histories reveal.

Consider the legendary—that is, the pioneers'—figure of Daniel Boone, about whom yarns were spun during many decades, an idol of three frontiers.   Daniel,
born in Pennsylvania, very early demonstrated remarkable talents.   As a youngster in a backwoods
school, little Daniel gayly flouted book larnin' by
mixing an emetic with the school-master's whiskey.
When the master, naturally riled, tried to wallop the
offender with a birch, the boy tripped him up and
escaped from school forever.   At fourteen Daniel was
a hunter of wolves, bears, and panthers, and when a
ferocious wildcat advanced upon a bevy of schoolboys,
though the rest ran away, Daniel calmly awaited the
charge and pumped a bullet into the beast's heart.
Before he was fifteen, he had abandoned his home and
had made a permanent camp in the wilds.   So his
father, seeing how talented the boy was, moved into
the wilderness with him.

Daniel, who could shoot a panther or a deer between
the eyes in the darkest forest, was hunting with a
torch one night.   He saw two eyes sparkling in the

torch light, but something told him they were not the eyes of a deer. They were, it soon developed, the eyes of a beautiful girl; the young hunter promptly courted her and married her. Daniel and his wife settled down to live in woodlands in which the ax of a white man had never felled a tree, but before very long people would move in a mile away and they would have to move on to get shut of their neighbors. "Too crowded—too crowded—I want more elbow room!" he would say—and off he would go.

He got into Kentucky in one of his searches for uncrowded country—that was Indian country then; he was the first white man to go there. He liked the solitude so well that he remained there for many months, alone. Indians tried to catch him there, but he avoided them easily by swinging on grape vines and throwing them off the trail. If they followed him with a hunting dog, he shot the dog. After a time his family and various settlers joined him, and he spent some time in one spot, bedeviling the Indians and hunting.

Boone had some right exciting scrimmages with Indians. They stole his daughter. Boone swore: "By the eternal Power that made me father, if my daughter lives, and is found, I'll either bring her back or spill my life's blood." He brought her back.

Indians, when they tried again and again to catch him, were at a disadvantage. He could wait for a musket to flash, then dodge the bullet. He could load his rifle as he ran, picking off his pursuers one by one.

And he could use cunning little tricks to fool them—
like throwing tobacco leaves in their faces. Once some
of them watched him as he ate a meal, preparing to
pounce on him. Daniel, seeing them, pretended he
swallowed his knife, though actually he merely put
it up his sleeve. Thinking he was a magician, they
slunk away. The redskins did manage to capture him
four times, and once he was adopted by a tribe—lived
with them for months. Always, however, he managed
to escape, getting away one time just soon enough to
avoid being burned.

A great explorer and a great hunter, Boone traveled
in all parts of the West, a forerunner of the frontier.
He went down from the Alleghanies into Tennessee,
and traced the Cumberland river. He wandered all
through Kentucky. He was carried prisoner by Indians through the forest land that was to be Ohio; he
found the headwaters of the Kentucky, the Wabash,
the Scioto, and other great rivers. In the end, an old
man, he went to Missouri, still ahead of the advancing
frontier, almost as spry a hunter as ever. He died
at a deer lick, with his gun in his hands, waiting for
deer.

One does not find all of this Daniel Boone in histories; this is Boone as he was re-created by the men
of his day. Though their portrait was not perfect, it
had distinct values: it mirrored the essential, the soul
of its subject.

In the campfire yarns which thus pictured him,
Boone was a typical frontier hero. He was typical

because he had the skill and the native wisdom the pioneers glorified, a skill almost superhuman at all times, often actually unbelievable. He was typical, too, in that he was a wandering figure and in that the story of his life was therefore an odyssey. It was told in a series of loosely linked yarns, because oral narratives built up episodes and anecdotes rather than plots. Frontier biographies had elements of picaresque narrative, likewise loosely constructed, for though most of the heroes were not—like those in similar continental stories—to be classed as rogues, they sometimes played rough practical jokes or used the tricks of sharp-witted rogues to outwit their enemies. In other words, created though they were in the Victorian age, stories about frontier characters were not moral as their creators presented them; they were a-moral. Most significant was the fact that though they emerged in the period of the development of American fiction which gave birth to little Eva, scores of genteel females with a talent for fainting, and gentlemen almost as full of sentiment, these pioneer idols were rough, tough, racy and rude. Their language defied grammar and the commandment which has to do with cursing, and they themselves stood up, on occasion, and defied the world to step over and take a licking. Thus, though we timid people of the twentieth century find them romantic and glamorous, for their contemporaries these frontiersmen were daringly real.

And none of them, in the time of his glory, was more

real, more representative, or more resplendent than
Mike Fink, King of the Keelboatmen. Like Boone,
he was a wanderer in the unsettled districts. Like
Boone, he shifted as the frontier advanced, resenting
the invasions of settlers who followed him, and also
like the great Daniel Boone, he was celebrated on three
frontiers. Historians happened to select Boone as a
symbol of the frontier. Their choice was a wise one,
but Mike was just as representative.

Born about 1770 on the Pennsylvania border, as a
boy he learned to shoot with an uncanny skill long to
be worshiped. As a boy, too, he pierced into the next
frontier, the Indian country, and took so many scalps
that he became celebrated as a ranger.

Then, the rivers open, during the days of the drift of
settlers down into Kentucky, he was the king of the
hardiest group of many lusty bands moving along the
frontier of the Ohio and Mississippi rivers—the boatmen. As colorful and dangerous as covered wagon
days were the days when a nation moved frontierward
by water—and Mike was a giant of those days. When
the land around St. Louis beckoned, he made his first
trip, in about 1814, to St. Louis, in the dawn of the
great fur-trading period, and thereafter he navigated
not only the older stretches of river but also the stretch
of the Mississippi between the mouth of the Ohio and
St. Louis.

Finally, as the fur-trade heralded the conquest of
new forests and prairies, as traders and trappers car-

ried whiskey and trinkets into the Northwest, traveling with them, tracing new trails into new lands, Mike Fink made his last journey westward.

Therefore when smoke from frontier fires drifted skyward, men told of the glorious adventures of this hero of three frontiers. He never quite became an authentic figure in history, and that fact may be fortunate. For, forgotten before historians had a chance to winnow away the great yarns about him, buried for decades in the old newspapers, almanacs, and books which preserved pioneers' tales about him, he is able to emerge to-day with some of the freshness that was his in the days of his creation. In the stories about him, there still lingers, after all this time, the scent of the forest and the smoke of campfires which eddied about him in the days of his splendor. These old-time tales bring back the strength, the exuberance, the roaring laughter of America in her glorious youth.

This book, then, retells the yarns about Mike Fink, without, it is hoped, the loss of too much of their flavor, their homely strength, or their beauty. In them is portrayed a hero of old America representative of a time-dimmed age. He seems worthy of a high place among the picturesque figures of the frontier who are still remembered and cherished.

ILLUSTRATIONS

MIKE FINK

KING OF MISSISSIPPI KEELBOATMEN

CHAPTER ONE

HOW MIKE FINK WAS BORN, HOW HE SPENT HIS BOY-
HOOD, AND HOW HE SERVED, DURING HIS YOUTH, AS
AN INDIAN SCOUT

I

Americans were marching westward with a determined sweep that later was to be compared, by many
writers, to a tide. The hosts of the movers grew in
force; they could not be resisted. Mountains blocked
their way, but they found a way to cross them. If
seemingly impenetrable forests baffled their search for
homes, they blazed trails or followed the trampled
paths redskins and wild animals had made through the
trees. Indians menaced their lives as they marched
or after they settled in clearings, but they gave the
savages blow for blow and kept off the painted warriors.

And when the government of his majesty the King
of Great Britain forbade them to enter the new lands
which had been promised to the Indians if only the Indians would live peacefully, they remarked, profanely
but vehemently, "To hell with his majesty's government!" Then they chopped off the bark of trees to
show the boundaries of their claims, rigged up tempo-
rary cabins which would keep out the rain until some-

thing better was built, cleared patches of ground, and planted corn, turnips, and potatoes, living chiefly on game until the first crops could be harvested.

"I have learned from experience," wrote woeful Governor Dunmore of Virginia, "that the established authority of any government in America, and the policy of the Government at home, are both insufficient to restrain the Americans; and that they do and will remove as their avidity and restlessness incite them. They acquire no attachment to Place; But wandering about Seems engrafted in their Nature; and it is a weakness incident to it that they Should forever imagine the Lands further off, are Still better than those upon which they are already Settled."

So the restless Americans moved forward into Indian territory as a tide moves forward on a beach. First there were little waves of trappers, hunters and scouts, then great waves of families seeking new wilderness homes. And the government would say to the people, "You have gone far enough. Stop here, for beyond this line is Indian country." It would assure the Indians that the whites would go no farther, and would give the Indians presents and assurances of peace. Meanwhile, the trappers would move forward, and the whites would threaten the military agents of the government or perhaps they would black up their faces and swoop down to rob pack-horse caravans bearing gifts to the Indians. And big waves of settlers would sweep into Indian country, and the Indians would be shoved back, while the government again tried to patch up a peace and to move over a boundary to accommodate those contrary American pioneers.

By 1770 the boundary had been pushed to the north bank of the Ohio and the Allegheny Rivers, and already a few forerunners of a new movement were pushing to the Indian side of those streams. The American colonies were agitated over a tax on tea and a row between troops and citizenry in Boston—the Boston Massacre. But they were also interested in western lands; they swarmed into the newly opened territory. And in 1770, a Virginia gentleman named George Washington went to Pittsburgh, which lay east of the Allegheny boundary, and his business was the purchase of western lands.

That same year, a baby first saw the light of day and greeted the world with a wail in one of the little cabins scattered in a cluster around old Fort Pitt. His parents, the Finks, promptly named him Mike, and he began a life which was to be lived on the frontier or in the wilderness beyond the frontier until he died.

Although nothing is known of Mike Fink's parents, it is probable that they were Scotch-Irish folk who with other Scots and Irish had raised their paltry little hovels on the east bank of the muddy Monongahela, calling their settlement Pittsburgh. Though Washington dismissed Pittsburgh in his diary by guessing that it had maybe twenty cabins, and hurried off to dine, four miles away, with Colonel Croghan at elegant Croghan Hall, Pittsburgh was a bustling frontier community of houses, huts, sawmills, lime-kilns, brick-kilns and trading-houses in addition to farms whose owners thrived by selling produce to the soldiers at the fort and to Indian traders.

Nevertheless, at the time Mike was born, and during his youth, Pittsburgh was a border town. For decades, Fort Pitt had furnished the chief refuge against savage Indian attacks; it had been under the protecting guns of this little stockade that the white man had established his first foothold west of the Alleghenies. The green forest still came close to the brown cabins, for only small sections had been cleared; a man occasionally could shoot game from his door. Life was primitive: most of the men of the settlement made a living chiefly by doing a little farming and by trading in skins and furs.

During Mike's boyhood, he lived in a dirty cabin, strongly scented with wood-smoke, which contained less furniture and fewer utensils than many modern camping places. He slept with his brothers on the floor or on a bed built on a forked branch, planted in the floor, from which other branches stretched to the side of the cabin, boards taking the place of bed-springs and mattress, bear or buffalo hides serving as covers. He sat on the floor or on a crude three-legged stool, eating his meals with a pewter spoon or a clasp knife, shared with his brothers, out of wooden trenchers or gourd bowls. A tin cup was as rare a luxury as an iron fork; he drank from a gourd. The table was a smoothed slab on four posts which had been set in augur holes.

His meat was bear meat, wild turkey breast, venison; his bread was Johnnycake or pone. For supper usually he had hog and hominy or mush with milk or bear's oil.

Around him eddied the work of the household. His mother washed and kept house, milked the cow, cooked the mess, prepared the flax, spun, wove, and made the clothes of wool or linsey. Her tasks lasted after sunset: hardly ever did the family talk in the evening by the crackling fire without the accompanying whir of a spinning wheel. At night Mike's father whittled out wooden bowls and noggins. During the day he put on his fur cap and cleared ground, plowed the rich brown soil, planted, cultivated, gathered corn, or dug potatoes. He disappeared into the quiet forests with hunting parties, spending days or weeks in the woods so that his family might have meat and clothing. Just as casually, on occasion, he went out and annihilated Indians, proudly bringing home their scalps. Young Mike hoed the garden, split and hauled in wood for the fireplace, carried water, and ground corn into meal at the hand-mill or pounded it into hominy in the mortar.

His sports were those of a boy in a community at war. At an early age he learned to use the bow and arrow; he was able to shoot an arrow into a squirrel or a bird at close range by the time he had learned to swear. Because the art was useful in hunting game or redskins, he soon mastered the trick of imitating the gobbling of turkeys, the bleating of a fawn, the hoots of owls. Not only did the boys of Pittsburgh have jumping and wrestling matches and foot races: they had contests, as well, with the tomahawk. At five paces from a tree young Fink could throw the weapon so that it bit into the bark with its handle downward; at seven and a half paces he could flip it into the tree so that it lit with its handle pointed upward. At night, before going to sleep, Mike, when very young, listened to stories about Jack the Giant Killer or old ballads which were "love songs about murder." In later years, at the family fireside, he heard yarns about hunting in which the spike buck, the three-pronged buck, and the barren doe figured frequently. And, of course, he heard much about Indians, and he learned to hate them worse than the devil—far worse, for Pittsburgh was an irreligious town in which the devil was seldom mentioned, except for vocal emphasis.

For there was an ever-present danger of an Indian attack. The beautiful Allegheny to the west, the boy learned, was still the uttermost boundary of civilization, for all beyond it was called "the Indian country" and associated with many a tale of scalping, hairbreadth escapes, burnings at the stake, and all the horrors of savage warfare. The outrages of the past were not easily forgotten. During Mike's boyhood, men still talked of how, seven years before Mike's birth, the Delawares and Shawnees "took Pontiac's bloody belt with wild delight" and spread destruction in the Monongahela country, burning crops and cabins, killing settlers, storming Fort Pitt.

Although this was the last siege of Fort Pitt by fully organized tribes, it was far from the end of Indian warfare. Indians frequently crossed the Ohio or the Allegheny to steal horses or to scalp settlers, and when whites went into the Indian country, they might expect attacks. As the Monongahela country became more densely settled, Indian raids, instead of ceasing, were more frequent. For now the Indians had learned the use of the white men's implements, and they fought against an incursion into their country with a hatred which was desperate. They were attracted by horses, by good crops, and by firewater, and they were spurred in their attacks by anger returned, full measure, by the settlers. Thus it was that in the Monongahela country the fury of scores of murderous raids was spent.

Sometimes young Mike would listen, enthralled, to the yarns of visitors who stopped for the night at the Fink cabin. Perhaps the traveler was a colonel, the commander of a station, resplendent in a golden new dressed deerskin hunting shirt fringed with shreds of buckskin dyed as red as blood-root could make them. The light from the fireplace touched his bronzed face as he puffed his pipe and told his story:

"I war a copporal then, and now I'm a kunnel. Lord! how the world is turnin' upside down. Well, you must know, we marched up the gully that runs from the river; an' when we neared the end bang went the savages' guns, an' smash went their hatchets; an' then it came to close quarters, a regular, rough-and-tumble, hard scratch! An' so I war ahead of the Major, an' the Major war behind, and the fight made him as ambitious as a wild-cat, and he war hungry for a shot; an' so he says to me, for I war right afore him, 'Git out of my way, you damned big rascal, till I get a crack at 'em!'

"An' so I got out of his way, for I war mad at bein' called a damned big rascal, 'specially as I war doing my best, an' coverin' him from mischief besides.

"Well! as soon as I jumped out of his way, bang went his piece, an' bang went another, let fly by an Injun:—down went the Major, shot right through the hips, slam-bang. He brushed against me as he fell, bleeding powerful bad, and cursing. And so said I, 'Major,'—for I warn't well over my passion,—'if you'd 'a' taken things easy, I'd 'a' stopped that slug for you.'

"And so says he, 'Bang away, you big fool, and don't stand talking.' An' so he swounded away; an' that made me ambitious, too, an' I killed two of the red niggers, before you could say Jack Robinson. An' then one of 'em took his tommyhawk, an' I saw it whirlin' above my head just in time, and I ducked a little—just enough, I reckon, for he hit me rather hard on the har, see?" He pointed to a scar. "It pays to have a thick skull, in Injun scrapes. I banged that varmint more harder than he hit me, an' his skull war split as neat as could be.

"I then felt that prehaps I'd better leave that place, for I war feelin' a mite weakish, an' blood war blindin' my eyesight. I helped to carry the Major off to the timbrels, wabbling like a new calf on the way.   Then I got some cloth tied about my wound, an' swallowed some whiskey, an' went back and finished off them there damned savages."

The colonel stooped for a coal, puffed his pipe, and flipped the coal back into the fire.   The boyish listener sniffed the strong, sweet smoke which swirled with the draft from the fireplace.   "I've shot varmints of all kinds," he said, "bar, an' buffalo, deer an' painters—but for a real scrimmage, give me red niggers every time."

And that night Mike dreamed of scalping Indians . . .

When the boy was five, the colonies launched their war against the mother country.   Weakened by the departure of men for the East, the people of the border were more harassed than ever by Indian incursions. The Tories, it was known in time, were inflaming the hatred of the Indians, providing them with guns and ammunition, even leading them.   Raids of the redmen increased in violence, and the whites came to loathe them with an almost insane fury.   When Mike was eight, there was talk of how Simon Girty and other traitorous whites had deserted the force at Fort Pitt and had allied themselves with the Indians.   Almost every day, Mike heard new stories of Indian violence.

One night, after the fire on the hearth had died down and the family had gone to sleep, they were awakened by a pounding at the door.   Mike's father, rifle in hand, rushed to the door, and stood there, listening. And outside, he heard a woman sobbing.

"Who's there?" he called.

"Betty Duncan. Let me in!"

Mike heard the grate of wood rubbing against iron, and the creak of hinges, and from his bed he saw a woman's figure in the moonlight. The door swung shut, and the cabin was dark again. But Mike heard sounds—the crying of the woman, the movements of his father and mother. Then a light was struck, and the boy saw the woman, crumpled against the wall, her hair disheveled, her gown torn and soiled.

"What are you doing here? I thought you was workin' out with the MacCrackens, ten miles away."

"They—don't need me any more," said Betty, and then she screamed with laughter. And the laughter was worse than weeping, fierce and insane. Mike's hair was chilled to the roots. She did not seem to be able to stop.

Mike's father splashed whiskey into a gourd and held it out to her lips.

"Drink, lass," he said.

She drank and wept again. But after a time she was quieted, though her eyes were opened very wide, and Mike could see the whites above and below the irises. Then, after a time, she spoke.

"The savages murdered them all," she said. "We chanced to leave the door open. And when I looked at the door, it was open, and three came in on tiptoe. Mr. MacCracken they shot. He was coming up with his rifle. Then Mistress MacCracken tried to seize an Indian's arm, for he was tommyhawking Danny, but she was stabbed, and little Danny was clubbed. Little Mary walked over to her mother—says she, 'Don't let them harm me, mammy,' but a savage laughed, and plucked her up, and killed her—the sweet babe! Oh, the sweet babe! And they took the new baby from his cradle, and flung him on the floor, and he stopped crying. They struck Mistress MacCracken as she crawled to his side. Then I lay under the bed, where I had been hiding, for a long time, while they took things from the cabin. And when they had gone, I came here, through the woods. It's very light to-night," she said, and shuddered.

Mike slept but little that night. His father had gone out to give the alarm, and there was no man in the house. And Betty retold her story in words filled with terror, failing to find sleep until the coming of the dawn.

II

When Mike was twelve, he was given a rifle, and though the weapon was somewhat heavy, he soon learned to shoot accurately. Always he and his companions played that they were shooting Indians. Two Pittsburgh boys Mike's age actually had killed Indians; they were as a result idolized. Mike stole some of their glory by beating them in shooting matches and in rough-and-tumble fights, but they continued to be the heroes among their comrades.

When Mike was thirteen, he was reckoned almost a man, for he could shoot well, and he was well grown. He was assigned his port-hole at the fort, and he even accompanied some of the larger expeditions against the redskins.

Now sometimes at the fort he saw and talked with famous Indian fighters whose very clothes smelled of mosses and leaves. Captain Jack, the Black Hunter, a swarthy giant who had killed four savages, single-handed, was at the fort once with a party of pioneers. To the fort also came the famous Lewis Wetzel, about six years older than Mike—a man with tub-like chest and huge arms, his face, pitted with smallpox, crowned with long black hair. His dark eyes sparkled as he played the fiddle for his friends. Though usually a silent man, now and then, thawed with whiskey, he told of his adventures—stories about his capture by Indians and his escape when he was but fourteen, about his killing three savages in a running fight during which he filled and fired his gun as he ran, about one unlucky adventure, when, said he, "I treed four Injuns, but one got away."

Greatest of all the Indian fighters, perhaps, was Sam Brady, who had devoted his life to Indian fighting following the death, at the hands of savages, of his father. There were many stories about Brady, but the most memorable told of his escape from Indians who had captured him. They took him to their camp, where they were lighting a huge fire in which they proposed to burn him, when Brady saw his chance. A squaw of

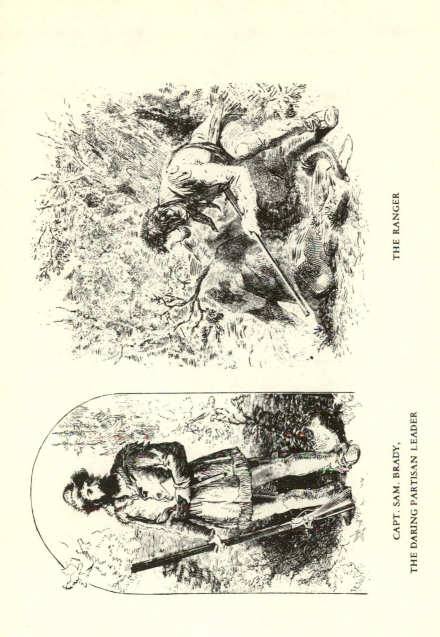

THE RANGER

CAPT. SAM. BRADY,

THE DARING PARTISAN LEADER

one of the chiefs came close to him, carrying a child in her arms. Quickly he snatched the infant from her, and threw it into the flames. As the Indians leaped to save the child, Brady broke away and ran, followed by a rain of bullets.

He at last reached the high banks of a stream, twenty-seven feet wide, as the Indians closed in on three sides. With all his strength he leaped across the gorge, barely catching overhanging bushes on the opposite side. But now as he ran, a bullet struck his leg, wounding him painfully, and he went more slowly. A little later, as he neared a lake, he heard the redskins shouting on his trail. He decided that unless he managed to hide somewhere, he would be killed. Splashing into the water, he made his way to a place thick with lily pads. He ducked as the Indians came to the shore. Desperation was the mother of invention; he broke off a water lily stem, and pushed one end to the surface. Then he placed the other end in his mouth, and sucked. Air came through, and he managed to breathe thus until the Indians, thinking he had drowned, went away.

Mike listened to the tales of border heroes with envy. He wanted to go with them on their exciting trips of retaliation against Indians who had shed the blood of whites. But, "Wait a bit; you're but a lad," they said, and Mike was left gazing after them as they set out on daring excursions. He had to wait, it seemed.

But meanwhile, Mike practiced with his rifle, accustoming his arm to its weight, his eyes to its sights, until he was the best of his contemporaries. And at last he went to his first shooting match for beef, competing against grown men who were the best shots in the town. He was unmercifully bantered by his rivals, for a boy was hardly a match for them in handling a long, heavy rifle.

But he came out very well. The match prizes consisted of "six quarters" of beef. The best shot won the hide and tallow, the next nearest the choice of the hind quarters, the third best the other hind quarter, the fourth a choice of the fore quarters, the fifth the other fore quarter, and the sixth the lead in the tree in which the targets were fixed. Mike had his choice of the fore quarters. Thereafter, he shot regularly, seldom failing to win a prize.

When Mike was seventeen, he engaged in a memorable match.

It was proclaimed in hand-printed advertisements which were placed on tavern walls: "David Neal offers a First-rate Beef, worth Eleven Dollars, to be shot for at his Farm, at Twenty-five cents a Shot, next Sunday."

When the day arrived, every good marksman in the neighborhood was at Neal's place with his gun. Mike went, his rifle draped over his wrist. At some distance, he heard the crack of rifles, and when he came nearer, he sniffed the air, pungent with the odor of black powder and wood smoke. A fire was blazing, and some of the buckskin-clad marksmen were burning their boards over the fire, preparing their targets; others were molding bullets or cleaning their rifles.

"Here's Mike Fink," said a man, squatting by the fire, "an' we'll now shoot for but five quarters, I suppose."

"You'll be lucky to get two," said Mike, "for I mean to buy five chances. Where's the paper?"

"You talk big for a lad not yet dry behind the ears," said David Neal, as he handed Mike the subscription paper.

"I shoot big," said Mike, as he wrote down: "Mike Fink puts in five shots. $1.25." "I," he continued, "have an eye as keen as a lizard, and when old Bang-all an' my shoulder gets together, the Fink family gets first-rate beef at low prices." He stalked over to the fire, and started to char his target.

"The shots is all taken," announced David Neal. The two judges took their stand near the tree on which the targets were to be placed, and the boards were piled around them. Then David paced off sixty yards northward, and marked the line with a log. He looked at his list, and called the first name. The judges fixed the target, a blackened board pegged with a white paper, in the center of which was a diamond shaped hole. The center was marked by a pair of lines scratched across the part of the charred board revealed by the hole in the paper. The man fired.

"Good shot!" said one of the judges. "Just on the right of the bull's-eye."

"Eb Keedy," called out Dave, and a gangly old man stepped up to the log.

"Gentlemen," he said, "I won't say I'll win beef, but I do perdict my piece'll eat the paper. My powder are not good powder, gentlemen, though I gin six bits a pound for it. But if it burns clear, Mrs. Keedy's husband eats paper."

With this prelude, Keedy twisted himself into the form of a question mark, took a long sight, and fired.

"I said I'd eat paper, and I done so," he said, after walking over to the target.

"Aw, shut up," said a bystander; "that's a long way from eatin' beef."

"But I eat paper," said Eb, obstinately.

Dave called out another name: "Hiram Byrd."

"Oh, Lord!" a marksman groaned, "put up another beef, an' we'll finish shootin' for it by the time Hiram takes his shot."

"If he ain't got his gun loaded, I'll go home, an' come back to-morrow to see him shoot," said another.

"I won't come back till to-morrow afternoon, after he's shot," said Mike. "That man's so near-sighted it takes him hours to see his front sight."

"You-all go plumb to hell," said Hiram, benevolently, and he went on with his preparations. He did not trust the judges with the task of hanging up his target: with his own hands he placed it on the tree. Then he wiped out his rifle, rubbed the pan with a special piece of flannel, drew a piece of tow through the touch-hole with his wiper, filled his charger with exquisite caution, flicking off a grain or two and then replacing a grain. Carefully then he poured the powder into the rifle. From his pouch, he drew a handful of bullets, and painstakingly he looked them over, choosing the most flawless. His patching he chose after pondering gravely. The other steps he took in preparing to shoot were performed as slowly, with the accompaniment of shakings of his head.

"Don't be hurried," said Eb sarcastically.

"You-all go plumb to hell," said Hiram, evidently well pleased with this phrase—and he went on with his work. At last he placed a curved piece of tin over the hind sight, to shade it, got a friend to shade the fore sight with his hat. For a long time he sighted; then he fired.

A judge bent to examine the target. At last he spoke: "Didn't eat paper," he said, and he doubled with laughter, while the others hooted.

"My piece war badly loaded," said Hiram.

"It shows you can't hurry your loadin' an' shoot well too," Mike preached.

Other shooters followed, some taking one shot, others taking two to five. Nearly all hit the paper, and several the black diamond in the center of the target, for these frontiersmen were great shots. When Mike came to the mark, the last man, six marksmen had cut into the black diamond.

"Have to shoot tolerable well to win beef in this here match, sonny," said Dave to Mike.

"Tolerable well!" echoed Mike. "The shot that

wins beef will have to be all hell-fired good, daddy. And that," he concluded, "is the shot I aim to make."

He walked briskly to the log, took aim quickly, and fired. The judges went to the target.

"Don't bother to look for that lead," said Mike. "It's where the lines cross. Jest move the paper, while my gun cools off, an' then I'll place another into the middle." Finding he was right in describing the shot, the judges moved the paper. Mike loaded with speed and skill, pouring his powder into the cupped palm of his hand until a bullet was covered, then wiping the powder into his charger, and dumping it neatly into the gun.

"O' course that war a chance shot, Mike," Hiram said, watching Mike's quick movements with agony. Then he blurted: "For God's sake, youngster, take pains with your loadin'."

"Hell," replied Mike, "loadin' a gun's an easy thing, granddaddy, once you've learnt to do it proper. I'll prove that was no chanct shot, by makin' another of the same kind. My eye's keen as a sarpint's to-day, an' my aim's plumb poison. I'll bet a quart o' whiskey my next shot's as good."

"Taken! You damned impudent calf!" roared Hiram.

"All right, it's a bet," smiled Mike. "Now if this old bull will stop mooin' I'll win drinks for the crowd." Cool, he aimed, taking rather longer this time. Then he fired. A knot of shooters surged around the target.

"Mike wins the whiskey, Hiram," called Dave.

"The hell he does!" said Hiram, incredulously. "Let me see it!" And he rushed to the target. He examined it carefully, for a long time. At last he said, shaking his head, "I'll pay the whiskey!"

"Whoop!" cried Mike, who had loaded his gun. "Want to bet, on the same terms, on this shot, Hiram?"

Hiram shook his head, but David Neal spoke up: "Damn it, Mike," he said, "you rile a body, the way you crow, and the wormwood from your mother's breast not yet dry on your lips. I'll wager a quart with you that you won't drive the cross."

"Taken!" cried Mike, as he raised his gun. "Clear the way, for Bang-all an' Mike Fink has got a powerful thirst!"

After the shot, Dave walked from the target to Mike, his hand outstretched. "You won fair, lad," he said, "an' here's my hand on it. You do rile a man, but, by God, you sure as hell can shoot."

Mike took his hand. "I'm hell on a target to-day, Dave," he said, "an' that's a fact. I aim to put lead into two more diamonds, though, for I've two more shots."

"You seem right sure, Mike," said Dave. "You wouldn't wager a quart on each shot with me, would you, so's I could win back a little firewater?"

"Don't bet, Mike," said several. "This can't last forever."

"Shift the paper, an' clear the way," Mike cried. "Bang-all can't miss the bull's-eye this Sunday, an' that's gospel. I'll take your bet, Dave, an' I'll take your beef as well!"

There was a deep silence as he took his stance. The rifle spat.

"It's in the diamond, Dave," a judge called. "That's right," chorused several.

"Move the paper!" cried Mike. "I'm eager to get that whiskey."

But David said, "Hell, there's no need to move that paper. This lad's been mighty lucky, but he's through now. Leave that paper where it's pegged, for he won't touch the diamond again."

"We'll see," said Mike, and, as he loaded his gun, his air was careless, but his lips were pressed tightly together. It seemed to some of the watchers that he sighted overlong before the sound of the shot broke the stillness.

Everybody thronged around the target, and at last Dave's voice boomed out. "Didn't eat wood, an' didn't eat paper; it's a clean miss."

"Stand out of my way, an' I'll find that lead for you, gentlemen," said Mike. He scowled as he bent his head close to the bull's-eye. "There it is: I put it on top of the other, so's it would be hard to find."

"Come, Mike, lad," said Dave, "admit you missed clean."

"If one of the judges will dig in there for lead, he'll find that there are two bullets cuttin' a dead four-point center. If he don't, hang me up and use me for a mark."

One of the judges dipped his knife-point into the wood. He held out two pieces of lead. "Damned if he ain't right," he said. The crowd shouted.

And now the judges drew aside to measure the shots, while a buzzing crowd swarmed around Mike. At last the judges announced that Mike had won five prizes— all of the awards with the exception of a fore quarter.

"We'll liquor up at the grocery," said Mike. "But first I want to say a thing or two. The next man that calls me a lad or a youngster is a-goin' to fight me, rough-an'-tumble. I can outshoot and outfight ary man in Pittsburgh, at ary time, at the drop of a hat."

"Come on," said Dave, twining his arm through Mike's "the drinks is on me, it seems. Come on— Bang-all."

III

Mike, it appeared in time, had become, as he claimed, the best shot in Pittsburgh. The settlers continued to call him Bang-all, in celebration of his skill. The shooting match was a rare one in which he did not win three or more prizes. At last, signs announcing matches ended with a significant line: "The Match is for five prizes, with Mike Fink excluded." For the exclusion, asserted a contemporary, Mike "claimed and obtained . . . the hide and tallow, for his forbearance. His usual practice was to sell his . . . quarter to the tavern or dram shop keeper for whiskey, with which he 'treated' everybody present, partaking largely himself. He became fond of strong drink, but was never overpowered by its influence."

And at seventeen, Mike was admitted to the irregular body of rangers who were the chief Indian fighters of the frontier, for his ability in rough and tumble fights and his skill with the rifle had been demonstrated beyond dispute. Broad shouldered, with huge muscles bulging on his arms and thighs, slightly over average height, he was every inch a man. His blue eyes sparkled in a rounded brown face which was usually good-natured, but which, in a moment of temper, became hard and stern; he was a man, it was clear, who would give no quarter in a battle. And no man who had heard him whoop as he leaped into a tavern scuffle could deny that he loved to fight.

The scouts had various duties. They were spies who penetrated into the Indian country to watch the Indians and to bring back news of threatened invasions of the white territory. Therefore frequently Mike went out alone into the wilderness, with a little parched corn and his rifle, living on the corn and game, creeping up to the edge of Indian camps to study the savages' activities. He moved through the forests with the silence of a snake, constantly watchful. At night, he slept on the ground, sometimes without a fire to warm him, ready to spring into action if the slightest unusual sound disturbed the quiet whisper of the leaves. Sometimes, too, the scouts moved in a body against the Indians, and fought bloody battles with

gun, tomahawk and hunting knife against enemies
skilled in the tricks of forest skirmishing.

Sometimes, with a companion, Mike would creep to
the edge of a camp wherein four or five savages were
preparing to spend the night. The scouts would lurk
behind bushes while the braves prepared to sleep, and
then when the Indians were wrapped in their blankets,
Mike and his companion would tiptoe to them and
cleave their heads with tomahawks or split their throats
with knives almost before any of them had managed
to struggle to wakefulness. Proudly the scouts would
bear the scalps to Pittsburgh with them, to exhibit the
trophies with something like the joy of a hunter who
to-day manages to bring home a few ducks or a deer.
At other times, alone, Mike would sally into Indian
country on horse-stealing expeditions. If he could kill
an Indian or two on the way, so much the better.

When the Indians became persistent in their raids on
settlements, the whites would organize scalping expeditions across the border. Once they decided, in a town
meeting, that the settlers needed some help from the
fort, and a committee of ten was appointed to visit the
commander and state their needs. The committee
shuffled across the brick parade ground, past the hewn
log barracks of the soldiers, and into the brick quarters
of the officers.

Sternly they faced the commander of Fort Pitt, and
their spokesman addressed him:

"Major," he said, "them God damned red niggers
has been scalpin' and burnin' all along the border, and

we aim to snuff out a few. And we thought we'd come to you, peaceful-like, and tell you what we want. We want a hundred musket, with cartridge boxes, if you would be so obleegin', and some powder and some lead."

"Gentlemen," said the major, "as you know, the government cannot approve of raids upon Indians with whom we are at peace. I must refuse to grant your request."

"Peace, hell!" said the spokesman, while the rest of the committee growled. "Them damned varmints have come twenty mile into our country, an' they have killed thirteen settlers. We figure we ought to scalp about twenty-five, to teach 'em a lesson."

"I cannot disobey orders, gentlemen. I give you good day."

Outside, the committee whispered a moment, then they entered the commander's quarters again.

"Sir," said the head of the committee, "I don't say we have any feelings in this matter, one way or the other. But you know there is in these parts a group of Black Men, whites, some say, who black up their faces so one won't know them."

"I know," said the major, his face steeled to show no expression.

"They're right friendly to the settlers, and sometimes they even attack the government if it crosses the settlers. And I suspicion that these Black Men may visit this post one day soon, and break into the stores, if"—and now his voice, painfully polite before, rose to a roar—"if you don't give us them pieces and that ammunition, by God!"

"I see," said the major. "I shall consider. Return in half an hour, and I will give you your answer."

And a few days later when he reported the incident in a letter to his superiors, the major concluded: "I thought it best to accede to their requests."

Meanwhile, guided by the scouts, the party of settlers had crossed the borders, had found and massacred a number of Indians, and had returned to Pittsburgh, loaded with scalps.

Indians, to the pioneers' way of thinking, were not human beings: they were pests, to be exterminated. One killed them, and one was pleased with the knowledge that he had done a good deed. Peace treaties meant nothing: the whites and the reds were fighting to the death, and that was the end of it. Even the flag of truce meant nothing. Lewis Wetzel shot an Indian named George Washington in the belly when the savage was riding to Fort Harmar under government protection. When Wetzel was captured, the settlers threatened war upon the soldiers so convincingly that he was released. Then Wetzel was treated to a banquet, and after the feast he was toasted by his fellows.

The most famous story about Mike as an Indian scout demonstrates the attitude. He was some distance from Pittsburgh in the Indian country, moving along quietly, with an easy stride, through the woods. It was spring, still chilly, and he was dressed for cool, wet weather. His moccasins were stuffed with deer's hair, and his feet were warm, but he knew that moisture would soon seep through the moccasins from the wet ground. At his belt hung not only his tomahawk, his scalping knife, and his bullet bag, but also his fur-lined mittens. On his head was his coon-skin cap, in his hands was his rifle. The fringe on his leggings beat softly against his moving legs.

He felt with his hand the bosom of his hunting shirt. Not much there—some tow for wiping the barrel of his rifle, a little parched corn, and some of the jerk he had dried when he first went into the woods. He was damned tired of parched corn and jerk, he reflected. His eyes rested smilingly on a dead tree: above his head, about a foot, were scratches where a bear had recently sharpened its claws, and there on the tree, about even with Mike's shoulder, it had cleaned its teeth. That bear would taste better than jerk. Then Mike stooped quickly and looked at the grass, and his keen eyes discovered the faint outline of a moccasin. On a bush nearby were drops of blood. Indian signs! That bear would not return again.

He moved in the open no longer, skulking instead, under cover of hazel and briar. At last he located the Indians, a hunting party, evidently, moving away from the Allegheny. But he followed them, eager to discover whether they were preparing to join a larger party. For several days he followed them, and at last the jerk was gone, but he dared not shoot more game.

Then one morning, as he was creeping along, his eye caught sight of a beautiful buck, browsing on the edge of a barren spot, about three hundred yards away. He shook his head sadly, then, a look of determination in his eye, he started to creep towards the animal. Whether the Indians heard him or not, he was going to have that buck.

As he approached the animal, he reprimed his gun and picked his flint. At last, within shooting distance, he saw a movement in the trees a short distance away. Watching closely, he caught a glimpse of a man moving toward the deer, not far from him. Quickly he shrank behind a trunk, just as a tall Indian, carrying a gun, came in view. Slowly the Indian raised his gun to his shoulder, aiming at the deer. At the same instant, Mike raised his rifle and pointed it at the savage. He waited: the Indian sighted for a long time. At last the Indian fired, and the instant the smoke rose from the red man's rifle, Mike's bullet sped through the Indian's heart. Indian and deer fell simultaneously. Mike waited a long time, reloading his rifle, watching the prostrate red man, listening for any sound which would show that the Indian's companions were approaching. At last, he walked over to the savage, looked him over carefully, then removed his scalp. Then he approached the buck, sliced off some of the pieces suitable for jerking. A few minutes later, he was on his way back to Pittsburgh.

Mike spent several years as a scout, killing his share of savages, enjoying many dangerous adventures. Pittsburgh grew to a sizable town, and the whites trickled into the west in ever-increasing numbers. At last he longed for new adventures.

In the Indian country, Mike met whites as well as Indians. He met scouts, sometimes, from other settlements, out after scalps, game or horses. Once, perhaps, he met a huge bandy-legged man who swaggered toward him, his bedraggled fur cap at a cocky angle:

"Stranger," said the man, "I'm from Kaintuck, I'm a gentleman, and my name's *Fight!* I fight agin all critturs, human an' inhuman, Christian an' Injun, white, red, black, an' party-colored! Foot and hand, tooth and nail, claw and mudscraper, knife, gun and tomahawk, or any other way you choose to take me, I'm your man!" And now he swelled out his chest, and flapped his bent arms as a rooster flaps its wings. "Cock-a-doodle-doo! Stranger, my name's Ralph Stackpole, and I'm a ring-tailed screamer!"

Mike listened with interest to the first example he had heard of the frontier boast.

"Well," said Mike, "I can't spout the way you do, but I'd have you know I'm brash as a new dog in a fight myself, an' I'll fight ary man at the drop of a hat. My name's Mike Fink, an' I'm right tough to chew too!"

"Well spoken," said Ralph, smiling, "and here's my hand on it. 'Tarnal death to me, I forgot myself. Here's no place for a scrimmage, in the heart of the Injun country. But come down into Kaintuck some day, and you'll find me waitin' for you. I'm your man in a rough-an'-tumble."

"I'll come down and fight you, sure enough," said Mike. "I'll come on a keelboat, for I mean to join a crew one day."

"Picked men run keelboats," said Stackpole, with a shake of his head. "Perhaps I won't see you again if you wait for that. You almost have to lick a keelboat-man to get his place at the poles."

"I might even lick a keelboatman," said Mike. "I'm a ring-tailed screamer, an' I take to fightin' like a babe to its mother."

CHAPTER TWO

HOW MIKE FINK BECAME A KEELBOATMAN, AND HOW
HE MADE HIS FIRST TRIP TO NEW ORLEANS

I

Mike, Indian scout in buckskins, strolled into a white public inn with a red-shirted boatman one spring evening in Pittsburgh, and crossed the smoke-filled, reeking room. There was much talk in the room—the talk of pioneers eagerly asking and answering questions about the Kentucky country, the talk of hunters and scouts who told tall yarns to credulous listeners, the rumbling talk of boatmen who were exchanging information about the river.

The boatman's face was bruised, one of his ears was slightly tattered, his red shirt was in shreds. Mike's clothes were covered with dust, and one of his eyes was swollen shut. The two stood on the sanded floor before the bar.

"Whiskey!" cried the boatman. "I'm buying drinks for myself and the best fighter, rough-an'-tumble, in Pittsburgh, or maybe in the world. He made me say enough, and by God! he had to fight tolerable well to beat this Mississippi screamer!"

"It was a good fight," said Mike, reflectively, sloshing the can of whiskey down his throat, and gulping water from a gourd as a chaser, "a good fight."

MIKE FINK

A Frenchman left a crowd near the bar and looked up and down Mike's muscular body. "Wat's zees you say, John?" he asked. "Zees man defeat you?"

The boatman whirled quickly. "Baptiste! Yes, this little feller made me cry quits, and I told him I'd bring him to you and ask you to take him on the crew. Name's Mike Fink. Here's the steersman, Mike."

"I'd like to go to New Orleans with you," said Mike.

"She's easy enough to go," said Baptiste, "mais coming back, zat's deeferant, oui. How tall are you, Mike?"

"Five feet, nine."

"Not very beeg, huh, John?" The Frenchman, himself far from huge, was smiling mischievously.

John, towering above six feet, shook his head with some shame. "Not big, but damn' if he ain't all bones and muscle."

Mike stood with his feet planted apart, his hands on his hips. "Try me," he said; "I'm a little bit the toughest varmint in these here parts."

The Frenchman's hands moved over Mike's limbs, testing the hardness of the iron muscles on his arms and legs. "Hum," he said at last, "what you do?"

"Tell him what you've been doin', Mike," interpreted John.

"Indian scout around Pittsburgh, hunter," said Mike.

"Peut-être you can use the rifle?"

"How about that, Obadiah?" Mike asked a by-stander. "He wants to know if I can shoot."

"That he can—no man in Pittsburgh can shoot against him. He's poison with his rifle."

"Wat you know about keelboats?"

"Not a damn thing. But I know what kind of a noise they make." Mike twisted his face, cupped his hands around his mouth, and imitated the blast of a boatman's horn. The men in the room listened and laughed. Some joined the crowd around Mike.

"By gar!" said the Frenchman. "I teenk we take you." His white teeth flashed. "Save money on horns!" The crowd laughed. Baptiste fumbled in his pocket, pulled out a pencil and a little book, turned the pages. "How ees it that you are called?"

Mike made a droll face, winked, as the steersman bent over his book. "M-i-c-h-e P-h-i-n-c-k," he spelled. The men around smiled, then looked very solemn, though their eyes sparkled as the Frenchman scrawled the name.

"Bon!" said he, shutting his book, then turning away. "John, you bring heem to the boat to-morrow morning."

"Ay, ay, sir," said the boatman.

"Whiskey," said Mike to the barman. "And you might as well bring me a full gallon, for I mean to do a little drinkin'."

II

It was when the Indians west of the Allegheny River had ceased to be amusing, and when Pittsburgh had become rather too civilized to be interesting, that Mike Fink started his first trip on a keelboat. "The witchery which is in the tone of a wooden trumpet called a river horn, formerly used by keel and flatboat navigators . . . entranced the soul of Mike while yet a boy; and he longed to become a boatman. This soon became his ruling passion . . . When Mike first set foot on a keelboat, he could mimick all the tones of a trumpet, and he longed to go to New Orleans, where he heard that people spoke French and wore their Sunday clothes every day."

For years thereafter he lived the life of a boatman, swaggering through the streets of bustling river towns, in his costume of buckskins and blankets, drinking rivulets of whiskey, loving the light women of New Orleans or Natchez-under-the-hill, playing rude practical jokes, making spectacular shots with his rifle, fighting giants of the rivers. And between orgies on shore were harrowing trips up and down turbulent streams, during which he risked his life daily, sweating and swearing as he and his comrades pounded their craft through river currents. And Mike Fink, boatman, was an important figure in the great westward sweep of pioneers, a hero in the thrilling saga of a growing nation.

At the end of the Revolution settlers straggled westward over Boone's Trace, or the Wilderness Road. In Conestoga wagons, on toiling horses, sometimes afoot, they scrambled through the Cumberland Gap, down into Tennessee, up into Kentucky. For the farmers and laborers of the South and New England the virgin soil of Kentucky was an El Dorado. When a minister, trying to describe heaven to his congregation and failing to find proper adjectives or similes, was at last suddenly inspired, he said:

"In short, my brethren, to say all in one word, Heaven is a Kentuck of a place."

But the most important path to the frontier was the water trail of two thousand miles from Pittsburgh to New Orleans. Down that gleaming trail after the War a flood of emigration poured toward new rich lands. Thousands of families piled their pathetically precious belongings—stock, furniture, farm implements —into weird new boats and moved down rivers swirling over sandbars and around islands where accidents seemed inevitable. Great was the pioneers' faith in God.

Less fervent was the faith of others who came to this outpost of civilization that was the frontier, for the westward tide of empire always carried with it its scum of rascals and outlaws, eager to move beyond the reach of the arm of the law. Sleek gentlemen, immaculately if flashily dressed, somehow found their way to taverns where some of the tables were used for gaming. Criminals, horse-thieves, murderers, found that, rough though life was on the frontier, it was more comfortable for them than life in the East. Prostitutes with carmined cheeks plied their trade in taverns, and prospered. Taverns flourished, some respectable, some vicious; travelers were advised to distinguish by looking for the landlord's ears; if one was gone, the chances were that it had been bitten off in a brawl or removed to punish a crime, and it might be better to try another tavern.

The most colorful of the adventurers who swarmed to the rivers were the men who worked up and down stream the unwieldy craft in which America moved westward—the boatmen. Ex-soldiers, whose taste for thrills had been developed during the War; former Indian scouts, like Mike Fink, well prepared to trade shots with Indians who might pop bullets from the shore or from canoes; the toughest farm boys, who longed for a life less drab than farms provided; jolly French Canadians, who loved the waters, became the cockalorums of the Ohio and the Mississippi.

These rugged boatmen were hated, feared, and admired by folk along the rivers. Mark Twain, who, as a boy, saw the pageant of their craft float past Hannibal, Missouri, spoke admiringly of these "rough and hardy men; rude, uneducated, brave, suffering terrific hardships with sailor-like stoicism; heavy drinkers, coarse frolickers in moral sties like . . . Natchez-under-the-hill . . . heavy fighters, reckless fellows, every one, elephantinely jolly, foul-witted, profane, prodigal of their money, bankrupt at the end of the trip, fond of barbaric finery, prodigious braggarts . . ."

Missionaries, less tolerant than Mark, testified that they had never seen more godless men. And one commentator who lived on the river said that "sober men began to regard the boatmen with apprehension, fearing that if their numbers increased with the increase of transportation on the western rivers, they would endanger the peace of the country. They might have continued for centuries, blighting the moral destinies of millions. But," he concluded gratefully, "the first steamboat that ascended the Ohio sounded their death knell."

"We believe," said another pioneer, with a sigh of relief, "that steam has done more in producing a moral revolution in the West than perhaps all the schoolmasters and most of the preachers combined."

Obviously, when Mike Fink won recognition as king of this crew of bruisers and roughnecks, he fought his way to leadership over a race of giants. These reckless savages with their flaunting scarlet shirts, their bright blue jackets, their leather caps, moccasins, knives, tobacco pouches, huge muscled, loud of mouth, always ready to brawl, were worthy carriers of the flinty pioneers, well qualified to fight and to win daily struggles against rollicking rivers.

Their fleet was perhaps the most heterogeneous aggregation of boats ever launched upon a dangerous body of water. It included boats of every kind imaginable and a few which to-day it is impossible to picture. As a youngster, watching the stream of vessels

on the rivers, Mike Fink learned to identify strange
boats of many kinds.

There were great canoes fifty feet long, lurching under burdens of families and household goods; arks—
massive thick-planked houseboats which blundered
with the current, the humans at one end, the stock at
the other; barges, sixty feet long, which moved like
water-bugs over the river, propelled by fifty oars. It
was a fine thing to see a barge moving down stream at
sunset through a haze drifting over the waters, while
the boatmen kept time to the tune they sang:

> Some row up, but we row down,
>   All the way to Shawnee Town,
> Pull away! Pull away!
>   Pull away to Shawnee Town!

And there were boats which had been hammered together any old way, crosses between various types of
boats; they looked sometimes like piles of lumber, as-
sembled willy-nilly, drifting erratically with the currents.

More important than any of these were the flatboats,
the type chiefly used by pioneers. Flat-bottomed boxes
of green oak plank fastened with wooden pins to timber frames, varying greatly in size and appearance,
they were usually about forty feet long, twelve feet
wide, eight feet deep—partly covered, the covered
boats which make one think of covered wagons, for
their use was similar. On each of the ends and the
sides of a flatboat projected an oar, not used to propel

the craft—the current did that—but to direct it. On each side was a thirty-foot oar, used to land the boat or to push it from the shore into the current; these horn-like projections caused boatmen to call the flat-boat a "broadhorn." A fifty-foot oar on the stern was used for steering, and in the front a short "gouger" helped in guiding the craft when the current was un-usually fast.

Coming to Redstone, to Pittsburgh, or to Wheeling, emigrants there bought boats, provisions, and farming utensils, moved their families and their stock onto the boats, and started to drift downstream, studying *The Navigator*, a book for emigrants which charted the river and warned of dangers. Landings, said this au-thority, were "attended with some considerable loss of time and some hazard," and therefore "you should con-trive to land as seldom as possible." The emigrant was warned against boats made of rotten wood which would be stove in by the first rock struck. On these drifting boats, the life of the farm was carried on in miniature as the current moved the unwieldy craft. Mothers cooked over stoves, children romped on the deck, sometimes splashing into the river. The mooing of cows, the cackle of fowl, the shouts of children and boatmen echoed from the hills. Sometimes two or three such boats "were lashed or fastened together, thus allowing the hands and passengers to while away the hours in holding converse together on the extended roof, or in each other's cabins."

Of course, there were accidents.   One traveler, for example, tells how his boat carried swiftly through a chute, stuck on a sandbar, and then dashed on the rocks of "Dead Man's Riffle" and almost capsized. Children shrieked, cottonstuffs and hardware fell from the shelves, nearly burying the emigrant's startled wife. And the excited captain tried vainly to find out what to do by thumbing the pages of *The Navigator*.

Davy Crockett, venturing down the river in a flatboat lashed to others, sat by the fire one night, thinking "how much better bear-hunting was on hard land than floating along on the water":

> The hatchway into the cabin came slap down, right through the top of the boat; and it was the only way out except a small hole in one side. . . . We were now floating sideways, and the boat I was in was the hindmost. . . . All at once I heard the hands begin to run over the top of the boat in great confusion, and pull with all their might; and the first thing I know'd after this we went broadside full tilt against the head of an island where a large raft of drift timber had lodged.   The nature of such a place would be . . . to suck the boats down, and turn them right under this raft; and the uppermost boat would, of course, be suck'd down and go under first.   As soon as we struck, I bulged for my hatchway, as the boat was turning under sure enough.   But when I got to it the water was pouring thro' in a current as large as the hole would let it, and as strong as the weight of the river could force it.   I found I couldn't get out there, for the boat was now turned down in such a way that it was steeper than a house-top.   I now thought of the hole in the side, and made my way in a hurry for that. With difficulty I got to it, and when I got there, I found

it was too small for me to get out by my own dower
[strength], and I began to think I was in a worse box than
ever. But I put my arms through and hollered as long as
I could roar, as the boat I was in hadn't quite filled with
water up to my head, and the hands who were next to the
raft, seeing my arms out, and hearing me holler, seized
them, and began to pull. I told them I was sinking, and to
pull my arms off, or force me through, for now I know'd
well enough it was neck or nothing. . . .

By a violent effort they jerked me through; but I was in
a pretty pickle. . . . I had been sitting without any clothing over my shirt; this was torn off, and I was literally
skin'd like a rabbit. I was, however, well pleased to get
out in any way . . . as before I could straighten myself on
the boat next to the raft, the one they pull'd me out of went
entirely under, and I have never seen it any more to this
day. We all escaped on to the raft, where we were compelled to sit all night, about a mile from land on either
side. . . .

We had now lost all our loading; and every particle of
our clothing. . . . In the morning about sunrise, we saw a
boat coming down and we hailed her. They sent a large
skiff, and took us all on board, and carried us down as far
as Memphis.

Here and there, all along the Mississippi, the traveler saw the wreckage of boats, and now and then he
saw red-shirted bodies of drowned boatmen floating on
the water. And there were graves of the boatmen,
marked with rude stones or crosses, on the shores of the
rivers.

Mike Fink worked infrequently on flatboats; most
of his boating was on keelboats, the pride of the river
in days before steamboats. The flats and the others

were only downstream drifters, which lasted a voyage, then were broken to pieces at their destination, and used for lumber, while their boatmen returned up the river on land over the Natchez Trace. But the slender pointed keelboat was an upstream boat, and Mike would fight the man who refused to admit that it was the best on the rivers.

These boats, averaging about fifty feet in length, nine feet or less in width, were ribbed vessels, built on a keel covered with plank, their draught only twenty to thirty inches. Raised over the boat a box-like structure served as a cover, leaving a narrow footpath on the outside all around. Keels shot downstream faster than the other vessels, carrying, despite their small draught, twenty to forty tons of freight. They could penetrate small streams, too shallow or narrow for flats, and they could navigate the rivers in low waters. But their proudest accomplishment was their triumph over the river currents on upstream voyages, when muscular crews, hairy chests heaving, with powerful pushes of their poles, nudged them along stubborn courses, crawling, by sheer strength, against relentlessly eddying waters.

Keelboats were sometimes used by pioneers, though broadhorns were more popular. Travelers, however, used them often for quick journeys, and wise merchants constantly sent their cargoes on them. "This method [of sending goods]," advised *The Navigator*, "is safest, if not cheapest, for . . . the cargo is confined to the care of an experienced and careful man, who perhaps descends and ascends the river twice or thrice in the course of one season, and of course must be well acquainted with all the difficulties in handling it."

Mike's life on keelboats was a joyous life, a life of broad practical jokes, tall talk, many orgies ashore, and much action on the deck of the boat. Always death was lurking around the bend of the river; meanwhile there was a savage struggle which rejoiced the heart of a giant, there were moments of beauty on a river twining through primeval forests.

III

It was early one April morning during the best season for travel on the river—for journeying was easiest when waters were high in the spring or the autumn—that Mike clambered aboard the keelboat on which he took his first trip down the rivers to New Orleans. The journey started with dawn, just as the black smoke which already had begun to mark Pittsburgh as a center which might become "one of the most considerable inland manufacturing towns in the United States" wafted skyward.

The patroon shouted a hoarse command: "Stand to your poles and set off!" And the crew, standing on two runningboards, one on either side of the boat, pushed the vessel into the current with their long poles. The steersman, "to scare off the devil and se-

A KEEL-BOAT ON THE MISSISSIPPI

(from a rare print)

cure good luck," blew a long blast on the boatman's horn. Mike imitated him.

"Well," said a poleman, "the new calf can bleat. Sounds as if he had horns."

"He's got horns," testified John, ruefully.

Many sounds were in the spring air, carried from other boats on the river. From arks and broadhorns came the disturbed moos of cows, the whinny of horses, the grunts of hogs, panicky because the world was moving though they stood still. Some boatmen on a flatboat already in midstream were singing:

> Hard upon the beach oar!
> She moves too slow
> All the way to Shawneetown
> Long time ago.

One of the trim galleys, a little light boat propelled by oars which carried passengers and mail, was moving with rhythmic sweeps, and the oarsmen caught the regular beat as the captain cried: "Pull! Pull! Pull!" The galley quickly left the rest, disappearing with flashing oars in the fog which smoked on the surface of the water, and after a time the keel left most of the more cumbersome boats behind.

"Put up your pole, Mike," said John, once the boat was in the current. "It's restin' time."

Now all the boatmen except the steersman and two oarsmen flopped to resting positions. The boat steered between the Monongahela bar and the Allegheny bar, formed by sediments which those two rivers had car-

ried into the Ohio, on, until, three miles from Pittsburgh, loomed the first of the Ohio's many islands—
Hamilton's Island.   Here, the boat came close to the
right shore at the head of the body of land, and after
passing the point bore towards the island, then kept
close to it all the way down, to avoid a sandbar projecting from the right shore.   But the steersman had
to keep a lookout for M'Kee's Rocks, which jutted
from the foot of the island on the left.

Mike watched the steersman and the gyrations of
the boat with puzzlement.

"See here, John," he said, "why don't Baptiste keep
a straight course?   Is he drunk?"

"Hell, no.   He knows the river like a book.   Matter of fact, here's the book."   John pulled a tattered
copy of *The Navigator* from a pocket, tossed it to
Mike.   Then he took it again and twirled its pages.
"Here's where we are now," he said, pointing to a page.
"Next we come to Irwin's Island.   It tells about it
here.   Read this book, like a good little boy, an' you'll
learn to be a steersman.   Me, I'm going to sleep."   He
stretched out again on the top of the cargo box, shutting his eyes.

Mike spelled through the directions for passing the
island:

> At the head of this island is a sandbar bearing towards
> the right shore, therefore keep about one-third of the breadth
> of the river to the right, and at the *first ripple* below and
> opposite Baldwin's mill, leave a big breaker or rock close to
> the right.—Now bear towards the island to avoid the *Second*

or *Horse tail* ripple, about half way down the island leaving a sandbar to the right and some breakers to the left.

Eight miles beyond was a serpentine stretch of river in which Mike distinguished Dead Man's Island, churned by foam. Here, weaving from the right side to the left and back to the right to avoid ripples, the boatman sailed along. Mike here sighted a stove boat, perilously poised on a rock which was a dark colored mass in the water roaring in Dead Man's Riffle. Some of the goods had been removed to the shore, and about it, shivering, bewildered, stood the bedraggled crew and the family.

The keel moved on, past Indian Loggstown, past Legionville, where General Wayne encamped in 1792, on down the river. The boatmen, for the most part, rested. Sometimes the steersman misjudged the extent of a sandbar, and there was a swearing session with the poles or the oars. But the wise Baptiste knew the river well, and there were few pauses. A fiddler in the crew brought out his fiddle and his bow, and played dance tunes, and one of the boatmen banged his feet on the cover of the boat, awkwardly jigging. One red-shirted, bewhiskered fellow trailed a fish-hook over the stern. A little group of boatmen played with a deck of greasy cards. Mike watched the menacing river.

The Ohio was a fine broad river, with a current for the most part uniform, smooth, and deceivingly placid. It was lonely, although a boat passed now and then. High banks stretched on either side, and there was no sign of life upon them, except now and then, at long intervals, a log cabin. But even the cabins, land cleared about them, as they rested beneath a hill, seemed to send lonely pencilings of blue smoke skyward. Most stood at the edge of a field from which black stumps projected.

And there was "an eternal foreground" which was menacing. "The river had washed away its banks and stately trees had fallen down into the stream. Some had been there so long that they were mere grizzly skeletons. Some had just toppled over, and having earth yet about their roots, were bathing their green heads in the river, and putting forth new shoots and branches. Some were almost sliding down as one looked at them. And some were drowned so long ago that their bleached arms started out from the middle of the current, and seemed to grasp the boat, and drag it under water."

Boatmen had names, Mike learned, for the various trees and logs which menaced the boat's passage. A grim black tree, destitute of leaves, which stood silent in the center of a boiling whirl of water, was a "planter" —a tree which had become attached to the bottom of the river, planted in sediment. More dangerous were "sawyers," which bobbed up and down in the currents, first submerged, then lifting their wet branches high above the surface.

One moment the steersman would see all the surface of the river gleaming peacefully in the sun; the next, right in front of the boat, a sawyer would loom, lifting menacing arms which threatened to crush the craft. Cursing prodigiously, the steersman would swing the boat around the obstruction—if he could—using all of his strength and all of his skill to save the vessel.

Not only did the steersman have to watch the surface of the river; he had to watch, as well, for obstructions beneath the surface—"sleeping sawyers," for example, their upper ends just beneath the surface, ready to rip into the ribs of the boat. It was easier, of course, to discern the "snags"—trees which lay upon the shoals of the river, branches gracefully rippling with the current; but even these might, by their very frequency or their position in the channel, bring disaster. Wooden islands—piles of entangled driftwood which floated with the stream or caught on rocks or island heads, were also easily discoverable and also menacing. Mike was not to learn all of the ingenious tricks of the rivers in one trip, or in many trips. The ever-changing streams had an infinite variety of snares for the frail crafts which moved through their waters.

Such were the natural menaces of the rivers. Mike knew, of course, that there were other dangers, Indians who sometimes swept down to capture boats freighted with whiskey, and "organized banditti, who sought every occasion to rob and murder the owners of these boats." In time, Mike was to have his share of trouble with these human menaces.

Surrounded, then, by dangers of many kinds, the keel floated down the Ohio, and Mike idly watched the river, or the red birds or vividly colored paroquets which flitted above the mysteriously silent banks. Sometimes the boatmen caught sight of a clearing, with a wildly clad pioneer pausing behind a team of oxen which had been pulling a plow through a stumpy field. Then perhaps there would be a joke.

Perhaps the plowman's nasal speech revealed that he was a Yankee, and when he asked what the boat's cargo was, the boatmen would name products which shrewd Yankee traders had palmed off on unsuspecting frontiersmen:

"Pit-coal indigo, wooden nutmegs, straw baskets, and Yankee notions."

Or perhaps a grinning rascal would shift his tobacco to the pouch of his cheek and entertain his fellows by hurling uncouth puns at a curious settler:

"Where are you from?"

"Redstone."

"What is your lading?"

"Millstones."

"What is your captain's name?"

"Whetstone."

"Where are you bound?"

"To Limestone."

More amusing was the torturous conversation which the jolly patroon carried on with a red-nosed plowman who stood thirstily in the sun watching the river:

"Hello, the boat!"

"Hello, the plow!" roared the captain. "Have you any potatoes to sell the boat?"

"None," said the crafty landsman. Then, "Have you any whiskey aboard the boat?"

The captain stooped and then stood erect, holding on high a cool looking brown jug, its top plugged with a corn-cob. "Plenty," he said, waving it.

The shoresman grew agitated, but tried to hide his impatience. "Well," he said, "I'll trade potatoes for whiskey."

The captain grinned at his men. "What do you ask for potatoes?" he asked.

"A dollar a bushel."

"Too much," said the captain, and he uncorked the jug, swigged the whiskey, smacked his lips.

"I'll let you have a bushel of potatoes for a gallon of whiskey."

The captain thoughtfully took another swig, and put the jug on the deck. The boat moved on.

"A half gallon!"

Then, as the voice grew faint in the distance, the settler wailed frantically, "A quart."

The captain thumbed his nose as the vessel disappeared around a bend.

All day the boat drifted along, the rivermen sleeping, singing, exchanging gossip with boatmen or passengers on other vessels encountered. Steersmen and boatmen took their turns working, and Mike fumbled with the oar and was initiated, with curses, into its mysteries.

At sunset, the boat put ashore for a time, and was tied to a log. The men gathered firewood, which was

abundant along the shore. Then they made a fire for
cooking in a big box filled with dirt, which was placed
on the roof. The evening meal consisted of salt pork,
bread, fire-baked potatoes, washed down with a fillee
of undiluted corn whiskey. The rivermen were proud
of their ability to eat and drink great quantities. Keelboatmen, said an impressed traveler, "must be fed with
double the quantity of food which would suffice American or English laborers. The meat which they prefer
is bacon or salt pork, of which they use daily about
four pounds each man, besides bread and potatoes."

Then, as a round white moon floated up above the
black trees, graying the river, the keelers pushed the
craft into the current again, for they were to float all
night, the waters being high, and the steersmen being
wise, even in the dark, in the ways of the stream. The
boatmen who were not at the oars wrapped up in blankets and stretched out to sleep on the cover of the boat,
while the red embers of their fire marked the movement
of the vessel through the blue moonlight. The boat
drifted down a silent lapping river, the quiet disturbed
only now and then by the weird baying of some
settler's dog in the blackness on the shore. And the
gnarled branches of planters, sawyers, and snags
seemed more menacing than ever as they loomed darkly
against the silver moving stream.

At twilight, seven days and a half after the start of
the journey, the boat reached Cincinnati, five hundred
and twenty-four miles below Pittsburgh. The boat
moored by the wagon-rutted landing for the night, and

in the morning put out in a noisy fleet of flatboats, arks, Allegheny skiffs, and keelboats. Most of the boatmen staggered aboard the vessel just before dawn, and they were heavy armed and large of head as they set their poles, for the taverns and brothels of Cincinnati had proved diverting.

Mike was awakened from his early morning nap by John, just below Cincinnati. "Look here, Mike, here's a new rig for you." He pointed to a curious boat—a keel of forty tons, pushed upstream by a horizontal paddle wheel. Six horses which circled on a galley above the boat, turning cog-wheels which in turn moved the paddle wheel, furnished the power.

"Hey, you old skinflint!" Mike yelled to the captain. "Them's not alligator-horses, them's just plain horses."

"Shut up, you damned son of a stuffed monkey!" said the captain, amiably. "These hosses eat hay, and it costs less to feed 'em."

Other queer boats appeared now and then—floating tinships, whereon tinners, with tools and irons, visited the settlements; blacksmith shops from which clanged the beat of hammer against anvil; heavily laden produce boats with a cargo of "Kentucky flour and hemp, Ohio apples, cider, maple sugar, nuts, cheese, and fruit." Sometimes a flatboat would take on the guise of a floating store, visiting river towns and settlements, and offering tempting bargains in crockery, paint, bonnets, boots, hardware and dry goods. Blasts on tin horns would announce that the store had arrived to conduct business, while a dignified admiral dashed around behind a counter, balanced a pencil behind his ear, metamorphosed into a merchant.

A few days' journey beyond Cincinnati, Baptiste said to Mike: "Now soon you see rough water. We come soon to ze Falls of ze Ohio."

Mike looked out on the waters, as glassy as any stretch along the river. They were passing through the calm waters near the harbor at Bear Grass Creek, where, as the pious author of *The Navigator* put it, "at one of the most dangerous places to the Navigator of the Ohio, Nature, in her wise and providential works, has been kind enough to place one of the safest and best Harbours that is to be found on the whole course of the river."

"It don't look very dangerous to me," Mike said.

"Not now, mais soon. Hear her roar!"

There was a mumble of water ahead. The keel whirled out of the calm water into a turmoil, and swirled speedily into the falls. Mike heard them roaring now, as he held tightly to the mast. For a moment the boat darted at a frightening speed, then Mike felt it move more slowly over unruffled water below the falls. He slowly relinquished his hold on the mast.

"By God, Baptiste, I guess maybe you was right. That was a mite disturbin'."

And now, the most exciting moments of the trip down this river past, the keel floated on towards the junction of the Ohio and the Mississippi. Drifting past Henderson, Cave-in-Rock, Three Sisters Islands,

LIFE ON A KEEL BOAT

and zigzagging through the four-mile Grand Chain of Rocks, it reached the mouth of the Ohio sixteen days after the beginning of the trip.

IV

The boat drifted into the broad muddy Mississippi, and the high banks, the abrupt cliffs along the shore, gave way to wide valleys on either side of the stream, stretching as far as eye could see, uninterrupted by hills or bluffs.   The current was swifter; treacherous sandbars, ever shifting, constantly threatened the progress of the keelboat; no longer was it possible to allow the boat to drift at night.   With darkness, the boatmen turned their craft to the shore.

And now Mike was initiated into the social diversions of the boatmen.   They were many.   Sometimes, after mooring on one of the hundred and twenty-five islands which dot the Mississippi, the navigators sat around the campfire and told tall tales of adventure with beasts or men or of the exciting towns which lined the river.   Mike celebrated his adventures as an Indian scout.   Some of the boatmen who had been at the wars told of the struggles of the colonials against the redcoats.   Some told tales of Daniel Boone and his great deeds in the wilderness.   Or perhaps they spoke wistfully of hilarious nights in the vicious towns along the Mississippi.   One of them may have described the wickedest of them all, Natchez, in words something like these:

"Natchez is a land of fevers, alligators, niggers, and cotton bales . . . where to refuse grog before breakfast would degrade you below the brute creation; . . . where bears, the size of young jackasses, are fondled in lieu of pet dogs; and knives, the length of a barber's pole, usurp the place of toothpicks; . . . where nigger women are knocked down by the auctioneer, and knocked up by the purchaser . . .

"The town is divided into two parts, as distinct in character as they are in appearance. Natchez on the hill, upon a high bluff overlooking the Mississippi, is a pretty little town . . . Natchez-under-the-hill . . . is . . . the jumping off place. Satan looks on it with glee, and chuckles . . . The buildings are for the most part brothels, taverns, or gambling houses, and frequently the whole three may be found under the same roof. Obscene songs are sung at the top of the voice in all quarters. I have repeatedly seen the strumpets tear a man's clothes from his back, and leave his body beautified with all the colors of the rainbow."

And he told of brawls in the thick-aired taverns, of lynchings, of the coups of gamblers, of amorous adventures, of squalid murders which the hardened ruffians of Natchez-under-the-hill viewed with bored indifference.

"Yes, that's a fine town," said another boatman, "but give me New Orleans any time. There you have as many nations as there are sandbars in the Mississippi, all congregated to raise hell—sailors from the seas with little girl pig-tails that can fight damn near as

good as a keelboatman, scum of the French and Spanish nations, that can't talk no English, but that can
brawl in any language, Creoles, Quadroons, Mulattoes,
Samboes, Mustizos, Indians, Niggers, all the colors of
the rainbow in one crowd, just spilin' to raise hell.

"And the females—" he became eloquent—"never
was there such wenches. They have clothes like—like
angels, by God, and hearts like devils. They spray the
fringes of their petticoats with gold, and they wear
gold slippers, and their stockings are decorated likewise
with the same precious metal, all sewed around in
pretty little God damned flowers on the prettiest legs in
the world. They're delicate—that's what I like about
'em—delicate and refined as all hell.

"They don't bury their murdered in New Orleans,"
he continued impressively. "They just dump 'em into
the river, or cart 'em into the cemetery in the heart of
the city, and leave 'em there to rot. I seen the cemetery; it was covered with human bones!"

And often, the boatmen talked of their most famous,
most joyous pastime, fighting. A mild narrative went
thus:

"I told him he lied; he told me I lied. I spit in his
face; he spit in my face. I kicked him; he kicked me.
I tripped him up; he tripped me up. I struck him and
knocked him down; he got up and knocked me down.
I then got mad; he got mad and we were going to fight
when the saloon keeper got between us."

The famed Davy Crockett has told of a fight with a
boatman in a story which was more typical:

"One day as I was sitting in the stern of my broad-horn, the old Free and Easy, on the Mississippi . . . who should float down past me but Joe Snag; he was in a snooze, as fast as a church, with his mouth wide open; he had been ramsquaddled with whiskey for a fortnight, and as it evaporated from his body it looked like the steam from a vent pipe. Knowing the feller would be darn hard to wake, with all this steam on, as he floated past me I hit him a crack over the knob with my big steering oar. He waked up in a thundering rage.

"Says he, 'Haloe, stranger, who axed you to crack my lice?'

"Says I, 'Shut your mouth, or your teeth will get sunburnt.'

"Upon this he crooked up his neck and neighed like a stallion. I clapped my arms and crowded like a cock.

"Says he, 'If you are a game chicken, I'll pick all the pin feathers off you . . .'

"Says I, 'Give us none of your chin music, but set your kickers on land and I'll give you a severe licking.' The fellow now jumped ashore, and he was so tall that he could not tell when his feet were cold. He jumped up a rod. Says he, 'Take care how I lite on you,' and he gave me a real sockdologer that made my very liver and lites turn to jelly. But he found me a real scrouger. I broke three of his ribs, and he knocked out five of my teeth and one eye. He was the severest colt I ever tried to break. I finally got a bite hold that he could not shake off. We were now parted by some boatmen, and were so exorsted that it was more than a month before either of us could fight."

Other nights, the keelmen fought among themselves to settle an endless argument about which of them was the champion. Their fights were a ritual, always preceded by crowings, neighings, and imaginative speeches about what each was going to do to the other. As a rule, each did plenty, for nothing was prohibited. "No natural weapon was barred: fists flew at faces, feet kicked wherever they could find a target; knees bucked at unprotected crotches; teeth sank wherever there was flesh; fingers clutched at throats and thumbs seemed to gouge out eyes from their sockets." Noses were battered, teeth splintered, and blood plentifully shed when boatmen squared off and shot fists at one another.

The cocky champion of the crew wore, sprucely perched on his hat, a red feather which proclaimed his high position. He had to fight often to defend it from ambitious rivals, and often, too, he battled with the similarly designated champions of other boats. Often the whole crew had a knock-down, drag-out scuffle with the crew of another boat—any crew would do, though the flatboatmen were the keelmen's chief enemies. And if one crew was larger than the other, the excess members of the larger crew stood by and watched.

When the boat docked at a river town, the boatmen swaggered down the street in search, first, of whiskey, and afterward, of fights. There was Little Billy, for example, six feet four inches, who came into a town one election day when the brown rutted streets were thronged with farm wagons full of produce and with broad-shouldered farmers. He staggered from an inn down to the town square near the court house, mounted a barrel which stood outside of a store, and started crowing and shouting, while townsmen, clad in great linsey hunting shirts and buckskin trousers, mighty men, gathered around.

"'Won't *nobody* come out and fight me? Come out some of you and die decently, for I'm *spilein'* for a fight! I han't had one for more than a week . . . I'm a poor man—it's a fact—and smell like a wet dog; but I can't be run over! I'm the identical individual that grinned a whole menagerie out of countenance, and made the ribbed nose baboon hang down his head and blush! W-h-o-o-p! . . . W-h-o-o-p! . . . One squint of mine at a bull's heel would blister it! Cock-a-doodle-doo! Oh, I'm one of your toughest sort—live forever, and then turn to a white oak post. Look at me,' said he, slapping his hands on his thighs with the report of a pistol. 'I'm the *ginewine* article . . . and I can out-run, out-jump, out-swim, chaw more tobacco and spit less, and drink more whiskey and keep soberer than any man in these localities! . . .'"

He paused, expectantly, looking eagerly, with watery blue eyes, over the crowd, which, excessively polite in its silence, avoided his challenging glare. Sighing, he leaped from his barrel head.

"'Darn it,' said Bill, walking off in disgust, 'if that don't make 'em fight nothing will . . . Well, I'll go . . . and have another *settlement* with Joe Sykes.

He's a bad chance for a fight . . . seeing as how he's but one eye left to gouge at, and an "under" bit out of both ears; but poor fellow, he's *willing to do his best*, and will stay a body's appetite till the next shooting match.' "

Perhaps there was a general militia drill in progress in town. In that case the boatmen gleefully descended in a body upon a mob of bumpkins who were making muddled attempts to execute military formations. Soon the streets echoed with roars and curses of militia-men and keelmen, and the squeals of an excited femi-nine audience. There were thuds and harsh snatches of deep laughter in a cloud of yellow dust scuffled up from the road. A little later, the militiamen, no longer splendid in their cocked hats and long-tailed coats, were in flight, kicking the dusty streets behind them, their hats askew over their ears or lying battered on the ground, their tattered coats trailing their tails in the breeze.

One evening when the steersman was looking for a place to moor for the night, Mike, standing by him, noticed a sprinkling of tents and wagons in a clearing in the forest by the river. As the boat drew nearer, re-ligious music wafted over the waters, and Mike saw men and women moving beneath the trees.

"A camp meetin'!" shouted Mike. "Baptiste, for the love of God, put her ashore here!"

The boat moored near two other boats which had been attracted by the religious festival. The crews grinned at one another.

"Hello, brothers!" yelled a keeler. "Coming to be saved?"

"We're here to do the work of the devil," said Mike, "and we're feelin' powerful cantakerous."

Other boats were hailed as they came into sight. "Camp meetin'! Come on an' help us poor sinners raise hell!" The boats swung to the shore. The crews mingled as they munched their evening meal and swallowed their whiskey. As darkness fell, about a hundred boatmen had gathered at the mooring place. In the distance they could see the gleam of lights through the black forest, and songs wafted through the trees, accompanied by the distant howling of wolves. The boatmen crept through the forest.

They came to the camp-grounds, two hundred and fifty yards square, lighted with flickering candles, torches, tied to trees, fires in front of the tents and wagons at the back of the grounds—dots of wavering flame against a black background. At the front of the space stood a speakers' stage, and at the other end of the space another. On both platforms leather-lunged preachers were shouting hellfire and damnation sermons. Below the speakers fifteen hundred listeners writhed on the benches, and the lights lengthened their squirming shadows.

Some of the listeners cried: "Hallelujah!," Amen!," and "Praise the Lord!" Some stood on the benches, chattering sermons of their own to a knot of listeners. Drunk with religion, some crawled on their hands and knees, barking like dogs. Others lay on the ground, twitching, jerking, foaming at the mouth. A few were chanting hymns.

The boatmen heard a few words of one of the preachers: "And the forces of evil shall descend upon you—"

"Come on, forces of evil!" roared a boatman, and whooping and howling, the rivermen descended.

Fifteen hundred religious folk heard their shouts drowned by the yells of a hundred red-shirted giants, who swept down like so many devils, scattering mourners' benches, setting the splinters afire. Women fled screaming to the woods, leaving parts of their dresses on twigs. Newly made converts were turned into frantically fighting demons. A minister stood panting and exchanging wallops with Fink, and in an instant a mob of figures swept down, engulfed the minister, and left Mike, for the moment, behind. Then Mike stormed into the center of the mob. It was some hours before the last of the godly fled before the wicked.

Then the boatmen limped and swaggered back to camp to sleep like angelic children at the end of a perfect day.

Other nights the crew would stretch a rope across a village street, several keelers holding each end. Then the boatmen would gallop down the street, roaring with laughter as "men, women and children, horses, carts and cattle" turned grotesque somersaults. Or perhaps the rivermen found a belligerent crowd in a tavern, and managed to fight until the barroom and its tables and mirrors were demolished, and reeking liquor pooled on the littered floor.

There were more peaceful amusements, shooting matches, for example, at which Mike, cub though he was, was victorious, or coon hunts. And there were country dances at which, accompanied by the scrape of the fiddle and the fiddler's cries, the boatmen hopped through square sets, reels, and jigs while red-cheeked buxom daughters of frontiersmen smiled up at their dashing escorts. Mike and his comrades wandered along gray trails through the trees to the boat as mocking birds imitated the songs of cardinals, lapwings or jays, then sang songs of their own. And as they walked, the boatmen chorused a song which boasted that it was their devilish habit to

> Dance all night, till broad daylight,
> And go home with the gals in the morning.

Thus they spent their nights. Each day, they moved farther down the river, hourly escaping perils. Sometimes caving banks of the Mississippi threatened to engulf the boat; planters, sawyers, wooden islands, more frequent than in the Ohio, were passed. "Wooden islands," warned *The Navigator*, "are more dangerous than real ones, the former being an obstacle lately thrown in the way of the current, and the bed of the river not having had sufficient time to form that bar or gradual ascent from the bottom of the river to the island, which divide the current at some distance from the point of the island above water, the current will hurry you against them, unless you use timely exertion." "There are also streams," admonished the help-

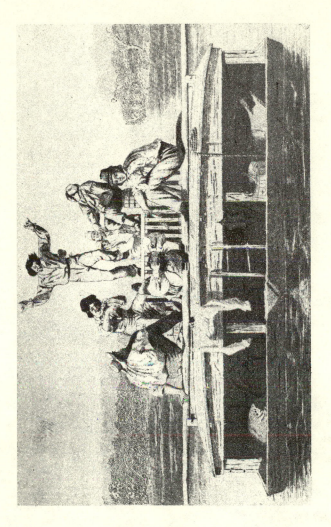

"THE JOLLY FLAT-BOAT MEN"

(from the original by G. C. Bingham, Esq.)

ful guide book, "which at all times sally forth from the main river with astonishing rapidity, and whose vortex extends some distance into the stream. Boats sucked into such bayous are next to lost, it being almost impossible to force so unwieldy a machine as a flat bottomed boat against so powerful a current. It will therefore be safest for boats, never to keep too close to shore . . ."

Mosquitoes from the swamps pestered them by day and by night. Mike's body and his face were blotched and red. One of the crew became very sick with fever, and fought for days before his mighty body threw off the illness.

The idling boatmen watched the shores and the river. The bottoms were green with sycamore, willows, gum-trees, bushes. Near the river, at times in the water, grew cypress trees covered with a thick green or buff velvety growth, often hung with Spanish moss. Near White River, water had inundated the bottoms, and the boatmen viewed a dense forest of huge trees, full of singing birds, buzzards, eagles "apparently rising from the bosom of the dark and discolored waters."

Now and then, seeing herds of deer leaping through the thickets, some of the boatmen went ashore, in order that venison might vary the monotonous diet. Or Mike's rifle bullet plowed through the head of a bear swimming in the stream, and there was bear meat. Often large flocks of ducks or other game birds rocketed out of the reeds; they were hardly frightened when Mike fired at them.

One day, when the boat had rounded a bend, blood-curdling shouts sounded from the shore. A white man, his clothing torn, his face matted with hair, stood on the shore and pleaded for help.

"Save me! For Christ's sake, save me!" he shouted, holding his arms out toward the boat, as if in prayer.

Mike watched his companions with amazement. They viewed the writhings of the wretch with the dispassionate interest of an audience watching a play. John called out to the man.

"That's mighty fine!" he shouted, and he spat into the river. "We ain't got no room for passengers."

"For the love of God," said Mike, "ain't we going to help the poor devil?"

"No," said John. "If we did, they'd be a covey o' redskins down on us like a cargo o' lead 'fore we could belch. It's an old Injun trick that catches none but yokels. They're stored away in the bushes, likely, sharpenin' their tommyhawks."

"But maybe he's not with Injuns," said Mike, still eyeing the woeful pleader.

"Maybe not. But he yells too loud, thinks I, and they're too many bushes there."

The boat moved on.

Two and a half days' journey above Natchez, the men found their hazardous way through the most dangerous part of the Mississippi—the Giant Gulf. It looked dangerous as the boat swept towards it: on the one hand a rocky bluff stretched into the swirling river, on the other lay a green point around which the muddied stream made a horse-shoe bend. The river, fiercely splashed against the rocks which blocked its flow, formed a caldron of sucking, seething waters below the bluff—a grave for many a boatman. Across the stream a counter current swirled, freighted with wooden islands and sawyers, past the forested point.

Baptiste sought the channel through the boiling yellow water, rather nearer the right shore, touching the tiller now and then, or calling on an oarsman to curve the vessel around a snag. At last the keel was clutched by the current. It sped like a shot through roaring waves while the men held tight to the mast or to the cargo box. Then in the path of the boat suddenly upreared the top of a huge black tree, dripping water which gleamed in the sun, and the boatmen's hearts sank. But the steersman at the instant when it seemed sure to crash the boat twisted the helm just enough to pass it, and its branches scraped against the running board. The boat swept on into smoother waters.

"Jesus to Jesus!" cried Mike, lost in admiration and wonder. "She dances like a lady!"

The steersman laughed with relief and clapped Mike on the shoulder. "Stay wiz zees boat, and, by Gar, I show you how to steer! I mak her float on heavy dew, or turn 'round on a dollaire!"

Sixteen days after the boat left the Falls of the Ohio, it reached Natchez, and Mike had an opportunity to test the truth of his companions' descriptions of that Sodom of the river. He found the descriptions slightly colored, but he had no complaint; Natchez was colorful enough in its own right. Natchez proper looked down upon the river from a lofty hill which rose so steeply two hundred feet above the river that it was called the Bluff. And Natchez proper was a pretty little town of three hundred homes, "several large Mercantile Houses," "two printing offices," and "a number of public inns," and, of course, some churches, all neat wooden buildings with many doors and windows, gleaming in the sun.

But Natchez improper—Natchez-under-the-hill— was an eye-sore. The bluff upon which Natchez stood was two hundred yards from the river, and the inter- mediate level space between bluff and river called the Landing, or Natchez-under-the-hill, was crowded with unseemly gray trading-houses, dramshops, gambling- dens, brothels. Natchez took some comfort in the fact that these battered structures below the gray and white cliffs were built on shifting sands, and now and then one slid into the river with a satisfying plop; but Natchez, try as it would, could not fail to hear the hub- bub which, day and night, echoed from the reeking re- sorts. Most of the skullduggery below the town Nat- chez ignored, though now and then an enraged group of vigilantes took from the teeming slums some over- bold rascal, tortured him with tar and feathers or ar- ranged a novel method of execution for him.

Usually a booming frontier created in time its bad town, its place of relaxation for frontiersmen, weary from the loneliness of the hills or the prairies. Thus

Deadwood, the heart of the Dakota mining district, at Mike Russell's famous saloon, ministered to thirsty miners. Thus, too, Dodge City became the tough town where bow-legged cowboys, after nerve-racking sessions with stampeding cattle, drank deep or shot out decisions on disputes over gambling tables. Natchez was the first haven of downriver boatmen. It marked the end of the hardest stretch of travel down the Mississippi. After leaving Natchez, boats again drifted at night as well as in daytime, and boatmen made only casual trips ashore until the time when they reached New Orleans, when another bender of gigantic proportions was in order.

So in Natchez the boatmen made merry with a frenzy almost desperate. Long into the night they boomed their songs, celebrating their conquests of treacherous streams, raw liquor, pretty wenches:

> Hi-O, away we go,
> Floating down the river on the O-hi-o,
>
> When the boatman goes on shore
> He spends his money and works for more,
> I never saw a girl in all my life,
> But what she would be a boatman's wife.
>
> Hi-O, away we go,
> Floating down the river on the O-hi-o.

Other verses were less printable. Other songs had the qualities of ballads, and were sung as plaintively as boatmen with rasping voices could sing them:

> And it's oh! she was so neat a maid,
>   That her stockings and her shoes
> She toted in her lily white hands,
>   For to keep them from the dews.

Then followed a chorus which celebrated the independence of bachelordom, the splendor of prodigal spending:

> Here's to those that has old clothes,
>   And never a wife to mend 'em.
> A plague to those that has halfjoes,
>   And hasn't a heart to spend 'em.

Boatmen in their cups unloosed their great treasuries of profanity. Some travelers were impressed by the novelty and splendor of their ripping curses; most were so shocked that they wrote brief sermons on profanity in their journals. Some pious gentlemen tried to reform the boatmen by lecturing them; one offended passenger even tried, on one occasion, to bribe an angelic-looking youthful boatman whose vocabulary was iridescent. "I offered him a dollar upon the condition of his not swearing for the remainder of the day. He was much pleased . . . but after controlling himself with much watchfulness, for about an hour, he became discouraged, . . . [and] returned to his long established practice." Unfortunately, there are no satisfactory transcriptions of the boatmen's profane remarks.

In the barrooms, too, boatmen strutted and chanted their challenges to battle. They were half-horse, half-alligator, they proclaimed; they were screaming eagles;

they were long-clawed wildcats. They would take on any one in the town, the valley, the nation, or the world in any kind of a contest, and beat him "quicker nor an alligator can chaw a puppy." Mike listened with interest, a poet of a sort composing a boast which he would utter in time in barrooms up and down the river. After the challenges came fights, fierce, uproarious, terrible.

"Generally," says a historian, "the boatmen expended their animal prowess among themselves, but they would occasionally break through the acknowledged boundaries of their own district [Natchez-under-the-hill], and carry the . . . city . . . by storm." Mike's crew and others swarmed up the bluff that night and took possession of the streets, mussing up the dandies of the city and cracking their rapier-canes, banging up the policemen and tying them to gate-posts, raiding orange shops and pelting scurrying people with the brightly colored fruit. They splintered mirrors in elegant barrooms and guzzled liquor free of charge. The keelers were cursed in three languages—English, Spanish and French—before they retreated down the winding road to the plateau.

There boatmen whooped, sang, and fought again. Meanwhile the prostitutes, the bartenders, the gamblers, carried on a thriving business until, when the morning sun tinged clouds with rose and purple, the keelers floated on drink-ballooned feet to their boat. Soon they were adrift on the current which was to bear them to New Orleans.

The tropical beauty of that city was heralded by foliage along the shore. The heavy fragrance of magnolias drifted over the river; scented flowers and vines with strange French names stirred with the breeze. Orange trees, billowy with fragrant flowers; bow-wood, decked with golden fruit against the green foliage, lined the banks.

Mike looked with wonder at the shore as they passed luxurious settlements, like Pointe Coupee, where piazza-ed, "elegant dwelling-houses" stood on lawns decorated with "ornamental trees." Negroes chanted plaintive songs as they worked together in the fields. At sunset one night, as the boat passed a charming plantation, Mike saw large herds of cattle feeding upon the banks of the river, and frolicsome negroes who had finished their work, some wrestling on the green grass, some fishing near shore, reflected in shining water, some swimming, some galloping upon their master's fine horses.

And at night, Mike heard two kinds of music. Sometimes the musical laughter of Southern belles, mingled with the delicate strains of old French music, floated through the candle-lit windows of great white mansions to the river. Other times, Mike heard the beating tom-toms and primitively weird songs of the negro quarters.

The downriver journey ended at New Orleans, where flatboats and keels tied up at the levee beside great sailing ships from the ocean. As far as eye could see, the margin was lined with flatboats, barges, keels—

loaded with ham, bacon, flour, corn, live stock, slaves, or "Old Monongahela Whiskey." The city's business was transacted by merchants on the squalid levee, which reeked with many odors, the most pleasant of which was the odor of tar. The merchants, some of them handsomely dressed, some of them in torn, soiled clothes, haggled among piles of cotton bales and produce. And here Mike caught his first glimpse of the handsome women of New Orleans, some of whom smilingly sold great baskets of luscious tropical fruits.

From the levee, Mike looked upon a city unlike any he had ever seen. "Some houses were adobe with half-cylindrical tiled roofs. Others were of brick covered with yellow stucco. Extraordinary wrought-iron work adorned the balconies, gates, and windows. Above the lesser buildings rose the Cabildo and the St. Louis Cathedral. Between them all ran unpaved streets, rough with the mounds of crayfish when the weather was dry, and covered by an inch or two of water by every passing thunder shower . . . New Orleans was pervaded with the leisurely atmosphere of a town on the edge of the tropics."

There were great crowds in the opulent markets, where strange fruits and vegetables and delicacies were sold by chattering merchants. There, too, one might see "Negresses and Quadroons, carrying on their heads and with solemn pace a whole table—or platform as large as a table—covered with cakes, and apples, and oranges, and figs, and bananas, and pineapples, and cocoanuts," chanting songs about their offerings.

The boatmen unloaded their cargo and took on an up-river cargo in the day-time and reveled at night. Now, in the evening, from the coffee houses to the levee strolled the immaculate silk-coated young gallants, to bow to the almond-eyed quadroons who, with chaperons, walked along the edge of the river. And the noisy keelers joined in frolics on the decks of the many vessels or invaded the tippling houses where "all colors, white, yellow, and black, mixed indiscriminately."

"There is," said one rueful visitor who was much shocked by what he saw in New Orleans, "in this city much female beauty; fine features, symmetry of form, and elegance of manners; but the virtuous man often perceives in these fatal testimony of moral aberration. Here the fascinations of accomplished dissipation move in the guise of delicacy, and captivate the youthful heart . . . Dissipation . . . is unlimited. Here men may be vicious without incurring the ill opinion of those around them—for all go one way . . . broad indeed is the road to ruin . . . Surrounded by the fascination of wealth, the blandishments of beauty, and the bewitching influences of music, they do not realize that they are losing the dignity of their nature, and preparing for themselves the most bitter self-reproach."

The keelers spent the night in the arms of the gold-shoed courtesans or rollicked in the dives—"in this corner a party staking their whole cash at a game of 'All-Fours'; here slaves, free people of color of both sexes, and sailors in jacket and trowsers hopping and capering to the sound of a fiddle; there a party roaring out some dirty song . . ."

And—"Many stabbings were reported, and shootings; many people falling into the river from flatboat or levee and drowning, while drunk . . ."

V

Then came the journey up the river, and the real work of the boatmen, the work which won for them the awed admiration of a generation of giants, began. The boat's crew was doubled in preparation for the long upstream battle. Mike learned why he had had to prove that he was strong before he was allowed to become a member of the crew. For none but giants could work a loaded keelboat through the strong currents of the Mississippi. There were three thousand pounds of cargo for each man on the vessel, and Mike, remembering the hazards of the river viewed on the trip with the current to New Orleans, may have groaned.

Every possible agency for moving the boat was used, the six oars which projected from the forward part of the cargo box, three on either side of the vessel; the square sail on the mast about a third of the length of the boat from the bow; the "cordelle" (rope) which was stretched from the mast to boatmen who struggled along the shore, their feet pressed against bowlders or trees; bushes along the shore, clenched and pulled by boatmen's fists; or when the water was shallow enough, the poles.

When the strong poles, each with a heavy socket, were used, the crew was divided equally on each side of the boat, standing on the foot-and-a-half running board which reached from stem to stern. The rivermen "set" their poles at the boat's head, then placed the sockets against their shoulders, pushing with all their might. Then "with their heads suspended nearly to the track of the running board," they walked painfully to the stern, hurrying forward, at the captain's command, when they had reached the end of the board, for a new set. Sometimes keelmen spent whole days thus laboriously shoving through currents.

"In ascending rapids, the greatest effort of the whole crew was required, so that only one at a time could 'shift' his pole. This ascending of rapids was attended with great danger, especially if the channel was rocky. The slightest error in pushing or steering the boat exposed her to be thrown across the current, and to be brought sideways in contact with rocks would mean her destruction. Or, if she escaped injury, a crew who had let their boat swing in the rapids would have lost caste. A boatman who could not boast that he had never swung or backed in a chute was regarded with contempt, and never trusted with the head pole, the place of honor among the keelboatmen."

Sometimes, above Natchez, where the going was roughest, many methods of shifting the boat along were used during two days. Starting in the morning, perhaps the men rowed to a point, keeping close ashore to avoid the eddy of waters around the bend. Then, the point reached, facing a heavy current, the keelmen had to slant their vessel across the river, heading into the current, fighting it, but nevertheless drifting some distance back down the river before reaching the other shore. Along this shore, the boatmen might "bushwhack"—drag the boat along by grasping overhanging bushes and trees and pulling. On the river side of the boat, the oars were used as an aid. And now they came to a sandbar, over which there was a swift current. The men took to their poles and began a struggling march along the running boards. Their bodies shook, their chests heaved, as they pressed every ounce of strength into the timbers; poles bent; the captain urged the men on, now coaxing, now swearing prodigiously. Then a pole snapped, and Mike had to do for a time the work of two, for wavering meant disaster. At last the boat floated into the calm water above the bar, and the bronzed keeler whose pole had broken spoke eloquently of his woes.

"I'll be fly-blowed before sun-down to a certingty," he said, "if that weren't harder nor climbing a peeled sapling heels upward. That there damn pole I used when I pushed a broadhorn up Salt River where the snags was so thick that a fish couldn't swim without rubbing his scales off."

Now the patroon of the boat considered how the boat might be moved along. The water was too deep for poles, too swift for oars, and there were no bushes to grasp. Therefore, the cordelle was called into use. The big rope "was stretched from the top of mast to the shore, with an auxiliary line to keep the boat from yawing, and was used to tow the boat through the troublous water.   This form of movement was both slow and arduous, with twenty or thirty men scrambling over the rocks and through the water to drag the boat. . . ."   When the sweating boatmen came to the mouth of a tributary stream, the men swam across, clinging to the line, or sometimes they carried the rope across in a yawl.   When progress was stopped by a bluff, the men had to "warp" or cross the river to the lower ground on the other side.

At last night came, and the men put ashore, swallowed their rations of whiskey, their suppers of "meat half burned and bread half baked," stretched themselves on the deck, and slept until morning.   The next day, perhaps, there was a good wind.   The sail was raised, and the boatmen rested while the keel skimmed over the water, covering as many miles as they had painfully traversed in two days and a half. That night there would be frolics ashore.

The next day, the wind died, and the men sweated and fumed, and sometimes sang, as they continued their painful march.

Thus the mighty men of the river fought upstream, stubbornly conquering, with crude devices, mighty natural forces.   When, several months—perhaps four— after leaving New Orleans, they reached Pittsburgh again, they unloaded a few bags of coffee, a few hogsheads of sugar.   For this the rowdies of the river had slaved, risked their lives.

"UP STREAM"

SUCCESSOR TO THE KEEL-BOAT

And now Mike Fink, back again in Pittsburgh after his journey down the river, was in his glory. Bronzed by the sun which had beat down on his naked body and which had been reflected upon him by the shiny river, dressed in the red shirt, blue jacket, the coarse butternut linsey-woolsey trousers and the tanned leather cap which proclaimed his trade, Mike swaggered down the street, a cock of the town, followed sometimes by envious boys, treated politely by citizens who did not want trouble.

He clambered to the tops of tavern tables and shouted the boast which he was composing, and occasionally he managed to find and to annihilate an opponent. He sang for appreciative audiences a song which he had learned in the long days of downriver drifting:

> There was a woman in our towdn,
>   In our towdn did dwell,
> She loved her husband dear-i-lee,
>   But another man twyste as wedl.
>
> Singing too, riloo, riloo, riloo,
>   Ri-too, riloo, rilay—ee,
> She loved her husband dear-i-lee,
>   But another man twyste as well.

The song had fourteen verses, and told an interesting story with a moral. He told tall tales about his adventures, some of them borrowed. He had attentive audiences wherever he went, and he was ready to be a keelboatman as long as he had enough strength.

CHAPTER THREE

HOW MIKE WAS A BOATMAN FOR MANY YEARS, WIN-
NING FAME UP AND DOWN THE RIVERS AS A JOKER
AND FIGHTER

I

Mike's first trip was followed by hundreds of trips up and down the rivers, journeys which carried him into the streams which cut into the Ohio and the Mississippi, voyages which took him out onto streams on which bobbing ice cakes were so thick that they had to be knocked aside before the boat might pass, streams dry with the drouth of summer, so meager that it was a task to find a channel deep enough for the boat. He rose in the world of boatmen—became a head poleman, a steersman, finally a patroon, having won eminence because of his courage, his wisdom in the ways of currents, his ability to command men. And meanwhile, he acquired the red feather which proclaimed him champion of the boat, and later he was recognized as the champion of the race of rivermen.

"From Pittsburgh to St. Louis, and New Orleans, his fame was established," testified a contemporary, the first to write of his exploits. "On the Ohio, he was known among his companions by the appellation of the 'Snapping Turtle'; and on the Mississippi, he was called 'The Snag.'" Says another writer, "Mike Fink

. . . was looked upon as the most fool-hardy and daring of his race.   I have heard Captain Jo Chunk tell
the story of some of his daring exploits.   'There ar'n't
a man,' said Captain Jo, 'from Pittsburgh to New Orleans, but what's heard of *Mike Fink;* and there ain't
a boatman on the river, to this day, but what he strives
to imitate him . . .   Mike was looked up to as a kind
of king among the boatmen, and he sailed a little the
prettiest craft that there was to be found about these
'ere parts.' "

Specific details concerning Mike's accomplishments
as a boatman are, however, remarkably scarce. A Captain John Fink, related to Mike, remembered that
Mike "generally had two boats" and that "in the man-
agement of his business Mike was a rigid disciplina-
rian; woe to the man who shirked," and we are told
(incorrectly, doubtless) that he was "the first boatman
who dared to navigate a broadhorn down the falls of
the Ohio."   And that is all.   One historian remarks
that Mike has "left the record, not that he could load a
keelboat in a certain length of time, or lift a barrel of
whiskey with one arm, or that no tumultuous current
had ever compelled him to back water," but that he
could lick any man on the river in any kind of a contest.

Perhaps pioneers did not bother to give specific information about Mike because the mere statement that
he was the greatest of the boatmen brought to their
minds vivid images of the great feats which he had to
perform to win his high place.   Pioneers knew how
great must be the strength of any man who coped with

the rivers and streams in the primitive boats of the day. They knew that with that strength was combined a technical skill with pole or boat-hook, a skill called instantly into play whenever, in boatman language, "hell was a-snortin'." They knew, too, as Mark Twain came to know during his resplendent days as a pilot, how miraculous was the riverman's knowledge of every sandbar, every curve, every island, in the long stretches of curving waters. He knew "Hog Hole" eddy, where "a drowned hog had floated for a coon's age," knew the intricacies of the passage around " 'Flour Island,' so called because wrecked vessels had sprinkled it white with flour, knew 'Sour Beer's Eddy' and 'Old Cow,' and the rest of the snags and bars and cross currents."

Pioneers knew, too, that the patroon of a keelboat, if he was to succeed with the rioting rascals who pushed poles, must know how to lead the obstreperous fellows. As a starter, he probably had to be able to out-fight them. In addition, he had, no doubt, to be able to out-drink them, to out-talk them, and to keep them in a working humor. Mike, a great bully among bullies, a prodigious drinker among men whose capacity was tremendous, and a rough-and-ready humorist preëminent in a band of roystering practical jokers, had fine qualities for leadership of the keelers.

He could even handle, it appears, the extraordinary keeler who was very different from his mates. Claudius Cadot, when an ancient gaffer reminiscing by the grocery stove in Portsmouth, Ohio, fifty years ago, proved the point by telling of his career as a keeler on

Mike's boat. He was in his twenties when he joined Mike's crew, shortly after the War of 1812, in which he had served. He went on the river to earn money, choosing to become a keeler simply because, in that day, about the only way to earn money was to push a pole.

He went to Mike, who was patroon of a boat owned by John Finch, operator of several keels running from Pittsburgh to all points along the Ohio, the Mississippi, and their navigable tributaries. Fink looked up and down Cadot's sturdy figure.

"Can you push?" he asked.

"I could try."

"Very good. I'll give you fifty cents a day—regular pay."

Cadot was a good keeler, and he remained with Mike's crew for four years. Unlike the other keelers, who prided themselves upon their ability to spend their money as fast as they earned it, he saved his wages. He turned over to Mike a great pile of silver, which was placed in Mike's trunk for safe-keeping.

"By God," said Mike, "since you've the greatest pile, you ought to keep the key!" And when Mike and the rest of the crew invaded a town for a spree, he patted honest Claudius on the head and told the lucky fellow that he was to have the honor of taking care of the boat and the trunk.

The contemporary of Claudius who took down his reminiscences completes the story thus: "Mike Fink was a very noted character in his day. He could scarcely be called a good man, although he had some good traits in his composition. He was one of the most wild and reckless rowdying men of his class. Yet he had respect for a man of different habits, and when a man like Claudius Cadot, whose sole aim was to do his duty and save his money [worked for him], Fink placed greater confidence in him and gave him greater privileges than the rest of his crew. When he paid him at the end of the year he gave him sixty-two and a half cents a day, when the bargain was for only fifty cents a day." And in the end, Cadot purchased a section of land with his savings, married, settled down, and became a respectable farmer.

Most of the pioneers' stories dealt, not with Mike's skill as a keeler, but with his practical jokes, his fights ashore, his skill with the rifle. These tales sometimes seem literally true, sometimes pass beyond the realm of probability. Always, however, they vividly reflect the life of the far-off period during which they originated.

Mike was famous as a joker, and most of his jokes were tinged with a lawlessness which the individualistic pioneers seemed to admire. "Every farmer on the shore," said a Cincinnati writer, "kept on good terms with Mike—otherwise, there was no safety for his property. Wherever he had an enemy, like his great prototype, Rob Roy, he levied the contribution of Black Mail for the use of his boat. Often at night, when his tired companions slept, he would take an excursion of five or six miles, and return before morning, rich in spoil."

To the keelboatmen, as one writer pointed out, "our merchants entrusted valuable cargoes, without insurance, and with no other guarantee than the receipt of the steersman ,who possessed no property but his boat; and the confidence so reposed was seldom abused." Mike, however, did not, it seems, always prove worthy of the trust of his employers, if his cargo was wine or brandy.

"A friend of mine," wrote a correspondent to *Cist's Cincinnati Miscellany*, in 1845, "one of the oldest and most respected commanders of steamboats to the Nashville trade, related to me . . . that, in 1819, he was employed to leave Pittsburgh, and go down the Ohio in hunt of Mike and his cargo, which had been detained by some unaccountable delay. At some distance above Wheeling he found the loiterer lying to, in company with another keel, apparently in no hurry to finish the trip.

"Mike did not greet our envoy in very pleasant style, but kept his fair weather side out . . . Mike was determined not to leave good quarters that night, and all went to bed wherever they could.

"In the night my friend was awakened by some noise or other, and before falling asleep again, he heard Mike say in a low voice, 'Well, boys, who's going to *still* to-night?'

"This question drew his attention . . . Watching for some time, he saw Mike take a tin bucket, that had apparently been fixed for the purpose, with a small pipe inserted in its bottom, about the size of a common gimblet. This was taken to a cask of wine or brandy, and a hole made in either end of the cask, the pipe put in, and then a couple of quarts of water turned into the bucket. Then the 'still' began to operate, as they drew from the head of the cask until the water in the bucket disappeared.

"Thus they obtained the liquor, and the cause of their long detention [was] ascertained. The very casks of wine that Mike drew from were returned to the merchant in Pittsburgh, more than a year afterwards, having soured."

One of Mike's tricks which obtained fresh meat and good liquor for his boat was frequently described to groups around campfires who roared as they heard of the keeler's shrewdness:

Drifting slowly downstream one day, Mike saw, dotting a green field near shore, a large flock of fine sheep. "Being in want of provisions, but scorning to buy them," Mike guided his boat to an eddy near to shore and tied her fast.

He went down into the dusk of the cargo box, rummaged around, and came on deck with a bladder of scotch snuff from which he took a handful of the finely ground tobacco. Ashore, capturing six of the sheep, he bent their faces into the snuff, rubbed thoroughly. Then he sent one of his men dashing up to the sheep-owner's house to tell him he had better hurry down to see what ailed his sheep.

Upon coming down hastily in answer to Mike's summons, the gentleman saw a portion of his flock very singularly affected; leaping, bleating, rubbing their noses against the ground and against each other, and performing all manner of undignified and unsheeplike antics. The gentleman was sorely puzzled and demanded of Mike if he knew what was the matter with the sheep.

Mike was gravely, portentously silent for a moment. "You don't know?" he asked somberly.

"I do not."

Mike leaned over and whispered: "Did you ever hear of the black murrain?"

Terrified, the sheep-owner managed to whisper, "Yes."

"Well," said Mike, "that's it! All the sheep up river's got it dreadful. Dyin' like rotten dogs—hundreds a day."

"My God! Is there no cure for it?"

"Only one as I knows on. You see the murrain's dreadful catchin', and ef you don't git them away as is got it, they'll kill the whole flock. Better shoot 'em right off; they've got to die anyway."

"But no one could single out the infected sheep and shoot them from among the flock."

Mike's eyes twinkled as he said impressively, "My name's Mike Fink." And he looked confidently into a group of white sheep, baa-ing, leaping, some of them packed together in a dense mass.

The man, impressed, begged Mike to shoot the afflicted sheep and toss them into the river. Mike pretended to be reluctant. "It mought be a mistake. They'll maybe get well. I don't like to shoot mannee's sheep on my own say-so. Mebbe you'd better go an' ask some neighbor ef it is the murrain sure 'nuf."

> The gentleman insisted, and Mike modestly resisted, until finally he was promised a couple of gallons of old peach brandy if he would comply. His scruples thus finally overcome, Mike shot the sheep, threw them into the eddy, and got the brandy. After dark, the men jumped into the water, hauled the sheep aboard, and by daylight had them neatly packed away and were gliding merrily down the stream.

The historian who recorded this tale commented, and told another:

> In all his little tricks, as Mike called them, he never displayed any very accurate respect to the laws either of propriety or property, but he was so ingenious in his predations that it is impossible not to laugh at his crimes. The stern rigor of Justice, however, did not feel disposed to laugh at Mike, but on the contrary offered a reward for his capture.
> For a long time Mike fought shy and could not be taken, until an old friend of his, who happened to be a constable, came to his boat when she was moored at Louisville and represented to Mike the poverty of his family; and, presuming on Mike's known kindness of disposition, urged him to allow himself to be taken, and so procure for his friend the promised reward. He showed Mike the many chances of escape from conviction, and withal plead so strongly that Mike's kind heart at last overcame him and he consented—*but upon one condition!*

"What's the condition?" asked the constable, wiping the tears from his eyes.

"I'm a boatman," said Mike, "and a boatman I'll be until the end of my days. Other mannees may feel at home with earth under their feet, but damned if I do. I can't stand up very good unless my boat's under me, and I feel a stranger unless my crew's around me. I'll go to the court house if you'll let me go on my yawl, with some of my crew!"

The constable wept again. "But Jefferson county court house is on the hill, seventy feet above the river. Oh, my poor family'll starve."

"There, there," Mike said, "don't carry on so. I don't care if the boat floats to the court house or not. Put the yawl on a wagon, and let some oxen pull her up. It's the feel of the boat that counts."

"Oh, Mr. Fink, will you go if I get a wagon and put the yawl on it?"

"I will."

"Wait right here; please do. I'll hustle."

The constable dashed away, procured a long-coupled wagon, and with oxen attached, it bumped down the hill at Third Street for Mike's yawl. The road, muddy and steep, slanted above the wagon, loaded with the yawl at last, when the officer went back to Mike.

"All right, mannees!" cried Mike. "Bring your poles along: we may strike a riffle."

The boatmen whooped as they boarded the strange vehicle. They stood with their poles poised as if on the running board of a keelboat.

"Gee!" yelled the little constable. Mike imitated the blast of a boathorn as the oxen tugged the wagon.

Laboriously they climbed halfway up the hill, when Mike suddenly gave a command.

"Set poles!" shouted Mike, and the end of each long pole was placed firmly in the deep mud.

"Back her!" roared Mike. The men heaved, the oxen slipped and stumbled backwards, and wagon, men, yawl and oxen did not halt until the bottom of the hill had been reached.

The worried officer trotted down the hill, his boots and trousers muddy. "What's the matter, Mr. Fink, aren't you going?"

"Well," said Mike, "I got to churning things around in my mind, and the farther we went the more snags I seen, so I thought maybe I'd better not take that chute."

"But you're safe, Mr. Fink. They'll do nothing to you. And my family, my family—"

"Oh, very well," said Mike. "If you're sure."

"Gee!" said the constable, and the oxen again began the ascent. They were nearly at the top of the hill, when Mike's voice rang out again:

"Set poles! Back her!"

And down the hill went the wagon, dragging the be-wildered oxen. And down the hill went the officer of the law, his clothes and his little face spattered with mud.

"What's the matter, Mr. Fink?"

"Constable, are you sure that there won't be any harm to me?"

"I'm sure, Mr. Fink. If I wasn't—"

"All right," growled Mike. "I wanted to be sure."

The weary oxen started the climb again, and this time reached the top. The courtroom was crowded with citizens eager to see the king of the boatmen. They heard the blast of a boatman's horn outside of the window, and Mike swaggered in beside the muddy little constable, who timorously marched with his hand lifted up on Mike's shoulder. There was the drone of lawyer's voices and the boom of Mike's voice as he answered questions.

"Case dismissed!" snapped the judge at last. "Lack of sufficient evidence."

"If it pleases your honor," said an oily voice, "there are three other indictments."

"To your posts!" Mike commanded. The crew sent officers and citizens sprawling as they made for the window. They climbed into the yawl.

"Set poles!" cried Mike to the boatmen. "Gee!" he shouted to the oxen, whacking them with his pole. The beasts trotted down the street. A posse dashed into the street, but the boatmen's poles brandished over their heads discouraged them.

Mike waved his red bandanna at the laughing faces crowding the courthouse windows.

"Had a pleasant time," Mike yelled. "We'll call again!"

The wagon jolted down to the tawny Ohio.

As strange as his ways with a court of justice were his ways with a woman. One night in November, 1820, Mike's keelboat joined a number of keels which

had tied up just below the broad mouth of the Mus-
kingum River. After making all fast, Mike, just under the bank, scraped together a heap of the dry brown
beach leaves which the winds of autumn were fluttering
to the ground. Curious boatmen gathered around.

"Building a house, Mike?"

"Out of chawing tobaccy?"

"Goin' to feed your keelboat?"

Mike made no reply; he continued his work until he
had heaped the leaves head high. Then he separated
the leaves, making them into an oval. Thoughtfully,
he spread his body in the hollow in the center, as if he
were interested in finding out whether or not the leaves
made a comfortable bed. Rising, he climbed aboard
the boat, found his rifle, ostentatiously primed it, and
then sternly shouted, "Peg!"

Dressed in homespun, a fine red kerchief about her
brown neck, her feet bare, a red-cheeked girl, who may
or may not have been Mike's wife, emerged from the
dusk of the cargo box. She followed the scowling
boatman, after a curt demand, to the structure of
leaves, anxiously trying to study his face.

"Damn you, get in there and lay down!" Mike commanded.

"Now, Mr. Fink" (she always called him "Mr."
when he was angry), "what have I done? I don't
know, I'm sure—"

"Shut up!" roared Mike. "You be as dumb as a
dead nigger in a mud-hole, and get in there and lay
down, or I'll shoot you." Mike swore a great oath,

and drew his rifle to his shoulder. Peg climbed into
the leafy pile, and Mike heaped crisp leaves over her.
Then he hurled a flour barrel crashing to the ground,
split a stave into slivers, lit some of them in the fire
in the earthbox on the boat, cracking for the evening
meal, growling threats that if Peg moved he would
shoot her. Now, with the blazing splinters in his
hands, he walked around the pile, stooping four times
to light the leaves. The wind fanned the flames, and
Peg moved uncomfortably.

"Lay still!" thundered Mike.

Peg remained as long as she could, then, screaming,
her clothing and her hair blazing, she ran to the shore,
leaped into the river. Bedraggled, pathetic, she stood
up, water streaming from her. Mike shifted his tobacco, sauntered to the shore.

"There," said Mike, "that'll larn you to be winkin'
at them fellers on the other boat."

Mike is said to have told, toward the end of his days,
a story about sufferings which he experienced and
which were as excruciating as those of Peg. "You may
talk of your scrimmages, tight places and sich like, and
subtract 'em all together in one almighty big 'un, and
they ain't no more to be compared to the one I war in
than a dead kitten to an old she b'ar," he said. "I've
fought all kinds o' varmints, from an Injun down to a
rattlesnake, and never was willin' to quit fust, but this
once, and 'twas with a bull.

"One hot day in August when I war nigh runnin' off
into pure ile, I decided to cool off by swimming in a

pool in a creek in Deacon Smith's meadow. Standing in the creek I was just hauling my red boat shirt over my head when I see the deacon's bull dashing at me. The varmint was a nasty one which had scared more people than all the parsons o' the settlement, and come mighty near killin' a few, and as he dashed up on the other side of the creek, he kicked soil behind him like he was digging one naked boatman's grave.

"I shouted, 'Come on, you bellerin' old heathen, and don't be standing there; for, as the old deacon says of the devil, ye're not comely to look on!'

"This kind o' reached his understandin', and made him more vicious, for he hoofed a little like, and made a drive. And as I don't like to stand in anybody's way, I gin him plenty of sea-room. So he kind o' passed by me and came out on t'other side, and 'bout faced for another charge. . . . I made up my mind the next time he went out it wouldn't be alone. So when he passed, I grappled his tail, and he pulled me out on the sile.

"The bull started to turn around; I pulled the other way. With fiery eyes the beast looked at me; then he started to paw and to bellow, kicking his hind feet high and handsome.

"But it warn't no use; he couldn't tech me, so he kind o' stopped to get wind for sumthing devilish . . . By this time I had made up my mind to stick to his tail as long as it stuck to his backbone. I didn't like to holler for help . . . 'cause it war agin my principle, and then the deacon was preachin' not far off, at his house.

I knew if they heard a noise, the hull congregation would come down; and as I warn't a married man and had a kind o' hankering arter a gal that war thar, I didn't feel as if I would like to be seed in that there predicament.

" 'Well, you old sarpint,' says I, 'do your cussedest.' Thereupon the dratted bull dragged me over briars and stumps in every part of the field, until he sweated and bled like a fat bear with a pack o' hounds at his heels. And my name ain't Mike Fink if the old critter's tail and I didn't blow out sometimes at a dead level with the varmint's back.

"At last the bull stopped by a stump and I snubbed the beast's tail around it. I sat down and thought, decided that maybe I had better shout after all. So I whooped for help, and soon the deacon's two dogs, who had a grudge agin me, ran out arter me.

" 'So,' says I, 'old brindle . . . I'll jest take a deck passage on that there back of yourn.' So I wasn't long gettin' astride of him, and if you'd been thar, you'd have sworn that thar warn't nothing human in that there mix. The sile flew . . . as the critter and I rolled around the field . . . one dog on one side and one on t'other, trying to clinch my feet.

"After what seemed to me 'bout an hour, the bull halted beneath a tree. I jumped up to a branch, and started climbing. I was nigh to the top of the tree, when I heard a vicious buzzing overhead. I looked up; a big hornet's nest war buzzin' above me. I felt the bull's back'd be more comfortable than the tree.

"So I jest drapped aboard him agin, and looked aloft to see what I'd gained in changing quarters; and, gentlemen, I'm a liar if thar warn't nigh a half a bushel of the stingin' varmints ready to pitch into me when the word 'go' was gi'n.

"Well, I reckon they got it, for all hands started for our company! Some of 'em hit the dogs—about a quart struck me, and the rest charged on old brindle.

"This time, the dogs led off fust, dead bent for the old deacon's, and as soon as old brindle and I could get under way, we followed. And as I war only a deck passinger, and had nothin' to do with steerin' the craft, I swore if I had we shouldn't have run that channel, anyhow!

"But, as I said before, the dogs took the lead—brindle and I next, and the hornets drekly after. The dogs yellin', brindle bellerin', and the hornets buzzin' and stingin'! I didn't say nothin', for it warn't no use.

"Well, we'd got about two hundred yards from the house, and the deacon hern us and come out. I saw him hold up his hand and turn white. I reckon he was prayin', then, for he didn't expect to be called for so soon, and it wasn't long, neither, before the whole congregation, men, women and children, come out, and all hands went to yellin'! None of 'em had the first notion that brindle and I belonged to this world. I just turned my head and passed the hull congregation. I see the run would be up soon, for brindle couldn't turn an inch from a fence that stood dead ahead.

"Well, we reached that fence, and I went ashore,

over the old critter's head, landing on t'other side, and lay thar stunned.

"And when the congregation got over the skeer started by seein' the parade of beasts, insects, an' me, arter hearing a sermon on hellfire, an' got up enough courage to investigate, they found that I had, for once, been worsted in a scrimmage. My courtship, for once, was sunk by a snag."

If a story dubiously accredited to Davy Crockett is true—and there are a few touches in the tale which make it seem a little tall—Mike was bested on at least one occasion by a woman, Mrs. Crockett.

"You've all on you," began Davy, "heerd of Mike Fink, the celebrated, an' self-created, an' never to be mated, Mississippi roarer, snag-lifter, an' flatboat skuller. Well, I knowed the critter all round, an' upside down; he war pretty fair amongst squaws, catfish, an' big niggers, but when it come to walkin' into wild cats, b'ars, or alligators, he couldn't hold a taller candle to my young son, Hardstone Crockett. I'll never forget the time he tried to scare my wife . . .

"You see, the critter had tried all sorts of ways to scare her, but he had no more effect on her than droppen feathers on a barn floor; so he at last bet me a dozen wild cats that he would appear to her, an' scare her teeth loose, an' her toe nails out of joint; so the varmint one night arter a big freshet took an' crept into an old alligator's skin, an' met Mrs. Crockett jist as she was takin' an evening's walk.

"He spread open the mouth of the critter, an' made

sich a holler howl that he nearly scared himself out of
the skin, but Mrs. Crockett didn't care any more for
that, nor the alligator's skin, than she would for a snuff
of lightnin', but when Mike got a leetle too close, and
put out his paws with the idea of an embrace, her in-
dignation rose a little bit higher than a Mississippi
flood, an' she threw a flash of eye-lightnin' upon him
that made it clear daylight for half an hour, but Mike,
thinkin' of the bet an' his fame for courage, still
wagged his tail an' walked out, when Mrs. Crockett
out with a little teeth pick, and with a single swing of
it sent the hull head and neck flyin' fifty feet off, the
blade jist shavin' the top of Mike's head, and then seeing what it war, she throwed down her teeth pick,
rolled up her sleeves, an' battered poor Fink so that he
fainted away in his alligator's skin, an' he war so all
scaren mad, when he comes to, that he swore he had
been chawed up, and swallered by an alligator."

Crockett's tall tale belongs with chaste narratives
of the sort men on the frontier told at night by wilderness fires. It represents a tendency to lift a hero of the
folk into the sunny realm of legend, where the hero, his
wife (Mrs. Crockett, for example), or his offspring per-
forms feats unfortunately beyond the skill of most
mere humans. In time, Mike, like the hero of the
Alamo, was presented with a lovely daughter possess-
ing supernatural strength and courage. She was named
Sal Fink, and she was, proclaimed the charming artistic
liar who outlined her story, indubitably "one of the

gals," "a Mississippi screamer."   On one occasion, "for she scorned the use of her side-arms," she killed a bear with her fists.

She fought a duel once with a thunderbolt, an' came off without a single scratch, while at the fust fire, she split the thunderbolt all to flinders, an' gave the pieces to Uncle Sam's artillerymen, to touch off their cannon with.   When a gal about six years old, she used to play see-saw on the Mississippi snags, and arter she war done she would snap 'em off, an' so cleared a large district of the river.   She used to ride down the river on an alligator's back, standen upright, an' dancing *Yankee Doodle*, and could leave all the steamers behind.   But the greatest feat she ever did, positively outdid anything that ever was did.

One day when she war out in the forest, making a collection o' wild cat skins for her family's winter beddin', she war captered in the most all-sneaken manner by about fifty Injuns, an' carried by 'em to Roast Flesh Hollow, whar the blood drinkin' wild varmints determined to skin her alive, sprinkle a leetle salt over her, an' devour her before her own eyes; so they took an' tied her to a tree, to keep till mornin' should bring the rest o' their ring-nosed sarpints to enjoy the fun.   Arter that, they lit a large fire in the Holler, turned the bottom o' thar feet towards the blaze, Injun fashion, and went to sleep to dream o' thar mornin's feast; well, after the critters got into a somniferous snore, Sal got into an all-lightnin' of a temper, and burst all the ropes about her like an apron-string!   She then found a pile o' ropes, too, and tied all the Injun's heels together all round the fire,—then fixin' a cord to the shins of every two couple, she, with a suddenachous jerk, that made the intire woods tremble, pulled the intire lot o' sleepin' red-skins into that ar great fire, fast together, an' then sloped like a panther out of her pen, in the midst o' the tallest yellin', howlin', scramblin' and singin', that war ever seen or heerd on, since the great burnin' o' Buffalo prairie.

Thus went one of the tales concerning Mike which seems slightly exaggerated. But even a story based upon an actual incident in Mike's life—the trimming of the negro's heel—is rather incredible. As one reads of this prank, he realizes that Fink lived in a day when attitudes and processes of thinking were vastly different from those of to-day. "Solitaire" (John S. Robb) told the story thus in a St. Louis newspaper, about a quarter of a century after Mike's death:

In the early days of St. Louis, before the roar of commerce or manufactures had drowned the free laugh and merry song of the jolly keel boatmen, those primitive navigators of the "Father of Waters" tied up their crafts beneath the bluff, which then, eighty feet in height, rose perpendicular from the water's edge in front of the city. On the top of the bluff then, as now, a number of doggeries [drinking places] held forth their temptations to the hardy navigator, and they were often the scene of the wildest kind of revelry.

At that time *Mike Fink*, the chief among keel boatmen, was trading to St. Louis, and he frequently *awoke* the inhabitants by his wild freaks and daredevil sprees. Mike was celebrated for the skill with which he used the rifle—then the constant companion of western men. It was his boast that he could "best shoot whar he'd a mind to with his Betsy," as he familiarly termed his "shooting iron," and his companions, for the pleasure of noting his skill, or exhibiting it to some stranger, would often put him to the severest kind of tests.

One day, while lying upon the deck of his boat below the St. Louis bluff, with two or three companions, the conversation turned upon Mike's last shot; and one of the party ventured the opinion that his skill was departing. . . . One of the party, at a distance of one hundred yards, had placed a tin cup between his knees, and Mike had, at that distance, bored the center of the cup.

"I'll swar I don't hold that cup agin for you, Mike," remarked the doubter, "for thur is the delicatest kind of a trimble comin' in your hand, and, some of these *yur* days, you'll miss the cup clear."

"Miss thunder!" shouted Mike; "why, you consarned corn-dodger mill, it war you that had the trimbles, and when I gin old Bets the wakin' tetch, you *squatted* es ef her bark war agoin' to bite you!"

"Oh, well," was the reply, "thar's mor'n one way of gettin' out of a skunk hole, and ef you kin pass the trimbles off on me, why, you kin *pass*, that's all; but I ain't goin' to trust you with a sight at my paddles agin at a hundred paces. . . ."

"Why, you scary varmint," answers Mike, bouncing to his feet and reaching for "Betsy," which stood by the cabin door of the boat, "jest pint out a musketeer, at a hundred yards, and I'll nip off his right hinder end claw, at the second jint, afore he kin hum *Oh, don't!*"

"Hit a musketeer, ha, ha! . . . Why, you couldn't hit the hinder part of that nigger's heel up thar on the bluff, 'thout damagin' the bone, and that ain't no shot to crow about."

The negro referred to was seated at the very edge of the bluff, astride of a flour barrel, and one foot hung over the edge. The distance was over a hundred yards, but Mike instantly raised his rifle, with the remark: "I'll jest trim that feller's heel so he kin wear a decent boot!" and off went "Betsy."

The negro jumped from his seat, and uttered a yell of pain, as if, indeed, his whole heel had been trimmed off, and Mike stood a moment with his rifle, listening to the negro's voice, as if endeavoring to define from the sound whether he was really seriously hurt. At last the boatman who had been doubting Mike's present skill remarked:

"You kin *leave*, now, Mike, fur that darky's master will be arter you with a short stick;" and then he further added as a taunt—"I knowed Betsy was feelin' for that nigger's bones jest by the way you held her!"

Mike now became a little wrathy, and appeared inclined to use *his* bones upon the tormentor, but some of the others advised him to hold on—that he would have a chance to exercise them upon the constable. In a short time an officer appeared with a warrant, but as soon as Mike looked at him he gave up the thought of either flight or resistance, and quietly remarked to his companions that the officer was a clever fellow, and "a small *hoss* in a fight."

"The only way you kin work him is to fool him," says Mike, "and he's a weazel in that bisness hisself!"

The warrant was produced by the officer and read to the offender, who signified his assent to the demand for his body, and told the representative of the law to lead the way. He did so, and when about to step off the boat he cast his eye back, supposing that Mike was following him, yet a little suspicious. The movement was a prudent one, for he discovered the tail of Mike's hunting shirt at the very moment the owner was retreating into the small cabin at the rear of the boat, which was immediately locked on the inside! All the boatmen, as if by previous concert, began to leave their craft, each bearing away upon his shoulder any loose implement lying about, with which an entrance into the cabin could be forced. The officer paused a moment, and then went to the cabin door, which he commenced persuading the offender to open, and save him the trouble of forcing it. He received no answer, but heard a horrible rustling within. At length getting out of patience, he remarked aloud:

"Well, if you won't open the door I can burn you out!"

and he commenced striking fire with a pocket tinder box. The door immediately flew open, and there stood a boatman in Mike's dress; but it *wasn't Mike!*

"You aint arter me, are you, hoss?" inquired the boatman.

The officer, without reply, stepped inside of the small cabin and looked around. There appeared to be no place to hide a figure as large as Mike, and there was a fellow dressed just like him. The thought immediately came uppermost in the officer's mind, that the offender had changed coats outside, while his back was turned to go off the boat, and one of the parties that had walked off was Mike in disguise! He was about to step out when a moccasin-covered heel, sticking out of a hole in a large mattress, attracted his attention, and when he touched it the heel vanished. He put his hand in to feel, and Mike burst out in a hoarse laugh!

"Quit your ticklin'!" shouted he. "Consarn your cunnin' pictur', I'll *gin in* 'thout a struggle."

The other boatmen now joined in the laugh, as he helped the officer to pull Mike out of his hiding place. He had changed his garments *inside* the cabin instead of outside. A crowd of the boatmen also gathered around, and they all adjourned to the bluff, where, after taking drinks, they started in a body for the magistrate's office, who, by the way, was one of the early French settlers.

"Ah, ha!" he exclaimed, as the party entered the door; "here is ze men of ze boat, raisin' ze *diable* once more time. I shall not know what to do wiz him, by gar. Vat is de mattair now?"

"Why, Squire," broke in Mike, "I've jest come up with the Colonel to collect a small bill offen you!"

"You shall collect ze bill from *me?*" inquired the Justice. "What for you do the city good to de amount of von bill? Ah, ha! you kick up your *heel* and raise de batter and de salt of de whole town wiz your noise so much as we nevair get some sleep in de night!"

All eagerly gathered around to hear what Mike would reply, for his having a bill against the justice was news to the crowd.

"You jest hit the pint, Squire," said Mike, "when you said that thar word *heel!* I want you to pay me fur trimmin' the heel of one of your town niggers! I've jest altered his breed, and arter this his posterity kin warr the neatest kind of a boot!"

The boatmen burst into a yell of laughter, and the magistrate into a corresponding state of wrath. He sputtered French and English with such rapidity that it was impossible to understand either.

"Leave ze court, you raskelle of ze boat!" shouted the Squire above the noise. "*Allez vous-en, vous* rogues, I shall nevair ave nosing to do wiz you. You ave treat ze court wiz *grand contempt.*"

The boatmen, all but Mike, had returned to the outside of the door, where they were still laughing, when Mike again, with a sober and solemn phiz, remarked to the Squire:

"Well, old dad, ef you allays raise h-ll in this way fur a little laffin' that's done in your court, I'll be cussed ef I gin you any more of my cases!"

Another roar from the boatmen hailed this remark.

"Constable, clear ze court, in *une* instant, right avay! *Les sacre* diables of ze river, no know nosing about how to treat wiz de law. I shall ave nosing to do wiz de whole what you call pile of ze rogues!"

"I ain't agoin' to stand any more sich law as this," remarked Mike. "Consarn my pictur' ef I don't leave the town!"

"Go to ze devil!" shouted the magistrate.

"I won't," says Mike; "mabbe he's anuther French Jestis!"

Amid a torrent of words and laughter Mike retreated to his boat, where he paid the officer for his trouble, and sent a handful of silver to the darky to extract the pain from his shortened heel.

"Here," the modern reader is likely to say, "is a story which cannot be true; its central incident obviously must be false." Yet when the St. Louis *Missouri Republican*, in July, 1823, printed the first news-story of Mike's death, it identified him as "the same who, sometime since, in this place shot off a negro's heel to enable him, as he said, to *wear a genteel* boot.' "

These were some of the tales of Mike and his pranks which spread his fame up and down the rivers which he plied as a boatman.

II

Mike was famous, not only as a practical joker, but also—as has been suggested—as a fighter. Whooping, crowing, slapping his hard thighs with palms which popped like rifles, the red-shirted king of the keelboatmen, stimulated by liquor (and he could drink, we are firmly told, a gallon of whiskey in twenty-four hours without staggering), would climb upon a tavern bench and bellow his boast:

"I'm a Salt River roarer! I'm a ring-tailed squealer! I'm a reg'lar screamer from the ol' Massassip'! WHOOP! I'm the very infant that refused his milk before its eyes were open, and called out for a bottle of old Rye! I love the women an' I'm chockful o' fight! I'm half

wild horse and half cock-eyed alligator and the rest o'
me is crooked snags an' red-hot snappin' turkle. I can
hit like fourth-proof lightnin' an' every lick I make in
the woods lets in an acre o' sunshine. I can out-run,
out-jump, out-shoot, out-brag, out-drink, an' out-fight,
rough-an'-tumble, no holts barred, ary man on both
sides the river from Pittsburgh to New Orleans an'
back ag'in to St. Louiee. Come on, you flatters, you
bargers, you milk-white mechanics, an' see how tough I
am to chaw! I ain't had a fight for two days an' I'm
spilein' for exercise. Cock-a-doodle-doo!"

Then another boatman, eager to wrest Mike's glory
from him, would reply with a roaring answer to the
challenge. And perhaps he would behave and talk as
did a character described by the inimitable Mark
Twain in a scene in *Life on the Mississippi* meant to
"illustrate keelboat talk and manners":

"The man [answering the challenge] . . . tilted
his old slouch hat down over his right eye; then he bent
stooping forward, with his back sagged and his south
end sticking out far, and his fists a-shoving out and
drawing in in front of him, and so went around in a
little circle about three times, swelling himself up and
breathing hard. Then he straightened, and jumped
and cracked his heels three times before he lit again
. . . and began to shout like this:

" 'Whoo-oop! bow your neck and spread, for the
kingdom of sorrow's a-coming! Hold me down to the
earth, for I feel my powers a-working! whoo-oop!
I'm a child of sin, *don't* let me get a start! Smoked

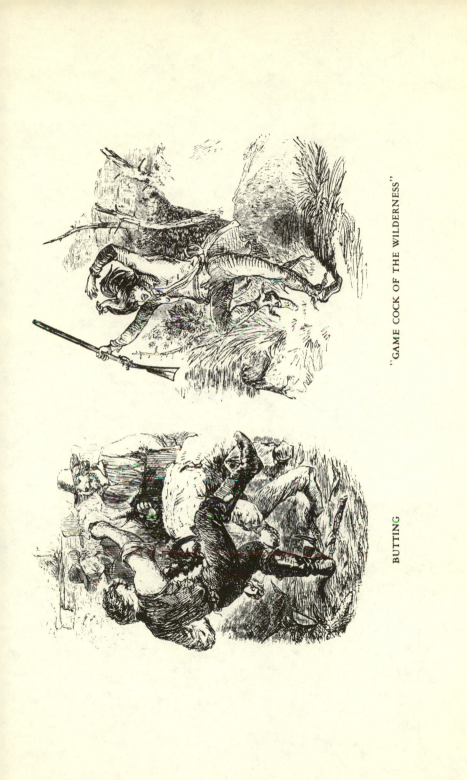

"GAME COCK OF THE WILDERNESS"

BUTTING

glass, here, for all! Don't attempt to look at me with the naked eye, gentlemen! When I'm playful I use the meridians of longitude and parallels of latitude for a seine, and drag the Atlantic Ocean for whales! I scratch my head with lightning and purr myself to sleep with the thunder . . . when I'm thirsty I reach up and suck a cloud dry like a sponge; when I range the earth hungry, famine follows in my tracks! Whoo-oop! Bow your neck and spread! . . . I'm the man with a petrified heart and biler-iron bowels! The massacre of isolated communities is the pastime of my idle moments, the destruction of nationalities the serious business of my life! . . .' He jumped up and cracked his heels together three times before he lit . . . and as he came down he shouted out: 'Whoo-oop! bow your neck and spread, for the Pet Child of Calamity's a-coming!' "

Then the Snapping Turtle sprang at the Pet Child of Calamity, while shouting spectators ringed the barroom floor. There were kicks, cuffs, roars of pain as a relentless finger gouged an eye, curses, heavy breathings, bear-like hugs, sometimes snapping bones, thudding blows. And at last the King of the Keelboatmen, disheveled but erect of head, strode to the bar and ordered a shifter of Race Horse whiskey, while the Pet Child of Calamity, bleeding, unconscious, was carried away.

Stories of the fights in river towns of that day are almost incredible. One may read an account by a Methodist clergyman of a company of a hundred road-

makers who, in sheer fun, divided into two teams and
pummeled one another with burning logs from a campfire until, says the reverend gentleman, "some were
severely wounded, blood began to flow freely, and they
were in a fair way of commencing a fight in earnest"—
when the captain told them to retire, and they all lay
down and went peacefully to sleep. One may read,
with amazement, also, an account of a fight which
shows vividly the methods of battling with which
Mike, in order to win the championship of the rivers,
had to cope. The fight took place in Wheeling in
1806.

"The quarrel was confined to a Virginian by birth,
and a Kentuckian by adoption. A ring was formed,
and the mob demanded whether they proposed to *fight
fair*, or to *rough and tumble*. The latter mode was
preferred . . . Bulk and bone were in favor of the
Kentuckian; science and craft in that of the Virginian . . .

"Very few rounds had taken place, or fatal blows
[had been] given, before the Virginian contracted his
whole form, drew up his arms to his face, with his
hands closed in a concave, by the fingers being bent to
the full extension of the flexors; and summoning up all
his energy for one act of desperation, pitched himself
into the bosom of his opponent. Before the effects of
this could be ascertained, the sky was rent by the shouts
of the multitude; and I could learn that the Virginian
had expressed as much *beauty* and *skill* in his retraction
and bound, as if he had been bred in a menagerie, and

practiced action and attitude among panthers and wolves. The shock received by the Kentuckian, and the want of breath, brought him instantly to the ground.

"The Virginian never lost his hold, like those bats of the South who never quit the subject on which they fasten till they taste blood, he kept his knees on his enemy's body; fixing his claws in his hair, and his thumbs on his eyes, gave them an instantaneous start from their sockets. The sufferer roared aloud . . . The citizens again shouted with joy. Doubts were no longer entertained; and bets of three to one were offered on the Virginian.

"The Kentuckian not being able to disentangle his adversary from his face adopted a new mode of warfare; and, in imitation of the serpent which crushes such creatures to death as it proposes for its food, he extended his arms around the Virginian and hugged him into closer contact with his huge body.

"The latter disliking this, cast loose the hair and convex eyes of his adversary, when both, folded together like bears in an embrace, rolled several turns over each other. The acclamation increased, and bets run that the Kentuckian 'would give out,' that is, after being mutilated and deprived of his eyes, ears, and nose, he would cry out for mercy and aid.

"The public were not precisely right. Some demon interposed for the biggest monster; he got his enemy under him, and in an instant snapt off his nose so close to his face that no manner of projection remained.

"The little Virginian made one further effort, and fastening on the under lip of his mutilator tore it over the chin.

"The Kentuckian at length *gave out*, on which the people carried off the victor, and he preferring a triumph to a doctor, who came to cicatrize his face, suffered himself to be chaired round the ground as the champion of the times, and the first *rough and tumbler*. The poor wretch whose eyes were started from their spheres, and whose lip refused its office, returned to town to hide his impotence, and get his countenance repaired."

In similar rough and tumble fights from which contestants seldom emerged without being mutilated, Mike won his reputation. Almost without exception, in scores of contests, he must have made good his boast; he went through life apparently without suffering a gouged eye, a torn ear, or an abbreviated nose, and that proved he was a champion. One old-time flat-boatman recalls that Mike introduced himself to strangers by licking them. Further evidence of his prowess—of a rather unfortunate kind—is the fact that the only extensive accounts of fights in which he engaged are those which tell how opponents, unusually strong or crafty, defeated him, as a rule by using some unusual trick. One gathers that Mike's victories were so usual that it was hardly worth while, except in a general way, to mention them.

The man who defeated Fink was likely to be remembered by his descendants, the story of his triumph handed down for generations. The late William E. Connolley, Secretary of the Kansas State Historical Society, remembered one such story. "In some of my manuscript writings," he said, "I have an account of a fight between three Big Sandy backwoodsmen who had taken some produce to Louisville in canoes, for sale. Mike Fink and his crew came along and attacked these . . . pioneers who lived in what is now Johnson county, Kentucky. They were powerful men and they completely defeated Mike Fink and all his keelboatmen. One . . . was Henderson Milum, who was six feet, six, and supposed to be the strongest man in the Big Sandy Valley in his day. I knew his descendants very well. Another man was a man named Hanna who had killed a bear on the Big Sandy River without weapons . . . on a bet. Another . . . was Peter Mankins, who lived many years on the . . . River but finally moved to Washington county, Arkansas, where he died at the age of 111 years . . . I know the descendants of Peter Mankins very well . . . This fight was on a wharf boat."

And as one remembers that the smallest crew a keelboat carried included at least eight men, one is inclined to suspect that the tale did not suffer in the telling.

Another tale, apparently circulated orally for years —for it did not find its way into print until 1895— told how Mike was quieted at the hands—or rather the feet—of the sheriff of the tiny town of Westport opposite Louisville on the Ohio:

Mike was telling jokes one day in the grocery (grog shop), and all of the drinkers laughed heartily, uproariously, at his yarns—all save one man, a little dried up fellow, whose pensive face suggested that he was contemplating death and eternity. Mike at last walked over to him.

"See here, Mister," he said, "these yarns I been tellin' is funny, and you stand there as glum as a dead catfish on a sandbar. I tell snorters for folk to laugh at in a good humored way, an' by God, I don't let no man make light of 'em."

"Is that so?" the little man asked, negligently, and he sank back into his gloomy contemplations.

Mike, at the bar, told another yarn, and the company dutifully howled. But the little man, sternly watched by Mike, looked positively tearful. Mike stamped across the floor.

"Whoop!" yelled Mike, "Calamity's a-comin'! I'm a Salt River roarer, an' I'm chockful o' fight. I'm—"

But in the middle of his boast, Mike was surprised. For the wizened mourner suddenly leaped into the air and as his body swooped downward, his fist smacked Mike below the ear, and the keeler fell sprawling.

"Is that so?" said his opponent, and he lay down as if to rest.

Mike staggered to his feet, blood in his eye, roaring with anger. But as he came forward, the little man doubled into a tangle of flaying feet and clawing fists.

Mike went into a whirl of flying arms and legs, and emerged with a scratched face and a sinking in his stomach where a swift kick had landed. Angrier than ever, he flopped on the man again, and again, against the torrent of claws and leaping boots, he was able to do nothing. Four times more he tried in vain to seize or to strike his rival, and each time Mike looked more as if calamity and desolation had struck him.

"Stranger," panted Mike at last, "I'm free to own I can't do nothin' with you. You're tougher to chaw nor buckskin."

"Is that so?" dreamily asked the visitor. "Listen to me. I'm Ned Taylor, sheriff of this county; and if you and your crew don't get the hell out of here in ten minutes I'll arrest the mess of ye!"

"Five's enough," said Mike, according to the tale. "You're a snag, a riffle, and a sawyer all in one."

And the people who handed down the tale maintain that the sheriff said, "Is that so?" and resumed his gloomy contemplation.

III

Several tales tell how Mike was defeated by a foeman worthier than the kicking sheriff—a mighty figure who won fame on the frontier as a circuit rider and as a political opponent of Abraham Lincoln—Peter Cartwright. This preacher was a child of the frontier who had gone with his family over the Wilderness Trail to Kentucky in 1790, when he was five. A circuit rider at eighteen, he went riding for years through forests and valleys, fighting through blizzards, thunderstorms and swollen streams, to preach homely sermons elaborating the text, "Behold the Lamb of God, that taketh away the sin of the world."

That was his text, but Cartwright did not look or act particularly like a lamb. Nearly six feet tall, he had a huge chest and arms and legs which bulged beneath his ministerial clothing. His head was crowned with shaggy coal black hair. Beneath his thick brows dark eyes gleamed from a swarthy, craggy face. A great joker, Cartwright, but when rowdies from the river or from the river towns came to disturb his meetings, he knocked their heads together, or dragged them away by the scruff of the neck.

One story says that when Cartwright was running for the Illinois legislature, Mike Fink, who was operating a ferry across the Sangamon River, became so angered by his political attitudes that he vowed he would drown him at sight. When Cartwright boarded Mike's ferryboat, Mike started arguing with him. Cartwright threw his horse's reins over the stake on the side of the boat.

"Lay down your pole, Mike," he said, squaring off.

Mike whooped and ran towards him. The two exchanged blows. Then Cartwright took hold with his mighty hands of the nape of Mike's neck and the slack of his breeches, and whirled him into the Sangamon. When Mike rose to the surface, Cartwright held him under the water until he at last promised "to repeat the Lord's prayer morning and night, to put every Methodist parson across the ferry free of expense, and to hear every one that preached within five miles."

Cartwright made Fink pray on another occasion, still another tale, told by a minister, reveals:

At the camp meeting held at Alton in the autumn of 1833, the worshipers were annoyed by a set of desperadoes from St. Louis, under the control of Mike Fink, a notorious bully, the triumphant hero of countless fights, in none of which he had ever met an equal, or even second. The coarse, drunken ruffians carried it with a high hand, outraged the men and insulted the women, so as to threaten the dissolution of all pious exercises; and yet, such was the terror the name of their leader, Fink, inspired, that no one individual could be found brave enough to face his prowess.

At last, one day, when Mr. Cartwright ascended the pulpit to hold forth, the desperadoes, on the outskirts of the encampment, raised a yell so deafening as to drown utterly every other sound. Mr. Cartwright's dark eyes shot lightning. He deposited his Bible, drew off his coat, and remarked aloud:

"Wait for a few minutes, my brethren, while I go and make the devil pray."

He then proceeded with a smile on his lips to the foes of the tumult, and addressed the chief bully:

"Mr. Fink, I have come to make you pray."

The desperado rubbed back the tangled festoons of his blood-red hair, arched his huge brows with a comical expression, and replied:

"By golly, I'd like to see you do it, old snorter."

"Very well," said Mr. Cartwright. "Will these gentlemen, your courteous friends, agree not to show foul play?"

"In course they will. They're rale grit, and won't do

nothin' but the clear thing, so they won't," rejoined Fink, indignantly.

"Are you ready?" asked Mr. Cartwright.

"Ready as a race-hoss with a light rider," answered Fink, squaring his ponderous person for the combat.

But the bully spoke too soon; for scarcely had the words left his lips when Mr. Cartwright made a prodigious bound toward his antagonist, and accompanied it with a quick, shooting punch of his herculean fist, which fell, crashing the other's chin, and hurried him to the earth like lead. Then even his intoxicated comrades, filled with involuntary admiration at the feat, gave a cheer. But Fink was up in a moment, and rushed upon his enemy, exclaiming:

"That wasn't done fair, so it warn't."

He aimed a ferocious stroke, which Mr. Cartwright parried with his left hand, and, grasping his throat with the right, crushed him down as if he had been an infant. Fink struggled, squirmed, and writhed in the dust; but all to no purpose; for the strong, muscular fingers held his windpipe, as in the jaws of an iron vise. When he began to turn purple in the face, and ceased to resist, Mr. Cartwright slackened his hold, and inquired:

"Will you pray, now?"

"I doesn't know a word how," gasped Fink.

"Repeat after me," commanded Mr. Cartwright.

"Well, if I must, I must," answered Fink, "because you're the devil himself."

The preacher then said over the Lord's prayer line by line, and the conquered bully responded in the same way, when the victor permitted him to rise. At the consummation the rowdies roared three boisterous cheers. Fink shook Mr. Cartwright's hand, declaring:

"By golly, you're some beans in a bar-fight. I'd rather set to with an old 'he' bar in dog-days. You can pass this 'ere crowd of nose-smashers, blast your pictur'!"

Afterwards Fink's party behaved with extreme decorum, and Mr. Cartwright resumed his Bible and pulpit.

Both of these are excellent stories which should not be rejected merely because one wonders how Mike's black hair happened to be "blood red" in the second story, for example, or because one considers the dates of the happenings they record. The election of Cartwright to the legislature took place in 1828, and the camp-meeting at which the boatman was humiliated is said to have taken place in 1833, and it may seem strange that Mike could have fought in those years, since he died in 1822 or 1823. And looking into Cartwright's autobiography, the student of the boatman's story finds Cartwright saying:

Somewhere about this time, in 1829-30, the celebrated camp-meeting took place in Sangamon County and Circuit; and, as I suppose, out of incidents that then occurred was concocted that wonderful story about my fight with Mike Fink, which has no foundation in fact.

"But," says Peter's biographer, "Peter himself admits that in order to quell Mike's violent verbal attacks upon himself when he first ran for the State Legislature, he threatened to baptize him in the name of the devil." It seems that it was a little late for that—in 1828—but why bother about mere dates?

But in cynical moments when one discovers inaccurate statements of this kind made by ministers of the gospel, one wonders how many other stories about victories over the king of the boatmen originated on the basis of an incorrect rumor which circulated after Mike's fame had lifted him into a realm of legendary splendor.

These were good tales, and there was at least one other story which also was a good one, whether true or not. The opponent who bested Mike in this tale is a folk hero in his own right, remembered for the great hardness of his skull and celebrated in several tall tales —the tough St. Louis flatboatman, Jack Pierce. This story of a defeat suffered by Mike was told in a book more or less appropriately called *Legends of the Missouri and Mississippi*, published by a physician in London in the seventies. This "legend" is somewhat suspect of having absorbed some of its flavor from Sunday School stories, for, though famous as a drinker and fighter—conqueror of the giant New Orleans boatman, Negro Jim—its hero, Jack, like many a character in Sabbath School fiction, loved his sick old mother so well that he promised her he would stop drinking and fighting. Then, in search of a crew which would help navigate a boat loaded with wheat down to New Orleans, he went into a groggery.

There he found his companions gathered around a man who "was a heap of flesh and blood, nerve and muscle, so firm, hard, and coarse in his general make-up that he looked of the consistence of iron. He had the reputation of being the strongest man that boated on the Mississippi, except Jack Pierce, and between the two, who was the strongest and best fighter, opinion was equally divided." Mike's gray eyes glared ominously at Jack as the two were introduced, for the keeler had heard of the flatboatman's smashing defeat of the New Orleans negro, and he was spoiling for a chance to hammer him with his fists.

"Come here, Jack," yelled a boatman. "Have a drink with Mike Fink. He's been in St. Louis often, but you never was here. There ain't a better man than Mike ever stood in a boat on the Massassip'."

Jack walked over to Mike, held out his hand in token of friendship, and Mike brought all of his strength to bear as he gripped the hand of Pierce, "but the bones and sinews were unyielding." Then Pierce returned the grip, using all his power, "and though the countenance of Mike Fink changed not, he felt a pain from the grasp that he never felt before, and it increased the prejudice . . . the hate for the man whose deeds were already eclipsing the fame which he had won in many a hard-contested fight."

Invited to drink, Jack chose—the narrator fails to indicate why—to forget one promise temporarily in order that he might keep the other; he touched glasses, peacefully enough, with Fink. But Fink was bound to start a fight. He turned the conversation to the topic of Negro Jim.

"By God," he said, "with fair play Nigger Jim could whop any man between St. Louis and New Orleans—excepting Mike Fink."

Mike emphasized the words "fair play." Jack, much to the surprise of his friends, kept his peace.

"Hell's bells and pickled panther tails!" shouted

Mike. "I can throw down any man that boats on the Ohio or the Massassip'!" He looked significantly at Pierce, walked over toward him, put his hand roughly on Pierce's shoulder. "Jack Pierce," he said, "you're a strapping young fellow. Have you got pluck enough to wrestle with the Snag?"

"The blood of Jack Pierce boiled in his veins at this second insult and the fire of battle was in his eye when" —says the moral narrator, approvingly—"when he recollected his promise to his mother. In an instant he calmed his fury, rose to his feet, and, throwing off a sort of round jacket worn by people of his class at that day, said, "I'll try you, Mike Fink." His promise, it appears, had not included wrestling matches.

The crowd went out into the sunny September air, up to the part of St. Louis, later occupied by the jail and the courthouse but then not built upon, the Hill. Encircled by spectators, the boatmen stripped to the waist, mighty browned men—Mike "broader across the shoulders, his muscles . . . firm and knotted as a gnarled oak," Pierce, more youthful and quicker, mighty in comparison with most men, but a stripling compared with Fink.

They stood an instant with arms locked, their feet wide apart, pushing one another, slightly twisting from side to side. Sweat stood out on the straining bodies. Pierce swooped down at Fink's right leg and Fink, not moving his feet, put his hands on the flatboatman's shoulder and shoved him away. Mike seized Pierce's wrist, tugging at it; Pierce twisted from him. The two

men threw aside pretenses of science, came abruptly together, each encircling the waist of the other, both
scowling. And Pierce tried to lift Fink from the
ground with an effort which made the blue veins stand
out on his temples, pulsing. Mike, roaring with laughter, stood as solid as a rock. Then Fink tugged upward on his opponent's body, his muscles bulging under the sheen of his bronzed skin. Suddenly Pierce's
feet left the turf and he sailed upward, and the crowd,
foreseeing a fall when Pierce was hurled to the earth,
shouted. But with lightning speed, the flatboatman
twisted a foot behind Mike's knee. Fink crashed to the
ground, Pierce, arms locked around the Snag's neck,
upon him.

It was the first time Mike had been thrown, and his
gray eyes were fiery as he rose to his feet.

"Hell and damn!" roared the Snag. "Now, you
flatter, you've got to fight! There's no cheating in
fightin' rough-and-tumble. The best man takes the
day, each one doing his best in his own way."

But Jack Pierce was putting on his clothes. "I
won't fight you, Mike Fink," he said. "If you want to
know why, I tell you I promised the old woman, my
mother, to be quiet for some time, and I want to keep
my promise."

"By God, I'll make you," shouted Mike. And he
walked towards Pierce, his hands clenched, his head
thrown forward.

"I'll fight you some other day, Mike Fink, but not
now," said Pierce. "Don't strike."

The spectators, crowded around Mike, held him in spite of his struggles. "Wait, Mike!" they urged, and, "Another time. He's promised to fight you another time. That's all you can ask. He ain't ready now."

Mike sneered at Jack's back. "Ask your old woman to give you leave. I'll whip her baby so bad that he won't leave her side again."

At home, Jack learned, by accident, a trick which was later to help him win his strange triumph over Fink:

> He had scarcely arrived at the cabin of his mother when he found one of the neighbors relating to her an accident that had occurred to a young man that morning from an attack made upon him by a vicious ram as he was crossing the common, and the owner of the ram, having heard of it, came to the cabin, at that moment to solicit Jack Pierce's assistance to capture the vicious animal. They went to the common, and on approaching the ram, the animal, by his movements, showed that he was ready to give battle.
>
> "Fight him his own way, Jack," said one of his companions, laughing; "your head is as hard as his horns."
>
> "I'll do it," replied Jack Pierce, feeling in one of his daredevil moods, and immediately approached the ram, which, giving an angry bleat, made towards him.
>
> To the astonishment of his companions, who thought he had been jesting, Jack Pierce dropped on all fours, and stooping his head to avoid the direct blow of the ram, raised it just in time to strike him under the lower jaw; and so sudden was the shock that the animal's neck was broken.
>
> This novel feat in twenty-four hours became the topic of conversation of the whole village, and such was the curi-

osity to witness a similar one, that quite a sum of money was made up to induce Jack Pierce to give battle to another ram. The feat came off in the presence of a large multitude of persons, Jack Pierce breaking the neck of the ram as he did in the battle with the first.

Time passed. Mike went down the river to New Orleans, remembering with anger his defeat, eager to return and erase the memory by annihilating Jack in a rough-and-tumble fight. And Jack, records the narrator, sorrowfully shaking his head, "found it impossible to resist the temptations by which he was surrounded. Though he was successful in many instances, in some unguarded moments he would yield to them, and becoming discouraged in his efforts at reformation, he no more tried to avert the moral ruin into which he was fast approaching." He went to the drinking shops, where, as a historian suggests, the beverages had names so enchanting that it was hard to resist their appeal—"Moral Suasion," "Vox Populi," "Shambro," "Pig and Whistle," "Poor Man's Punco," "Split Ticket," "Virginia Fence," "Deacon," "Ching Ching." And again he caroused. But there was still that fine Sunday School story touch in his make-up. "He strove to keep continually employed, so that his mother should have every comfort during her helplessness. His happiest moments were when he laid the money he had received from his wages upon her pillow, and whatever might have been his frailties, no unkind word or look added to the sufferings of his parent."

Mike, having brought his boat up to St. Louis,

walked into a saloon through the smoke-filled air to
Pierce, sitting by a table. Loudly he slapped Pierce's
face with the back of his hand, and loudly he shouted:

"How's mamma's baby now?"

Jack stood up, his cheek red, flung his chair clatter-
ing to the floor, retreated a few steps, taking off his
coat. "I'm in for a big fight," was all he said. And he
walked toward Mike who, crouched, awaited him.

The barkeeper bustled from behind the bar, and
pushed both combatants toward the door. "Go out of
the house," he said. The crowd, the barkeeper among
them, piled out behind them into the street, and the
two boatmen cautiously sparred in the road dust.

Mike came in crouching, his arms rigid. Then a
blow, swinging from the ground, thudded against
Jack's shoulder. Jack hooked a short blow between
Mike's eyes, but Mike came on. Pierce's fist cut
Mike's eye, and blood trickled from the keeler's face,
but Mike kept marching toward him. He seized Jack
with mighty arms, braced, heaved him to the ground.
He chuckled as he flung himself on the flatter. His
fingers sought an eye and started gouging, his knee he
tried to plant on Jack's chest. But Jack placed his
arms behind him, writhed, pushed, staggered to his feet.
A solid blow to the face rocked the flatter. Another
blow followed, and Mike's hand curved around Jack's
cheek, the thumb gouging an eye. Jack turned his
head, his mouth open, and his sharp teeth bit into the
flesh of Mike's forefinger. He lifted his hands to
clutch Mike's throat. Mike's face was harrowed with

pain as he tugged his finger from Jack's mouth, bleeding; Jack spat out flesh and blood. The keeler closed in, lifting Jack with a convulsive effort, and again flung him sprawling. But as the Snag came, panting, to kneel by his opponent's side to fetter his arms, Pierce's fist flew into Mike's face, and both rose together.

By this time "it was evident that the brute strength of Mike Fink was superior to that of Jack Pierce, and he was gradually getting his opponent more and more at his mercy." The flatter was staggering; the crowd was urging Mike to throw him again.

"Again the combatants closed, and again Jack Pierce would have been thrown, but he thought of turning the hardness of his head to some account, overmatched as he was in the combat. With both hands he caught Mike by the ears, and brought his forehead against Mike's three times in quick succession, the blows sounding like a maul upon timber. The knees of Mike Fink trembled, his head drooped, his hands relinquished their hold, and when his adversary released his grasp he fell senseless upon the ground, sputtering white froth and blood . . . He, however, did not die. He recovered, but Jack Pierce had gained the victory."

Not long after, the celebrator of Pierce records, the flatter had his brains knocked out by a ram when, engaged in his most spectacular pastime, the man lifted his head an instant too soon. And again, Mike Fink was the king of the boatmen, for hard-headed Pierce had been the only man on the rivers who could beat him.

CHAPTER FOUR

HOW MIKE PERFORMED MARVELOUS FEATS OF MARKS-
MANSHIP AND HUNTING

I

Mike and his men had just negotiated the Falls of the Ohio, and they lounged about the boat, which had been moored to a tree on the shore, panting and resting. Fink had had several stiff drinks of raw whiskey, but he was still thirsty.

"Whew!" said Mike. "That pull makes a feller's whistle as dry as a mud creek in a drought, and I could stand about a quart of whiskey for to dampen my smolderin' innards. Who wants to bet me the whiskey on sixty paces?"

"I'll do it!" cried a tall, lanky keeler. "Jest to see you shoot, Mike, for it actually does a feller good to see that thar rifle o' yourn come up to your peepers, and then get solid like, and blaze away. Come ashore, mannies: Mike's going to shoot the cup." The crew stood up and moved shoreward.

"Where's Carpenter?" roared Mike.

"Here, sir!" yelled a youngster of fourteen, as he came from the cargo box.

"Is your skull fit to butt a nigger's to-day, son?" asked Mike.

"I'm afraid it's not so thick as all that," said the

126

boy, "but if you want to shoot the cup, I reckon it's bullet-proof."

"That's the talk, my bully boy! Hurry ashore now, for I'm as dry as a salt herring."

On shore, the man who had made the wager with Fink was taking sixty paces across the grass. He was a tall man, and the paces were long, but Mike, coming up with his long rifle resting on the bend of his left arm, made no complaint.

"Just moor there where Jabe Knuckles wants you, sonny," he said, "and stand a whiskey cup on top of your hair for to pertect you from the sun."

The boy walked to the spot, poised a tin cup on his head, looked calmly at Mike, and said:

"Blaze away, and take care you don't elevate her too low, or you'll have to pay, you know."

"True as gospel," said Mike, "an' it sure would hurt me to have to part with good liquor."

As he spoke, he threw back his right foot, took a firm stance, and slowly raised his rifle to his eye. There was a moment of heavy silence. All of the men looked steadily at the cup gleaming on the boy's head. They started as the rifle cracked. The cup bounded to the grass twenty feet behind Carpenter.

The audience shouted:

"Well shot!"

"That's an easy way to get a drink!"

"Mike gets the whiskey, Jabe!"

And Jabe said: "I guess I'll have to pay you, Mike. But damn me if I ain't ornery enough to keep on bettin' with you on that shot.   Some day maybe you'll lose a quart to me."

But Mike was busy swallowing whiskey, and he did not answer . . .

.   .   .   .

Of all the tales about Mike which impressed the pioneers who told them, the tales of "shooting the cup" obviously were the favorites.   Details varied.   Sometimes Mike shot at thirty paces, sometimes at sixty, sometimes at a hundred.   Sometimes he shot on a bet with a fellow boatman, sometimes he shot for a reward in the form of liquor.   At times, too, shooting the cup was a ritual.   After a session of drinking, Mike and a companion would stagger out of a tavern at dawn, determined to demonstrate their affection.

"By God, Andy," Mike would say, his arm around his companion's shoulder, "we're friends for life, and I'd like to pledge by shootin' the cup with you."

"Shoot as many cups as you like—sheven, forty-'leven, a hunnerd.   Glad to shoot cups wish ole Mike Fink."

"Here's a puck—a cup.   Fill it full whiskey—good old whiskey.   Put it on your head.   I won't spill it. Stand there."

Andy tried to stand still, but his head swung around, and the whiskey splashed on the grass.   "Sorry," he said, "the cup's crooked.   Here; I'll pour in s'more whiskey, an' hold it anyhow.   I'll hold the handle with my finger.   Now shoot."

FEAT OF MIKE FINK

"Carpenter and Mike used to fill a tin-cup with whiskey and place it by turns on each other's head and shoot at it, with a rifle, at the distance of seventy yards. It was always bored through without injury to the one on whose head it was placed."

Mike had weaved his way through thirty paces. He turned and faced Andy, and lifted his rifle slowly. A few seconds passed as he drew a bead on the unsteady cup. Then the rifle banged, and Andy lifted the cup from his head.

"Never spilt a drop!" he said. "Now you stand for me!"

Mike stood steady, a cup poised on top of his head. Andy straightened, and the traces of drunkenness faded from him as he took aim. Then a bullet crossed the top of the liquor, splashing out a few drops.

The two met, cups in hand, lifted the vessels, clanked them.

"Friends forever!" said Mike.

"Damn' right!" said Andy.

They drank.

Such was the ceremony with which Mike pledged his friendships, a ritual which combined the bravado with the skill of the frontier. The feat caught the fancy of Mike's contemporaries, and as tales of shooting the cup and other yarns demonstrating his skill were told during the years when Mike was boating and the decades after his death, he became famous not only as a jokester and fighter but also as a marksman and hunter. Hence, even though Mike's skill has heretofore had frequent mention in this book, a more detailed consideration of his feats now seems necessary.

To win fame in these fields, the keeler had to win over competitors worthy of his rivalry. With the rifles of the day, awkward, heavy, unwieldy weapons judged by modern standards—though the peer of any of modern make in accuracy—the men of Mike's time could perform feats which, performed by men with modern rifles, would be sensational. Loading a gun was an art which required exactness and even genius. And sheer muscle was needed to aim the long-barreled rifles at a mark.

As the story of Mike's first shooting-match hints, great skill with the rifle was far from unusual. From a point forty paces away, Mike and his contemporaries shot at the head of a nail driven into a target. A marksman who missed the nail head was considered an indifferent shot; it was better to bend the nail; but a good shot would hit the nail squarely. A frontiersman could hit a wild bird on the wing with a rifle shot, or could snuff a candle, without extinguishing the flame, at fifty yards on a dark night. Daniel Boone and others of his and Mike's day could, at fifty yards, "bark" squirrels—knock the animals off branches by clipping the bark from beneath their feet.

Mike was intensely proud of his Kentucky rifle, Bang-all, as he humorously called it. His well-worn old .45 caliber flint-lock was his faithful companion, provider and protector for well over twenty-five years. Rifles were not strange to Mike: he knew a good one the moment he clapped eyes on it; indeed he had himself known many of the old gunmakers and had watched them boring those long barrels in their mountain-home gunshops. In his years on the Ohio Mike had actually handled hundreds of flint-locks and knew by that sixth sense of an expert rifleman their many little peculiarities of action. Each was different, the product of some pioneer American gunsmith's genius; and each had its "fussy" peculiar individuality. But of all the rifles that Mike had handled and shot, old Bang-all suited him best. It was "slicker'n a wildcat and quicker in action," he claimed, and handled like a "willow sapling in spring." The barrel length and the drop at the heel just suited his stumpy shoulders, while its hair-trigger action particularly pleased Mike's snapping-turtle temperament.

But Mike's rifle even exceeded his own fanciful effusions: it was one of the finest products of the old Lancaster gunmakers in Eastern Pennsylvania and had been made to Mike's order. Mike himself had selected the tree that produced the beautiful full curly maple stock; and Mike sat on an old stump swapping tall tales while the gunsmith forged the crude iron bar into the long octagon barrel. With its heel on the ground leaning against Mike, Bang-all measured 58 inches, its tip almost touching Mike's coonskin cap. The stock was plain but what it lacked in scroll-work it made up in a dazzling display of 47 brass and silver inlays. On the cheek-plate was Mike's lucky six-point star inlaid in brass; and on both sides of the stock were etched figures of Indians in silver, crescents, diamonds, dogs, deer, hearts, the American Eagle and many other such figures. But this ornateness did not hamper Mike's marksmanship—these were his lucky signs—for with old Bang-all in good working order Mike could pile one lead ball on top of another at fifty yards or spill a cup of whiskey off his comrade's head.

Frontiersmen for many years told stories about Mike's skill with Bang-all.

II

One spring Mike's boat was moving up the Mississippi above the mouth of the Ohio, its sails rounded by a breeze which made it dart up the brown stream. Mike, looking over to the green shore slanting from a settler's cabin, shouted joyously and seized his gun.

"Pork!" he yelled. "My mouth's been waterin' for fresh ham for months. And damned if there ain't some of the finest fat pork I ever see! I want a pig!"

"Don't shoot, Mike," said a keeler. "Them pigs belong to your old friend, Riffles Dixon. That's his place."

Mike sighed. "Riffles did me a favor once in Natchez," he said, "and I'll cheat my stomach out of gratitude for it. But it is a shame."

"Hell, Mike," the keeler said, "you couldn't kill any on 'em anyhow. They're a good fifty yards away, and this here boat's dancin' like a nigger at Christmas."

"Hell and damn," said Mike. "I'll show you."

He raised his rifle to his shoulder, pulled the trigger. On shore, a pig squealed and ran. Its tail had been chopped off close to its rump.

"And that," said Mike, "wan't no accident."

To prove it, standing on the deck of the dancing

boat as it sped upstream, he fired eight more shots, and each time the gun spat, a bewildered pig lost its curly tail.

"Pretty good," said a keeler.

"Just a de-tail," said Mike.

Another time, Mike met the famous Davy Crockett in a strange shooting match. Here is the story told of the match by Davy Crockett, as printed in *The Crockett Almanac for 1840:*

"I expect, stranger," said Davy, "you think old Davy Crockett war never beat at the long rifle; but he war, though. I expect that there's no man so strong what he will find some one stronger.

"If you haven't heerd tell of one Mike Fink, I'll tell you something about him, for he war a helliferocious fellow, and made an almighty fine shot. Mike was a boatman on the Mississip', but he had a little cabin on the head of Cumberland, and a horrid handsome wife, that loved him the wickedest that ever you see.

"Mike only worked enough to find his wife in rags, and himself in powder and lead and whiskey, and the rest of the time he spent in knocking over b'ar and turkeys, and bouncing deer, and sometimes drawing a lead on an Injun. So one night I fell in with him in the woods, where him and his wife shook down a blanket for me in his wigwam.

"In the morning says Mike to me, 'I've got the handsomest wife, and the fastest horse, and the sharpest shooting iron in all Kentuck, and if any man dare doubt it, I'll be in his hair quicker than hell could scorch a feather.'

"This put my dander up, and sez I, 'I've nothing to say agin your wife, Mike, for it can't be denied she's a shocking handsome woman, and Mrs. Crockett's in Tennessee, and I've got no horses. Mike, I don't exactly like to tell you you lie about what you say about your rifle, but I'm damned if you speak the truth, and I'll prove it. Do you see that are cat sitting on the top rail of your potato patch, about a hundred fifty yards off? If she hears agin, I'll be shot if it shan't be without ears!"

"So I blazed away, and I'll bet you a horse, the ball cut off both the old tom cat's ears close to his head, and shaved the hair clean off the skull, as slick as if 'd done it with a razor, and the critter never stirred, nor knew he'd lost his ears till he tried to scratch 'em.

" 'Talk about your rifle after that, Mike!' sez I.

" 'Do you see that are sow off furder than the end of the world,' sez Mike, 'with a litter of pigs around her?' And he lets fly.

"The old sow gave a grunt, but never stirred in her tracks, and Mike falls to loading and firing for dear life, till he hadn't left one of them are pigs enough tail to make a toothpick on.

" 'Now,' sez he, 'Colonel Crockett, I'll be pretticu-larly obleedged to you if you'll put them are pigs' tails on again,' sez he.

" 'That's onpossible, Mike,' sez I, 'but you've left one of 'em about an inch to steer by, and if that had

COL. CROCKETT, BEAT AT A SHOOTING MATCH

a-been my work, I wouldn't have done it so wasteful. I'll mend your host.' And so I lets fly, and cuts off the apology he's left the poor cretur for decency. I wish I may drink the whole Mississip', without a drop of the rale stuff in it, if you wouldn't have thort the tail had been drove in with a hammer.

"That made Mike kinder sorter wrothy, and he sends a ball after his wife as she was going to the spring after a gourd full of water, and knocked half her comb out of her head, without stirring a hair, and calls out to her to stop for me to take a blizzard at what was left on it. The angeliferous critter stood still as a scare-crow in a cornfield, for she'd got used to Mike's tricks by long practice.

" 'No, no, Mike,' sez I. 'Davy Crockett's hand would be sure to shake, if his iron war pointed within a hundred mile of a shemale, and I give up beat, Mike. And as we've had our eye-openers a-ready, we'll now take flem-cutter, by way of an antiformatic, and then we'll disperse.' "

Mike's marksmanship won triumphs for him in more orthodox shooting-matches in Pittsburgh in his youth and later when he visited river towns where matches were in progress. And on journeys up and down the river, when boatmen went ashore or popped at birds or animals from the boat, his rifle brought down game for the boatmen. He became famous in legend as a hunter, celebrated in the Crockett almanacs not only for his prowess with a rifle but also for his victories without a gun.

One day, fishing in a yawl on the Mississippi, says one tale, Mike was attacked by a monster wolf. "A most terrible struggle ensued, and in a most dangerous place for the brave Fink. But our indomitable hero was not to be daunted by anything that threatened him —and he wrestled and tugged with his sturdy antagonist, till the beast foamed at the mouth, and howled —as if more under the efforts of pain than rage. Fink next contrived to secure the forepaws of the wolf within the powerful gripe of his two hands—and by a quick and most herculean effort, he flung him from the side of the boat into the water. The animal slipped from his gripe only to come at him with renewed fury. Fink kicked and pelted him with the oar; but still he managed to bound back at him, as if determined to overcome his intended prey, or die in the effort. At last, Fink, taking advantage of his approach at him, seized his forepaws again, and pressing them upon his head, plunged him back into the torrent, and held him fast there, till he was completely drowned."

Another time, Mike killed a wolf in a fashion even more spectacular:

During the life of Mike Fink, the great roarer of the Mississippi, large and ferocious wolves were the terror of those regions to both the natives and the settlers: and although the government offered high rewards for their extirpation, yet few persons were found with sufficient daring and courage to go far in their pursuit, or even venture in the vicinity of their known haunts. One of these monsters, belonging to a pack, had become a particular terror—and this one the celebrated Mike Fink determined to seek out, and, as he said, "spiflicate him hull."

But it happened that Mike fell in with the object of his adventure when he did not expect him; for, being out one morning strolling, for an appetite, he suddenly encountered the identical-monster wolf in a spot well known ever since as "Wolf's Den," and the furious beast, being urged by hunger, sprang upon the defenseless intruder with a howl and a bound that made the spot fairly groan.

The daring Fink received his antagonist with nothing but his huge fists. At almost every blow, the animal was disengaged, and thrown upon his haunches. Finally, the wolf succeeded in getting Fink down upon the earth, where the struggle, if possible, became more desperate—while the hideous howls of the beast would have terrified any human being out of all consciousness but the indomitable Fink.

Just as the wolf, with distended tongue and jaws, was making a death bite at him, Mike gave one terrible blow under the pit of the stomach, which rolled him over harmless and defeated.

Another tale recounts a thrilling adventure with a moose. "The celebrated Mike Fink, the great admiral of flat-boatmen on the Western river, the William Tell of marksmen on land, and the most daring of all wild-forest adventurers, was the Prince of moose-catchers," began the narrator of this yarn. Then, for the edification of his Eastern and English readers, he made a short excursion into natural history: "A moose, reader," he explained, "is a very large species of deer, with a body like a fat horse, without the tail, and a head something like that of a jackass, to which is appended a large pair of horns, weighing sometimes as much as ninety pounds. They are higher than an ordinary horse, and sometimes weigh more."

"A mammoth specimen of one of these brutes" had long escaped skilled shots and hunters, partly because he was fierce and quick, dashing from a hiding place at a hunter and crushing him before he could shoot, partly because of his ability to get away from pursuers by fording the swiftest streams.

Fink, trailing this giant, had wandered far from his companions as night fell. His friends, alarmed, built hunters' signal fires along the edge of a ravine by which they had hunted, shouted his name, but heard no answers to their cries. Below them lay the black ravine, its rocks and trees touched here and there by the light of the fire, and below these rushed waters which sparkled as they passed below the flames, then moved into the darkness.

Suddenly, above the roar of the torrent, there rose a human cry, accompanied by a tremendous snorting. The men looked below, and saw Fink clinging to the horns of the huge moose, which was beating through the waters towards an island. The animal was jerking his head, trying to shake off the unwelcome burden.

The animal struggled ashore, and Mike faced him, aware that his gun—which, miraculously, he had carried with him—and his pistols were wet and useless. The watchers saw Mike swing his rifle, saw the butt descend on the animal's head. Twice he struck, and the second time the weapon was splintered as it battered against the heavy horns. The moose staggered forward for another attack. Fink dodged, fell upon his knees. Then he turned quickly, and the blade of his knife flashed and came away from the animal's throat, dripping blood. Again the knife darted. The moose fell to the ground, and Mike stood above it . . .

III

The tales of Mike's adventures as a marksman and hunter included still another, more elaborate than the rest, a story told in print by T. B. Thorpe, whose "The Big Bear of Arkansas" was a classic among hunting yarns. "The Disgraced Scalp Lock" was the title of Thorpe's tale, and it recounted a strange adventure with an Indian.

Mike for once (thus the tale began) had been persuaded to take a flatboat down the Ohio and the Mississippi to New Orleans. "A keelboatman lowers himself when he runs a flatboat," he had said. "I wouldn't do it nohow—except for the money." So he carelessly lolled by the sweep that guided the boat as it moved along with the currents of the Ohio. He looked sternly at the numerous signs of civilization along the banks.

A boatman clapped him on the shoulder. "God Almighty, Mike," he said, "you look sour as a merchant that's lost a cargo when prices is high. What the hell's the matter?"

Scowling, Mike waved a hand towards the shore. "I knew these parts, Jabe," he said, "afore a squatter's ax had blazed a tree. 'Twasn't then pulling a God damned sweep to get a living, but pulling the trigger done the business. Those was the good old days; a man might call himself lucky to live in those days. But now—" He squirted tobacco juice contemptuously, and did not bother to finish the sentence.

"Hell, Mike, look at the improvements! Houses, mills, towns, scattered all along the river!"

"Improvements! What's the use of improvements? When did cutting down trees make deer more plenty? Whoever cotched a b'ar by building a log cabin, or twenty on 'em? Whoever found wild buffalo or a brave Injun in a city? Where's the fun, the frolickin', the fightin'? Gone, gone! The rifle won't make a man a livin' now. He has to turn hisself into a nigger and work." He looked indignant, and settled his muscular body to a more restful position.

"Forests goin' up in smoke all the time, just to let folks raise hogs." He pointed an accusing finger at a lonely farm, where a few pigs were visible. "I may yet die of smotheration—smothered by a settlement! To hell with improvements!" He spat again. "This life won't do. I'll stick to the broadhorn accordin' to contrac', but once done with it, I'm off for a frolic. If the Choctaws or Cherokee or the Massassip' don't give us a brush as we pass along, I'll grow as poor as a strawed wolf in a pit-fall. Six months an' no rumpus would spile me worse nor a dead horse on a prairie."

Mike ended, for the boat was drifting up to the landing below Louisville. He called out: "Stand by to moor the boat!" He stood carefully watching the currents, turning the broadhorn toward the shore, while the men bustled about making preparations to tie her. A crowd on shore watched the approaching vessel.

Among the throng that crowded around the boat on its arrival were several renegade Indians, dirty loiterers in the town, cast out by their tribe for committing some crime or getting drunk too often. They lived by hunting a little and stealing as much as possible, spending most of their money on firewater. Mike's eyes were attracted by the bedraggled warriors.

"Injuns!" he cried. "I've jest finished wishin' for a tribe or two of redskins, so's I could devastate somebody."

He gave a terrific war-whoop, wrapped a piece of canvas, blanket-like, around his shoulders, and strode towards the ragged braves, pausing now and then to do a few steps of an Indian dance. He halted before the knot of redskins, swooped down with a gesture that resembled a curtsey, and then began a mock oration:

"Me Snappin' Turkle, chief of the keelboatmen! Ugh! Ugh! Whoop! Me push damned boat up river many moons, push any damned boat up any damned river, any number of moons, or suns either. My tribe catch Injuns, feed 'em to cat-fish. Maybe make cat-fish sick. Braves too fat, no can drink firewater, no can run, jump, fight, kiss 'em like heap big Chief Snappin' Turkle! And," said Mike, eyeing the Indians eagerly, "if ary moth-eaten redskin doubts that, I'll be in his hair quicker'n hell can scorch a feather."

The braves were disdainful. "Ary two redskins!" said Mike, still hopeful. But the Indians were silent. "Ary tribe o' redskins! Oh, hell!" Mike remarked, for the braves still were haughtily silent.

Mike's hand slapped the seat of a warrior's buckskin trousers. "Ow!" wailed the brave. Mike bumped another Indian with his shoulder, and the man sprawled on the ground, murder in his eyes. Mike's companions and some of the crowd joined him, bumping the Indians, tripping them, pulling off their blankets, hooting and jeering at them. At last the Indians ran from the landing, while the whites shouted insults.

One, however, refused to run. His head back, his proud face as calm as if he were walking in the forest, he started to stalk away. Mike noticed that he had a carefully ornamented scalp lock, noticed, too, the pride of his bearing.

"Well," said Mike, "look at this one! Who's this little feller?"

"That's Proud Joe," a bystander told him.

"An' why does he wear this har on his head?" said Mike, as he took hold with one hand and pointed with the other.

"He's keepin' it so some day his tribe kin scalp him."

"It's right handsome," said Mike, and benevolently he tugged out a hawk's feather and a few hairs. Proud Joe glared horribly at the boatman, snatched the feather from his hand, shook a fist in the air, and then retreated after his friends.

"Well, Mike," chuckled Jabe, "it looks as if you riled Proud Joe a leetle."

"So it does," said Mike. "Injuns is all-fired proud o' their top-knots, an' even that flea-bit varmint ain't lost all his pride."

"Maybe he'll want to get even, Mike."

"I'm afeared not, Jabe. But I'll fix it up, by God. I'll chop off that scalp lock close to his head the first chance I get. Meanwhile, I could do with a drink or two. Come on!"

The following morning, the crew of the flatboat made preparations to move on down the river. Mike had taken his position at the sweep, and the journey was about to start when Jabe shouted to Mike:

"There's your old friends, Mike! Maybe you'll have time to scalp Proud Joe now."

Fink looked up and beheld at some distance Joe and his companions making hostile gestures in his direction. "I wonder," said the keeler, "if maybe they've come to think better about fightin' me." But as he spoke, all of the aborigines except Proud Joe disappeared.

Joe looked sternly down at Mike, and then up and down the river. As the boatman turned his head up to view the Indian, he noticed that the head and the shoulders of the redskin were boldly outlined against the sky. Joe turned toward the river, and the keeler saw his profile, the scalp lock and its adornments more strongly outlined than ever.

The boatman reached for his rifle, drew a bead on Proud Joe, and pulled the trigger. The rifle ball whistled through the air; Joe leaped, then fell to the ground.

About fifty people at the landing, many of them on other boats, started to shout. There was a great hubbub as their voices were lifted in protests and accusations.

"Cold-blooded murder; that's what it was!"

"Damned dirty boatmen, always raisin' hell."

"He ought to swing for that!"

"Let's get him."

Mike merely said, "Well, I'll be damned!" He reloaded quickly, then, as a number of men rushed towards the boat, he flung his coat off, took his powder horn in his teeth, and jumped, rifle in hand, into the river. From the boat, the crowd saw him swimming for the opposite shore.

"To the skiff!" shouted some one, and several men piled into the only skiff at hand. They pulled swiftly after the swimmer, who turned around now and then to look at them. When they were about a hundred yards away, Mike, treading water, raised his rifle.

"Stop!" yelled one of the men in the skiff. "For God's sake, stop!"

"Hell, he couldn't hit us. He's in the water, and it's a hundred yards."

"That's Mike Fink, you fool!"

"Mike Fink!" he raised his voice. "Don't shoot! We'll go back."

Mike waved a hand towards Louisville, then turned

and continued his swim across the river. His pursuers rowed back to the landing.

The firing of Mike's rifle, the pursuit, and the return of the hasty pursuers all took place in a few minutes. On the bank stood the crowd, now gaping with astonishment at Joe. For Joe was staggering to his feet, dazed and bewildered. In a moment more, he had fully recovered his senses; he was standing upright, looking down at his scalp lock, which lay at his feet. The ball had cut it from his head; the cord around the root of it in which were placed feathers and other ornaments had held it together. Joe had been stunned merely by the concussion; he had escaped bodily harm.

Members of the crowd babbled their admiration for Mike's shot. He never missed, they said; he had done the job clean as a whistle; he was the best shot on the river, and this shot had proved it. Others jeered at the Indian.

But Proud Joe paid little attention. His face was stern, he breathed deeply, as he looked towards the sky, raised his arms. He spoke a few words in his own language, and the crowd, for a moment, impressed by the rapt appearance of this ragged savage, listened. They watched him in silence as he strode away.

"What did he say, Bill?"

"He said that he vowed by the Great Spirit of his forefathers he'd be revenged."

"The hell he did! Well, he'll need plenty o' help to get Mike Fink!"

The crowd broke up, still chattering about the keeler's marksmanship. The boat which Mike had deserted was got under way, and dashing through the rapids of the Ohio, it wended its way downstream. Soon the river carried the men into unsettled country. The waters were high with the floods of spring, and the clear sunlight teased out a thousand shades of green in the new leaves and buds. Mallards skimmed above the river, unafraid of man; noisy spoonbills splashed in shallow waters near the shore, and myriads of wild birds were singing in the forests. Occasionally the man saw a bear stepping along the shore as if dainty of its feet and, snuffing the intruders, retreating rapidly into the woods. For a day and a half the boat moved through country which seemed deserted.

"The Snappin' Turkle would like this," said one of the crew. "No improvements here."

"Yes," said Jabe Knuckles, who had taken Mike's post as steersman, "an' that smoke over there looks to me like an Injun sign. He'd like that, too, though I don't go for it."

He pointed to a thin column of smoke struggling upwards through the river mists along shore. The fire from which it rose apparently had been built upon a projecting point of land near which the main current twisted.

"A darn good place," the first speaker remarked. "Our broadhorn has to go right close to it, an' redskins hid in bushes might be tolerable dangerous."

"Get your shootin' irons ready, men," said Jabe, "an' get out o' sight! There's Injuns on that point!"

BEAR HUNT

The boat swept around the point as the men, scrambling for hiding places, loaded their rifles. The men's eyes eagerly scanned the shore. Then the flatters laughed. "Chief Snappin' Turkle!" said Jabe.

There on the grassy point, near the water, lay Mike, sonorously asleep, his feet toasting at the fire, his pillow a huge bear. There were several deer and wild turkeys scattered around him. It was obvious that Mike had selected a place on the bank from which he could hail the boat, and that while waiting he had spent his time hunting.

Mike's companions shouted hilariously. At the sound, Mike leaped to his feet, and his rifle swept to his shoulder even as he looked around.

"Put down your shootin' iron, you wild critter!" "Proud Joe ain't with us; don't be skeered!" "Come help us with this flat, you lazy critter." The men shouted greetings as the boat swung to the shore.

"My God," roared Mike, "I thought you was never comin'. You'll never get to New Orleans at this rate."

Mike and the men jibed at one another as they lugged the game aboard and started down the river again.

"We thought you'd killed Joe," said Jabe, "but you jest took his scalp off. He's tolerable spry ag'in, and he's lookin' for you."

"I didn't think I'd snuffed him," said Mike. "I ain't made a bad shot in twenty year. But I couldn't wait to make sure."

IV

A month passed during which the boat drifted several hundred miles down the Mississippi. The journey had been uneventful after the incident at Louisville, and time after time Mike had complained about the monotony of the banks and the stream, about his unsatisfied longing for excitement. "I'm as miserable an' helpless as a wildcat without teeth an' claws," he groaned.

He was complaining as the boat moored one evening not far from Natchez by a shore from which a few abrupt hills towered like monuments above the lowlands. The boat was tied for the night in the shadow of a high bluff.

"Cheer up, Mike," Jabe told him, "this is Injun country, you know. The Choctaws hunt here, and there may be a scrimmage."

"Small likelihood," growled Mike. "I've had nary a brush with the Choctaws. A cursed time whites must have of it livin' here. Now if I lived in these here parts, I'd declare war on the Injuns, just to have something to keep me from growin' dull. I could build a cabin on that there hill, an' stand off a whole tribe if they came arter me. I never was pertic'ler about what's called a fair fight. I just ask half a chance with the odds ag'in me; and if I don't keep clear of snags and sawyers, let me spring a leak an' go to the bottom."

"Sometimes, Mike, I think you're a little fond of a row."

"Well," said Mike, "I walk tall into varmint and Injuns. It's a way I've got, an' it comes as nat'ral as grinning to a hyena. I'm a regular tornado, tough as hickory withe, long-winded as a nor'-wester. I can strike a blow like a fallin' tree, and every lick makes a gap in the crowd that lets in an acre o' sunshine. Whew, boys!"—and Mike twirled his rifle around his head as if the weapon were a walking stick—"Whew! If the Choctaw devils in them there woods would give us a brush, just as I feel now, I'd call 'em gentlemen. I must fight somethin', or I'll catch dry rot, an' burnt brandy won't save me."

But as the evening passed, no Indians appeared. The boatmen therefore divided into two teams and fought and wrestled during most of the evening. Tired at last, they lay down to rest, some in the confined interior of the boat, others in the open air. It was a quiet night, the only sound being the lapping of water against the boat or the shore, a silver night, too, for a full moon poured its white light down upon the hills and upon the boat.

The silence was interrupted by the crack of a rifle, followed by the war-whoops of Indians. One of the boatmen who had been sleeping on the deck groaned, turned upon his face with a spasmodic motion, and died.

The crew clutched the rifles by their sides, sprang to their feet and peered into the darkness for a sight of their foes. And as they looked forms swooped through the air from the hill, and moccasined feet thudded on the deck. The Indians grappled with them before they had a chance to shoot. Knives flashed in the moonlight, arms flailed, there were screams and grunts and groans.

And above these sounds was lifted the joyous voice of Mike Fink. "Give it to 'em, mannees! Cut their hearts out. Choke the devils. Here's hell fire an' the river risin'! Whoop!"

One blow felled one redskin, and Mike leaped and clenched with another one. The huge Indian and Mike sprawled on the deck together. They writhed and twisted, one on top and then the other. The boatman pushed his head from beneath the smothering weight of the Indian's body in time to see flashing steel. The Indian had lifted a knife; Mike seized his wrist and twisted. Fink's muscles knotted, and his hand slipped —then he twisted the wrist of the savage sharply. The knife clattered to the deck. Mike's fist shot in an arc to the redskin's face. The Indian grunted, blindly reached out his arms, caught on, hurled the boatman to the deck, and reached for the knife.

And the other boatmen were battling other opponents. In a few minutes, two Indians lay dead on the deck. The others broke away and splashed into the water. There were spurts of flame as the boatmen sent bullets after them, but the dark heads sank below the surface, and did not appear again on the moonlit river. The mooring ropes were slashed by one of the crew, while another, manning the sweep, steered the flatboat into the current. The boat bobbed on the water.

Again the knife was poised above Mike's heart, slowly sweeping downward, though Mike pushed against it with all his might with one free hand. Mike's face was bathed with sweat, and he was breathing heavily. Then Mike shifted, pulled free his other hand, and bent back his opponent's wrist. A bone cracked, Mike's hand clasped the sweaty knife handle, twirled the blade. The Indian grunted and lay still. The boatman staggered to his feet, wiping his wet hand on his leg.

"By God," said Mike, "I ain't been so busy in a long time!" He drew a deep, quivering breath. "By God, that feller fought beautiful. If he's a specimen o' the Choctaws that live in these here parts, they're screamers. The damned possums!"

"We got the best on 'em," said Jabe. "Two on 'em was downright weak an' keerless with their knives, an' four ran away on us."

"Looks as if your friend tried to give you a shave," said a boatman.

Mike put his hand up to a wound on his cheek. "Blackberry scratch," he said. "Who'd they get?" He stood above the dead boatman. "By God! Poor old Andy!" A torch lit up the face of the flatter, and Mike bent closer.

"Hum," said Mike, "four bullets in him. Them redskins sure wanted to make sure of him!"

"Let's have a look at 'em, Mike," said Jabe. "This is an onnatural business, 'pears to me—four wounds in one man, an' no one else shot at. An' I don't recollect ever hearin' o' Choctaws startin' a scrimmage."

The light was carried over to the Indians Mike's companions had slain. "Them's not Choctaws," said Mike, "but I don't rightly know what tribe paints like that." He turned the torch toward the big Indian with whom he had fought, lying on his face. Then:

"I'll be damned an' fried crisp in hell!" he exclaimed, pointing.

The Indian had no scalp lock. Only the stump, stiffened with symbolic red paint, was left.

"Proud Joe!" said Mike. "Poor Andy was mistook for me!"

"By God!" said Jabe. "That Injun was riled! He went nigh onto a thousand mile, through swamps an' forests an' rivers, an' among hostile redskins, to get your scalp."

"Injuns is queer," said Mike. "They don't like to lose their scalp locks 'less they die."

"Sometimes," said Jabe, "you shoot too damned good, Mike!" And as he spoke, he looked at the silent body of Andy.

CHAPTER FIVE

HOW THE KING OF THE KEELBOATMEN ROUTED THE
DANGEROUS OUTLAWS OF CAVE-IN-ROCK

I

On the northern bank of the Ohio, twenty miles
above Shawneetown, is Cave-in-Rock, famous in frontier history as the rendezvous of river pirates. A large
cave in wilderness country, its wide mouth screened by
trees and columbines, it was an ideal lair for the outlaws. From it, the pirates could see far up and down
the river; a party attacking the inhabitants of the cave
could be seen at a distance, and boats which were to
be plundered were discoverable long before they
reached the hiding place.

At one time or another, the cave in the high limestone bluff was the dwelling of some of the most cruel
criminals in pioneer history. There, as early as 1797,
Samuel Mason lured thirsty boatmen ashore by adver-
tising a "Liquor Vault and House for Entertainment"
in a huge sign on the river bank. Once the men were
in the huge cave, they were robbed and murdered, and
their boats were stolen.

Other outlaws were in the cave in later years, while
Mason moved to the Natchez Trace, where he held up
travelers through the wilderness. Mason and his suc-
cessors used various tricks to wrest cargoes and gold

from river travelers. Sometimes a bedraggled man or woman shouting desperately for help would cause boats to turn ashore, and when the rescuers were near enough, the outlaws pounced upon them. Above the cave, a man shouted offers to pilot boats through the dangerous passage running by Hurricane Island. The bogus pilots, if given a chance, would land a boat at the cave or wreck it on Hurricane Island. Captured boats were sold or were piloted to New Orleans, where their cargoes were sold.

Counterfeiters, thieves, gamblers and murderers gave Cave-in-Rock a bad name in frontier annals. There for a time lived two monsters, the Harpes, of whom a historian wrote: "Neither avarice nor want nor any of the usual inducements to the commission of crime seemed to govern their conduct. A savage thirst for blood—a deep-rooted enmity against human nature, could alone be discovered in their actions." Between them, before they were killed by irate pioneers, the two Harpes murdered perhaps twenty people. Such were the inhabitants of Cave-in-Rock.

Historians have told the thrilling story of the famous outlaws of Cave-in-Rock in several fine books. No historian, however, has told how Mike Fink routed one bloodthirsty gang of outlaws who inhabited the cave, a gang as cruel as any discoverable in the tales of those desperate days. The story, told by a writer of fiction, once famous, now forgotten, records a feat of the king of the keelboatmen highly worthy if not of belief at least of celebration.

II

A storm had driven down over the river at nightfall, and Mike, patroon of the keelboat *Lightfoot*, carrying freight and passengers down the Ohio from Pittsburgh, had been forced to moor his craft for the night in a small cove just below Cave-in-Rock. Black clouds, low hanging, had blotted out the sky, and the wind roared over the river and through the trees on shore. Rain splashed down on the boat as it was made fast. Mike and the crew knew, of course, of the ill repute of Cave-in-Rock. However, for several years no river pirates had been reported active there, and the landing place of the *Lightfoot* seemed safe.

Mike climbed atop of a whiskey barrel, called his crew around him, and made a speech.

"Boys," he said, "this here's a night. How the wind rolls an' tumbles about, like a dyin' crawfish, an' sprinkles the water in your faces, my hearties! And all for your own good, too, if you warn't so thunderation blind you couldn't see it. Why, if the rain didn't wash you off now and agin, what in natur would become on you, my angels? You never get water nearer to you nor the river, an' you're afearder o' that nor a maddog! Hurray for a storm, then, say I! Whoop!"

Mike stopped and looked questioningly at the drenched boatmen, who looked rather mournful as the rain dribbled down their faces and seeped through their clothes.

"Why in hell don't you holler, when it's all for your own good?" Mike demanded sternly. "Holler! Don't stand there shiverin' like a set o' babboons!"

Obediently, though somewhat unenthusiastically, the crew cried, "Huzza for the rain."

"Well," said Mike, "that's better. An' now huzza for me, you scapegoats! I'm a land-screamer—I'm a water-dog—I'm a snappin' turkle. I can use up Injuns by the cord. I can swallow niggers whole, raw or cooked. I can out-run, out-dance, out-jump, out-drink, out-holler, an' out-lick any white thing in the shape o' a human on the Massassip'! Holler, damn you, or I'll jump down your throats quicker nor a streak o' greased chain-lightning!"

"Huzza for Mike Fink," the crew shouted, shivering in the storm.

"Them's the kind as makes a mannee feel good," said Mike, grinning. "Now what'll we do, boys? Shall we go ashore, an' try to hunt suthin' cantankerous, or shall we go below for an extra fillee an' a game o' cards?"

"Below, below! Licker and cards!" shouted the crew, almost in unison, and they crowded toward the cabin in the stern of the boat. Mike laughed, and started after them, beginning a song in which the others joined:

> The boatman is a lucky man,
> No one can do as the boatman can,
> The boatmen dance and the boatmen sing,
> The boatman is up to everything.

> Hi-O, away we go,
> Floating down the river on the O-hi-o.
>
> When the boatman goes on shore,
> Look, old man, your sheep is gone,
> He steals your sheep and steals your shote,
> He puts 'em in a bag an' totes 'em to the boat.
>
> Hi-O, away we go,
> Floating down the river on the O-hi-o.

The crew gathered around a table, circulating whiskey, playing with a dog-eared deck of cards, pausing now and then to join in a song. Feeling very jolly, they sang some doleful ditties. They wailed:

> Oh, it's meeting is a pleasure,
>   Parting is a grief;
> But an onconstant lovyer
>   Is worse nor a thief!
>
> A thief and a robber
>   Your purse he will haave;
> But an onconstant lovyer,
>   He will bring you to the grave!

Within an hour, some of the crew were neglecting the cards and roaring songs. Others were slumbering on the floor or with arms outstretched on the table. Mike was standing unsteadily, waving a bottle, and singing, while his companions beat time on the table:

> Here's to you, an' all the rest,
> An' likewise her that I love best;
> As she's not here to take part,
> I'll drink her health with all my heart.

Mike sucked at the empty bottle, looked at it sternly, and smashed it on the table. Genially he threw the neck of the bottle at the head of a boatman, missing by an inch.

At this instant the door flew open, and a young man, dressed in the civilized clothes of a passenger, stepped from the darkness, breathing hard.

"Up and arm—or you're all dead men!" he shouted.

A boatman rose unsteadily, his round green eyes blinking. "Be howly Mary!" he exclaimed. "What's that?"

"Robbers!" the passenger shouted. "A deserter warned us. They're nearly here."

"Huzza!" Mike shouted. "A fight!" He seized a brace of pistols hanging on the wall and a heavy iron bar lying on the floor, and led about half his crew toward the bow of the boat. Despite the racket, the other boatmen continued their slumbers.

On the deck, the keelers saw that the assailants had already arrived: pistol shots, screams, and the sound of scuffles came from the passengers' cabin in the bow. Roaring, Mike moved forward, and he was soon discharging his pistols and swinging his iron bar at dark figures who closed with him.

The outlaws, outfought, broke, if they could, from the crew, and splashed into the water or leaped ashore. Mike roared after them: "Come back, you infernal cowards, runnin' away afore I got half o' my jints in playing order!" He moved around the boat. "Only four on 'em knocked down," he said.

Just then, down the shore, a woman shouted for help.

"They've borne off a female!" exclaimed a passenger.

"Aurelia!" It was the young man who had carried the news of the attack to the crew. "I'm going to go ashore!" he said, and in a moment he had leaped to the ground, and moved in the direction of the shout.

"Shall we go arter 'em, Mike?" asked a keeler.

"Arter 'em!" said Mike, then, "no, 'twon't do. This is their country, an' this night is as black as pitch. Later, maybe, we'll walk tall into 'em when we get the lay o' the land. But now we'd better care for ourselves."

"Be Saint Pathrick, I think so," said a keeler. "And our hands full we've got, sure, with the living, the dead, and the dead drunk."

"Let's rouse them sleepers first," said Mike, and he went to the cabin and splashed water over the drunken boatmen.

"Man the oars!" he shouted. The boat pulled across the river to a point where it would be safe from another attack. The deserter who had warned the boat was tied up, for safety's sake, and placed in the cargo box. The wounded were cared for, and the dead were prepared for burial.

Then crew and passengers went to their resting places, while the storm roared over the river, and the *Lightfoot* rocked on the wind-swept waves. The storm passed a little before dawn.

III

The following morning was blue and gold and green, a fine clear day in spring. Soon after sunrise, the people on the boat were astir.

Mike called his crew together and addressed them:

"You're a purty set, you land-lubberly ragamuffins, what gets drunk jest when you're wanted for a fight! What'd 'a' happened to you if a few on us hadn't been able to drink whiskey an' hold it too? You'd 'a' had your soaked whiskey-pipes slit up, that's what. Whiskey's a curse." Mike looked at a boatman sternly. "Dick," he said, "I'll jest trouble you to hand me that jug on the shelf there. I feel drier than a sun-baked mud-turkle that ain't seen water since the flood." He drank deep and smacked his lips. Then, looking at the woeful crew, "You might wet your whistles a bit," he said, and passed the bottle around.

"Now," he continued, "all I've got to say about the matter is that we've got to scuttle that band o' outlaws and send 'em to Davy Jones' locker, an' no mistake. To come to the p'int, I'm a-goin' to walk tall into them fellers, and I want to know which o' you suckers is goin' to sneak out an' stay behind. That there young bride that war taken off, an' her husband that went arter her has got to be brought back, or I'll be split on a sawyer. Who's goin' to sneak out on't—who?"

"Niver a damned one of us!" answered the Irish keeler.

"Not me! Not me!" said the crew.

"Good," Mike said. "Now let's talk with the passengers."

He led the way to the fore part of the cargo box, where the passengers, three men and a woman, were standing. The woman was weeping; her husband had been killed the night before.

"Good morning," Mike said. "The crew and me has decided that we must finish off them outlaws."

"We'll be right glad to join you, Captain Fink," said one of the gentlemen.

"Good," said Mike. "I thought as much, Mr. Hamilton. Those mannees that was killed last night, prehaps we'd better sink their bodies in the Ohio, eh?"

"I presume that will be best," said Hamilton.

"Well, do you think 'ud be a right decent trick to give them damned cutthroats Christian burial alongside?"

"I'd spend little time with their carcasses," the passenger replied, bitterly.

"Well, I feel the same. Here you, Jack and Dick, go an' snake 'em out here, an' pitch 'em overboard!"

"But hadn't you better push into the stream first?" asked Hamilton.

"Prehaps I had. Hold on, then, boys! But let me see—one on 'em's not dead yet, I reckon."

"He died this morning, a little before sunrise," reported a boatman.

"So much the better," Mike said. "We won't have to string him up, then. So, then, that makes four, don't it?"

"Four of the robbers, and three of our own party," said Hamilton.

"A tough fight, an' no mistake. Why couldn't I gotten into it sooner? My bones was achin' for a fight, an' here one was close to me an' I drunk as a nigger on a holiday. An' these damned angels," added Mike, pointing to the crew, "was some on 'em even worse. Well, prehaps we'll make up for it later."

"Do you have any plans?"

"Let's talk with that deserter," said Mike. "Bring him up, Pat."

Pat returned shortly, followed by a bewhiskered giant in a picturesque costume. On his head was a coarse red skull-cap, and he wore a ragged shirt striped with red and black. Around his waist was a broad belt from which dangled a holster and a knife case, and his legs were covered with loose linsey trousers and heavy boots.

Mike looked at him sternly. "See here, you belong to that damned band o' pirates, don't you?"

"I *did* belong to 'em. We had a fracas, an' I left 'em."

"A fracas, huh? That may be. We ain't a-goin' to harm you, so long as you don't try no tricks. Then it'd go hard with you—but I'll see to that, I'll see to that. What we want to know is how many is there in that gang, an' how can we get at 'em?"

"There's no more nor ten on 'em there now—the rest are down the river; an' I shouldn't, for my part, be afeard to venter what force there is here agin 'em."

"But," asked Hamilton, "what would be our best plan?"

"Drop down the river, and then come up on land, in the night, and surprise 'em."

"But do you think we can surprise them?"

"I knows it; it's jest the easiest thing in the world. I'll lead you; I know the gang's habits."

"I'm not sure that you're the best possible guide," objected Hamilton. "You were one of the outlaws."

"I *was*," said the man, "but Camilla—he's the leader —ordered me shot for breaking an order, and I cut loose. No fear of my serving you bad—I hate 'em as bad as you do."

"Good," said Mike. "We'll walk tall into 'em then. Untie this mannee; I'll tend to him. First we'll drop downstream. Boys, stir your trotters! Cast off the bow-line and push off!"

In a few minutes the boat was swung from her moorings, and was floating down with the current. As she gained mid-stream, Mike pointed to some black figures high on the rocky ridge of the Illinois shore. "They're on the lookout for us, the infernal possums!" he exclaimed.

"Be me sowl! an' it'll be afther doin' 'em good to look out," Pat remarked.

Around the first bend, out of sight of the cave, the king of the keelboatmen took charge of the consignment of the dead to their graves in the river. The four outlaws were cast without ceremony into the water. The three remaining bodies were sewed in sacks and lowered into the water while the passengers and crew stood with heads uncovered. And the widow of the murdered passenger wept tempestuously.

IV

For some time the *Lightfoot* glided down the turbid and swollen river, keeping near the center of the stream. The crew talked gleefully about the coming fight.

"Well," said Pat, "all I've got to say about it is—jist let 'em give Michael Flanegan's son Pathrick a fair shake, and if he don't walk clean through 'em, like wather through a—a—"

"Oh, hell," said Mike, rumpling the Irishman's hair, "why don't you talk about somethin' you know about —whiskey?"

"And is it whiskey you're afther spaking about? If I'd but been lookin' at you, whiskey's all I could ha' thinked on, jist."

"You damned hoss," said Mike. "What'll you take for your body, Pat, when the hangman's done with it?"

"If you want to buy I'll not bargain with ye."

"Why not?"

"Jist for the rason that it'd be chating ye."

"How so? I think it'd be a grand speculation, for arter stillin' out the whiskey, I could sell your carcass to the doctor for full value."

"Could you jist? Blatheration! I don't think you'd be wantin' it then."

"And why not?"

"For the same reason that Jimmy Stady wasn't at his brother's wake in the oulden time—'cause he was hung up himself before his brother!"

Mike roared with the crew, and whacked Pat a powerful blow over the shoulders. "Come," he said, "I'll licker on that." The bottle was produced and was passed among the crew.

Mike, smacking his lips over a second swag, saw Hamilton approaching.

"What are your plans for the attack?" he said. "Shouldn't we go ashore soon?"

"Why," said Mike, "we're going to turn in soon to a creek a bit below, an' then hide the boat thar, an' take it afoot back through the country, so we can reach 'em about dark. Meantime it might be good to get ready. Boys, get out your shootin' irons, and have 'em cleaned, ready to go ahead when the time comes."

In a few minutes members of the crew who could be spared from other tasks and the three masculine passengers were cleaning their arms and new-flinting and repairing such locks as were out of order. They were interrupted by Mike.

"Where in hell's our guide?" he asked.

"Damned if I've seen him this two hours," said a boatman.

"Me neither," said another.

"Maybe he's down below," suggested a third.

"Carpenter," said Mike, to a youthful member of the crew, "go down an' see, an' if you find him, tell him he's wanted up here instanter."

The boy departed, and in a few minutes returned to report that nothing could be found of the man.

"By God!" cried Mike, "if he's left us over the runnin'-board, then it's all up, for we can't do nothing unless we take 'em by surprise."

"I don't think he's left the boat," said Hamilton. "Let's search for him."

A hunt was started, but for some time no trace of the deserter was found. At last, however, a shout from the cargo box, followed by a rippling stream of cuss words, brought the crew to a point amidships. There lay the missing man, so motionless that at first it appeared that he was dead. But a straw protruding from a gimlet hole in the barrel and the perfume of whiskey indicated that he was only dead drunk.

"It appears this here poor robber's been led astray by this damned drunken crew," said Mike. "We'll teach him a lesson. Here, boys, up with him on deck, an' don't spill him on the passage."

As soon as the order had been obeyed, Mike, who had kept close behind the outlaw, said:

"Now some o' you fetch me a long rope, an' we'll show this angel how to be a fish."

"Howly mother!" exclaimed Pat. "Is it drownding him you'll be after doin'?"

"No; ducking."

Fastening a rope around the waist of the deserter,

CAVE-IN-ROCK, ON THE OHIO

INTERIOR OF CAVE-IN-ROCK

Mike gave an order to heave him overboard. The drunk man splashed into the stream, and Mike and two keelers held the rope so that the man kept above the surface. At first he slept tranquilly, but in time his eyes opened, and he looked with terror around him. Then he began to struggle desperately.

"Don't be afeard o' that stuff!" Mike cried. "That's water!"

In a short time the man was hauled to the running-board, dripping water and woeful of countenance, but nearly sober.

"You're a pretty sucker now, ain't you?" said Mike. "To get drunk at this time, an' float belly-up'ards, like a double-damned dead sun-fish."

"Why, you see, captain," said the man, "I seen the barrel and the straw, and I was powerful dry—"

"I see, in course," said Mike, "but we're goin' ashore now, an' we want a guide. You might look close at this here pistol, which will put lead into your hide if you try any tricks." He raised his voice: "Run her into that creek, lads!"

This creek, or inlet, set back from the river some two hundred yards, between steep hills, and was rendered dark by the dense foliage of the trees overhead. The crew rowed the boat into a hiding place where the branches completely concealed her from the view of any one standing five paces away, and there made her fast. There a boatman, one of the male passengers, the boy Carpenter, and the feminine passenger were to be left while the party of ten went to attack the outlaws.

When the party was ready to leave, Mike gathered them around him and spoke to them: "We're goin' to hit some snags maybe," he began, "an' some on us won't come through with whole timbers. But by God, we're goin' to have a sweet fight. If I don't jump into somethin' every so often, I'll die, an' so I mought as well die in a fight, as through not fightin' is how I feel about it. I'm in for a fight, I'll go my death on a fight. I'm an out-an'-out sea-hoss! Wet your whistles, boys, an' we'll be on our way."

So the bottle was passed, and the dangerous expedition to Cave-in-Rock was started.

V

As the party moved toward the cave, Groth, the deserter, told about the lay of the land. The robbers then at the cave, he said, used the cavern for a storage room and a hiding place. They lived above the cliff in a group of old log cabins which had been erected many years before by early French settlers. The robbers used simple but effective methods: they lured a boat's crew and passengers ashore if possible, gave them liquor, and then murdered them. Soon after some of the band took the boat and its cargo down the river. Their pleasant motto, "Dead men tell no tales," had been so efficiently followed that the boatmen had not heard of their activities. Their leader, Camilla, sometimes went up the river to find promising boats. On such expeditions, said Groth, he used the name of Hardick.

"Hardick!" exclaimed Mike. "He was a passenger on the *Lightfoot* that left the boat up the river!"

"You was expected," said Groth, "though it was hardly thought you'd moor right below the cave."

"By God," said Mike, "the damned storm fixed that. But we can manage a right good storm ourselves, and Camilla's my man, sure as hell."

The attackers pushed forward as quickly as they could, and reached their destination about an hour before darkness. They rested at some distance from the cabins occupied by the outlaws, and then when black night, sprinkled with stars, came down, the men moved towards the cabins.

They heard the sound of singing and shouting, and Mike chuckled. "We turn the tables," he whispered, "for they seem as happy as we were t'other night when they sneaked up on us."

A window in the building from which the sounds came was open, and Mike and his followers moved toward it, careful not to snap twigs which lay on the grassy ground, soft beneath their feet, carefully feeling their way through the darkness. They might as well have walked boldly up to the window, for, as was soon evident, the robbers were not in a state which aided vigilance. Mike divided his forces, remaining near the window with four of his men and sending

Hamilton, at the head of four more, to watch at the rear door. Standing near the window, Mike and his followers saw clearly into the cabin.

The robbers for the most part were seated on benches around a rickety table on which stood a pale light. Its gleams touched haggard, unshaved faces, from which stared bloodshot eyes. The outlaws drank from cans which sat on the table. A few were standing upright, cursing or roaring.

Their costumes were similar to that of Groth: 'they wore red skull caps, tight-fitting shirts striped with black and red, linsey trousers, and heavy boots. Their clothes were dirty and torn.

There was the explosion of a pistol, and the talking stopped. From the shadows, walking somewhat unsteadily, moved Camilla, a tall, swarthy man, his hair and his beady eyes jet black, his thin lips crookedly smiling.

"We'll have a trial and a hanging," he said, "to liven up things. I'll send for our prisoner, shall I?" He cut short a joyous shout. "Where's the nigger that has him in charge?" he asked.

"He's not been with us for an hour," said one of the gang.

"Hell crisp his black hide! By God, I'll have him tied and whipped! Anthon, go out and call Cato."

Outside, Mike whispered a few words to one of his crew: "Jack, follow him a ways an' dispose of him."

The rest of the crew fell back, and the keeler moved silently behind the robber. There was the sound of a

fiercely pushed knife as it struck Anthon's chest, then
silence. Jack came back swiftly and silently, cleaning
his knife. "Didn't even groan," he said.

Within, Camilla was speaking: "Damn him, why
doesn't he call?" he exclaimed. "By God, I'll have
him whipped too!" He moved toward the door, but
as his feet touched the threshold, Mike shouted:

"Set poles for hell!" And he presented a pistol to
his body and fired. Then, blinking, Mike watched
Camilla with wonder, for Camilla staggered but did
not fall. Instead he turned and roared at his men.
The bullet had struck the robber leader's knife, and
had been deflected.

"Out with the light, you fools! Follow me out the
back door!"

The light disappeared, and there was the sound of
buffeted furniture in the pitch darkness. Then a pistol
shot echoed in the cabin, and Mike roared with delight:

"Arter the hellions, an' give no quarter! Chawr 'em
like a Virginia nigger does cabbage! Whoop!"

Shouting, the boatmen followed the patroon, kicking
over the table as they went, and sending pistol shots
after the robbers. And now Hamilton's party began to
yell and shoot, and two of the robbers fell.

"Surrounded, by God!" cried Camilla. "Hell's
curses! Turn, and tear 'em to pieces!"

The outlaws discharged their pistols, then closed
with Mike's followers. The forces were about equal,
and each outlaw engaged an opponent. They fought
on wet grass, their feet slipping now and then as they

strained and tugged. Knives clashed, fists banged against faces; there were groans, yells, and the stamping of feet.

Mike's opponent came toward the roaring keeler, a pistol leveled at him. Mike seized his arm as the bullet left the gun, coming so close that powder singed his cheek. Mike's face pressed against the rough shirt of the outlaw, and his nostrils were assailed by the mingled smell of sweat and whiskey. Mike's hands moved over a huge arm, as he twisted his hips to escape a knee which came swiftly towards his crotch. He tugged at the wrist, and a knife fell from the man's grasp. The man stooped, and Mike fell upon him. His hand searched the wet grass as his weight held the man down. "Ha!" he bellowed, and he lifted the knife. The man tried to seize his arm as it swept down, but failed. Mike felt the warm blood of his rival gush over his hand. The man lay still.

The patroon of the *Lightfoot* moved toward the house, struck a flint, and fired the tablecloth. On the table he heaped benches and chairs. The fire grew, crackling, sending tongues of flame up the log walls, and Mike ran outside again.

Aided by the light of the fire, Mike could see that the ground was strewn with the dead and the wounded. Groth lay, locked in the arms of an outlaw, besmeared with blood: both were dead. Anthon lay staring at the fire with wide eyes, his face white and motionless. Other bodies cast black shadows on the green grass.

Pat and Hamilton, the passenger, were the only living men in sight.

Then out of the darkness staggered a boatman, his face as crimson as his boating shirt, his eyes staring wildly.

"It's all over, Mike," he said, as he sank to the ground. "God forgive——" and he died at Mike's feet.

"All the rest have gone, I guess," said the Irishman.

"Where's Camilla?" Mike asked.

"I seed him runnin'," answered a voice behind Mike.

The patroon turned round, and recognized one of his crew. "Where'd you turn up, Lewis?" he asked.

"Oh, I fout one on 'em clean out here, for a quarter mile, an' damn me if he didn't get away from me, drat his soul!"

"Hurt any, Lewis?"

"A few scratches."

"Then keep with me, for there's more business. Where'd Camilla run to?"

"Thought he ran into one o' the houses."

"Got to burn him out, then, sartain."

"Howly murther!" said Pat. "Somebody's ahead uv us, in the burnin' line!"

He pointed. Flames were leaping out of the window of one of the cabins. Before the boatmen and Hamilton had reached the building, the fire was darting through the crackling roof. They stood near the house.

"God," said Mike, "was the prisoners in there?"

A voice behind them shouted: "Save her! For God's sake, save her! She's—"

Looking around, Mike saw the passenger who had left the boat to rescue the woman the night before, accompanied by a negro, dashing from the direction of the river.

"St. Vincent! Heavens," said Hamilton, "we thought you lost!"

"I was released from the cave—by this man—but, God, too late—is it?" He ran towards the door, staggering, for his run had exhausted him. The door was in flames. He struck it with his shoulder, and it fell in. Hamilton and Pat pulled him back as he started to enter. He struggled for a time, then groaned as he failed to free himself.

Suddenly the group was startled by the sound of a woman's voice, shrieking for help. It seemed to come from the river.

"Her voice!" exclaimed the young man, and he darted toward the river. The others followed him.

From the cliff, the group looked down on the river, sparkling in the red light of the fire. Far below them they saw the tall form of Camilla, a woman in his arms, climbing into a boat. He dropped the woman and pushed the boat from the shore. He started to row as St. Vincent leaped over the rocks to the shore.

"A rifle!" cried Mike.

"Here's one!" said Pat.

Mike caught and loaded the piece quickly, and brought it to his eye. His companions watched him in silence as he took aim. The boat was dancing away towards the black part of the water. In a moment it would be no longer visible.

The rifle barked. Camilla rose, his hand over his heart, then toppled into the water, tipping the boat. The woman screamed. St. Vincent leaped into the water, and moved rapidly toward her.

The men rushed down to the shore and peered across the water, red in the firelight, with traceries of black. They saw the swimmer come to the surface, carrying the woman, saw him coming shoreward. They carried the two up on the bank. The woman was breathing.

.   .   .   .

Shortly after sunrise, the party arrived again at the boat, and found all aboard safe. After a hearty breakfast, they went again to Cave-in-Rock, where they buried their companions as well as circumstances would permit.

They explored the outlaws' quarters, and found that the two buildings which they had burned had been the only ones which had been occupied. They entered the huge cave, and found there much plunder, and many knives, pistols, rifles, and powder flasks scattered over the floor. As many of these as they could, they carried with them back to the boat.

The next day the *Lightfoot* was again floating down the river as smoothly and quietly as if nothing had occurred to interrupt her passage.

And the man who told the tale said: "Of the outlaws

of Cave-in-Rock, but little more was ever known. With Camilla died their leading spirit; and though they banded together somewhat afterward, and sought to revive old customs, yet their efforts failed, and they gradually became scattered abroad."

CHAPTER SIX

HOW MIKE FINK BECAME A TRAPPER, AND HOW HIS ADVENTUROUS LIFE ENDED WHEN HE MET VIOLENT DEATH IN THE WESTERN WILDERNESS

I

Mike Fink's life was associated with three frontiers: the Pennsylvania frontier of his boyhood and youth, where he served as a scout in the hazardous conflicts with the Indians; the Kentucky frontier, touched by the winding Ohio and Mississippi rivers; the Missouri Valley frontier, into which during his last days Mike penetrated with one of those vanguards of westward expansion, a fur-trading expedition. Through his colorful life, one feels death must have pursued him—in the Indian country, into which he ventured so bravely alone; up and down the dangerous rivers, where snags and riffles and sawyers menaced his life; in the savage gambling dens and saloons, where death at last came to many a mighty boatman. Death, melodramatic, violent, caught up at last with Mike Fink in the winter of 1822-23 in a remote trading post by the mouth of the Yellowstone River in the western wilderness.

Just how he died, it is no longer possible to discover. For something about the life, and more especially the death of the king of the keelboatmen attracted the fancy of the western pioneers, and so many tales were

177

told about the end of his picturesque career that now the truth about his death is so tangled with legend that no one can untangle the skein.

Although Mike Fink lived but once, according to legend he died at several different places and in a number of different ways. He was almost as versatile in dying as were the famous James brothers, of whom, at the height of excitement about them, Bill Nye wrote:

> James boys have died in Texas and in Minnesota, in New England and on the Pacific coast. They have been yielding up the ghost whenever they had a leisure moment. . . . The men who have personally and individually killed the James boys from time to time, contemplate holding a grand mass meeting and forming a new national party. This will no doubt be the governing party next year.

Other great legendary figures of America had a similar tendency to die more than once—Frankie and Johnny, Billy the Kid, and, on another plane, J. Wilkes Booth. To some extent, the importance of these persons is indicated by the number of their deaths.

On this basis, Mike Fink was a very important legendary figure. At least fifty times, the story of the end of his life has been told in print, and at least eleven versions have been the sources of these numerous and varied narratives. The first of these original versions appeared a few months after the boatman died, and the last, it seems, appeared in 1860. During the interval, the story must have been told orally hundreds of times.

What, so far as may be ascertained, are the real facts

about Fink's death? The bare facts—and they are very unsatisfactory facts, in a way, for they leave many important things unexplained—are to be found in the government report concerning the fur-trading party of which Fink, in the year of his death, was a member—"Volume XXXXII, Record Book Containing Copies of Letters from Indian Agents and Others, to the Superintendent of Indian Affairs at St. Louis, September 10, 1830, to April 1, 1832." Here, grudgingly, unimaginatively, in a section, "deaths of men caused by accidents and other causes not chargeable to Indians," a few stiff sentences bristling with drama tell that, in 1825, "Marshall was lost in the willow valley near Salt Lake"; in 1823, "Holly Wheeler died from wounds received from a bear"; in 1824, "Thomas, a half-breed, was killed by Williams, on the waters of Bear River . . ."; in 1828, "Bray was killed by a blow from the hand of Mr. Tullock," and, in addition—

In 1822 Mike Fink shot Carpenter—Talbot soon after shot Fink, and not long after was himself drowned at the Tetons.

This report was written after September 10, 1830; it was not printed, it seems, until 1902. Meanwhile, many versions of the story had been published.

A slightly more detailed version, the first, in fact, to reach print, appeared in the *Missouri Republican* of July 18, 1823:

By a letter received in town from one of General Ashley's [fur-trading] expedition we are informed that a man by the name of Mike Fink well known in this quarter as a great marksman with the rifle, and the same who sometime since, in this place shot off a negro's heel to enable him, as he said, to "*wear a genteel boot,*" was engaged in his favorite amusement of shooting a tin cup from off the head of another man, when aiming too low or from some other cause shot his companion in the forehead and killed him. Another man of the expedition (whose name we have not heard) remonstrated against Fink's conduct, to which he, Fink, replied, that he would kill him likewise, upon which the other drew a pistol and shot Fink dead upon the spot.

Here, one might say, is an account which may well be the true one. It comes, it would seem, from a man who either saw Mike die or who soon after the event heard the tale from those who had seen the death. It was printed, furthermore, before the story had been mulled over, twisted, and embellished, by inventive spinners of tales who yarned dramatically by hundreds of wilderness campfires. But it leaves several interesting questions unanswered: Why had Mike, who never missed, failed to hit his mark this time? Was there anything back of the phrase, "or for some other cause," which might explain Mike's inaccuracy or which might explain the strange readiness of the bystander to shoot the keelboatman? What was the relationship between the three men who had a part in the tragedy?

The next published story (1829) of the death purported to come from a steamboat pilot who had once been a keelboat patroon. He told Morgan Neville

NEW ORLEANS WATER FRONT IN 1827

MISSOURI RIVER IN 1827

that Mike missed because he "had corned too heavy," and then "a friend of the deceased . . . suspecting foul play, shot Mike." And again there were doubtful features in the yarn. Mike had almost always performed his favorite trick when he had drunk deeply of corn whiskey. He was used to shooting while drunk, and it does not seem probable that a few swags—or many, for that matter—would cause him, as this story holds, "to elevate too low." Further, why should the friend "suspect foul play," especially if it had been evident that Mike had missed because he was drunk? And one is a little dubious about the authority cited: Not on the scene, the pilot must have heard the story from others, and perhaps the tale had been twisted before it reached his ears.

The same year the pilot's tale was printed there appeared a yarn which was more satisfactory, more convincing. Told by "an intelligent and respectable fur-trader of St. Louis," it gave details about Mike which had not appeared in print before, true details about his death which appeared for the first time. After a quarrel about a squaw—thus the story ran—Mike and Carpenter (here first named) agreed to show friendliness in the customary fashion, by shooting the cup. Carpenter, suspecting foul play, made his will and declared he was sure Mike would kill him. Mike shot Carpenter, but pretended it was unintentional. Several months later, when Fink boasted that he had intentionally murdered Carpenter, Talbot (here first named) drew Carpenter's pistol—left to Talbot in his will—and shot Fink. Talbot was later drowned.

This story names the principals of the tragedy for the first time, points out the actual scene of the killing, and adds the important fact of Talbot's death by drowning. It furnishes a not improbable motive for a quarrel; for the death of Fink occurred in the Indian country, where traders and trappers frequently consorted with Indian women. But it presents the puzzling spectacle of a man who, knowing that he was to be killed, willingly stood and allowed himself to be shot. That is a hard detail to swallow. And how neat is the justice of the touch that makes Mike die of a wound from the gun of his victim! It is too neat, perhaps; one scents the Nemesis motif which threads its way through many legends.

There are other stories which pretend to solve this century-old mystery. Most of them are, for some reason, unsatisfactory. Some of them are palpably false —this one, for example, of 1842:

> Mike Fink was an extraordinary and real character. He was shot somewhere on the Mississippi. . . . As we have heard the story, Mike engaged, for a wager, to knock a gill cup of whiskey off a man's head at fifty yards with a rifle ball—a feat he had performed a hundred times! On that occasion, owing to the man's moving his head, Mike's ball grazed his skull, and stunned him for a moment; a brother of his being present, thinking Mike had killed him, and intentionally, shot Mike dead on the spot.

So the tale varied and changed through the years. There were disagreements concerning the shooting of

Carpenter. Mike shot him by accident in stories of 1823, 1829, 1838, 1844, 1847, 1848. He killed him (1829) because he remained angry after a quarrel about a squaw. In 1842, Mike did not kill Carpenter; he merely stunned him. In 1855, a story had it that Mike, trying to shoot an apple off a friend's head— perhaps under William Tell's influence—grazed the skull, "evidently from mere wantonness." In 1844 and 1847 Mike missed the cup and killed Carpenter because he had been unnerved by the suspicion that Carpenter was treacherous. In 1845 it was said, with venom, that he killed "an unarmed youth, whom he had raised as a child, in a fit of drunken jealousy, probably without cause . . ." In 1856, the name of the person killed was not Carpenter, but Joe Stevens, and the keeler killed him because he was angered when he learned that Joe had enjoyed the favor of Mike's sweetheart. Then there was a melodramatic miss in a yarn of 1860, wherein, after a quarrel, Mike shot the victim in the head though he held the apple which was supposed to be the target in his hand. And naturally, as Mike raised his gun, "his countenance changed to a demon's hue, black and fearful."

Mike died for many reasons. He was killed, in 1823, because he threatened a protesting bystander. Somewhat similarly, in 1845, "when reproved . . . by one of his comrades," Mike "drew his rifle to his shoulder to kill him also, provoking the quicker movement, which . . . deprived him of his life." But in 1829, Mike was killed with Carpenter's pistol after he had boasted that he killed the youth purposely. In 1838, the person who killed Fink did so because he had an old grudge against him. In 1842 and 1856, the victim's brother avenged his death. In 1844 and 1847 Talbot shot Mike because he feared him. And the boatman died most interestingly, perhaps, in 1860, when, far up the Missouri where he had fled "to escape from the meshes of the law," after drunkenly boasting, he was "overtaken by a boon companion of Carpenter" who "followed the murderer to his wild haunts and stabbed him in the heart."

Fink shot Carpenter on the Arkansas River once, on the Missouri several times, on the Mississippi now and then, "at Smithland, behind the Cumberland bar" once, and once—as late as 1874—on the banks of Chouteau's Pond near St. Louis. The boatman and his victim were related in several ways; they were old friends, they were brothers, Carpenter was Fink's adopted son. Carpenter's avenger was, at various times, the victim's father, his brother, his friend.

Thus the tales changed, tangled skeins of truth with skeins of inventive fiction, and the years reared a splendid monument to folk ingenuity. One sees how some of the features of the tangle crept in. One sees, for example, contamination, when the apple trick is stolen from William Tell by Mike, the whiskey cup discarded. Or was the change made in the interests of temperance? One sees dramatic economy in the interrelating of all of the characters. The elaborate details about places are perhaps results of efforts to attain verisimilitude—

to convince, or perhaps they are meant to honor certain communities by allowing Mike to die in them.

II

No one can decide definitely what the facts are, what the fictional details are; one may merely have preferences. The authors of this book have two preferences among the stories of the death of Mike Fink, both of them stories told by Joseph M. Field of St. Louis, Missouri. One they like because it seems to them the most believable, the other because it ties together, ingeniously, many of the legends about Fink in a story which has a strange splendor. For them, the latter is the finest tale, true or false, about the king of the keelboatmen—open to many criticisms, perhaps, but glamorous nevertheless. Here, modernized, a few of its least probable incidents deleted, abbreviated or filled in now and then, is Field's yarn, published in the *St. Louis Reveille* in 1847, "Mike Fink, the Last of the Boatmen."

"Fifteen years ago," says Field, "the writer listened to some stories of Mike, told by the late Morgan Neville, Esq., of Cincinnati, a noble old gentleman, whose pen has done much towards transmitting to posterity the fame of the 'Last of the Boatmen.' In Louisville, subsequently, many 'yarns' respecting the early river hero were repeated to the writer; and since that time, in New Orleans, Natchez, and, finally, in St. Louis, anecdotes and stories, and, above all the ac-

tual facts which are to form the frame-work of this history have reached him till, between truth and fable, he
is amply supplied with material.   The writer, though,
is conscientious to a painful degree, and he wants to
'fix things right'; above all, he is afraid of . . .
'stretching things out' . . . and therefore he intends
to be very careful.   After the story shall be written,
though, he gives fair notice he will swear to every word
of it; when if anybody knows more of the matter than
he does, let him meet the same test."   Then he plunges
into his tale, which follows the strands of Mike's destiny through the years which lie between his youth and
his death.

The events of the story began one evening "in the
fall of the year 179–," in a little settlement on the
banks of the Monongahela "not far from where stands
at present the bustling little town of Brownsville."
There a little group of pioneers had carried into the
wilderness their household and farming implements,
some muskets, a little food, a little seed, and had hewed
their homes out of the virginal forests.   The fort—a
group of stockaded cabins and blockhouses—stood in
the center, fringed by little farms which had been
painfully cleared of brush and stumps, industriously
plowed with unwieldy wooden plows, planted with
grain which was laboriously cut with cradles.   In that
settlement Mary Benson, the daughter of old Benson,
was to be married.

Old Benson, an Englishman by birth who had lived
once in New Orleans and on the lower Mississippi, was

one of the successful figures in the settlement. Furthermore, he was respected in the community; he had been
the leader in the erection of the log meeting-house, and
he was called "Deacon."   But there was much talk in
the settlement about the marriage.   Mike Fink, the
settlers guessed, would create a stir when he came back
from one of his hunting expeditions.

Mike was the handsomest and strongest young man
in the section, the best shot, the best student of "Injun
ways"—an admired favorite of the community.   He
had been courting Mary for more than a year, her
escort at the weddings, the house-raisings, the husking
bees which were the festivals of the frontier, and it had
been generally understood that the two were engaged.

But suddenly, while Fink had been away on one of
his long hunts in the Alleghenies, old Benson had announced that his daughter was to marry immediately
an Englishman, Taggart, who but lately had wandered into the settlement from the lower country.
Heavy, dark browed, sulky, he had soon won the dis-
like of most of the people of the settlement.   Moreover, he was thirty-five, Mary but eighteen.   Mary,
handsome, dainty, called "the Lady" by the folk of
the community, would not, thought gossips, disobey
her father.   With the dawn she would move with her
husband towards the south, a sacrifice, doubtless, to her
father's avarice.

And so on the night of the wedding, a group gathered with Jabe Knuckles in his saloon by the river
bank, drank, waited for Mike, and discussed the affair.

"By God," said Jabe, filling a can. "It's a down-right cruelty to the young."

"That it is," said a gaunt frontiersman, frowning, "and Mike Fink is jest nat'rally bound to make a widow of Mary, so as to set things agreeable agin."

"By rights he ought to choke Taggart's fat throat."

"And that old hypocrite, Deacon Benson, ought to be scalped."

Jabe looked sternly out of the window at a round yellow moon floating above black trees. "Injun Pete couldn't 'a' struck Mike's trail," he said, "or he'd 'a' been here 'fore now. I sent Pete off towards the mountains more than a week ago, when I first smelt out the plot." He paced the floor. "Makes my blood boil," he said. "Let's drink."

They drank; they watched the hand of the clock creep past the hour of the wedding; they swore; they drank more. Stories started—yarns of Indian fights, hunts, fights between frontiersmen. The eyes of the group were glazed, their faces flushed, when, at three o'clock, a shout outside interrupted a song. The door flew open, and in stalked Mike Fink, scowling, blinking as he came in from the darkness followed by the wiry half-breed, Indian Pete.

"Mike Fink!" yelled Knuckles, "and too late!"

"She's Mrs. Mary Taggart, and in bed, at that, since nine o'clock," growled one of the men.

Another staggered from his chair, waved his beaker, and started to mumble the conventional toast of the backwoods: "Health to the groom, not forgetting myself; and here's to the bride, thumping luck and big chil—" But the toast died on his lips as Mike pushed him aside and he saw the blackness in Mike's face. Mike seized a can, lifted it to his mouth, jerked his head back.

"Poor Mary," said Knuckles. "They forced her into it."

"She's been lookin' like a ghost for two weeks."

"And expectin' you'd get back in time to stop it."

"By God!" cried Mike. "I'm in time, I tell you! I tell you I'm in time, and you'll see it! Who'll go with me to drink the health of the groom in good Monongahela whiskey?"

The men shouted approval. They had one more drink all around, then started up the bank, past the silent cabins of the settlement, black in the moonlight, their lantern throwing long shadows. Some of them staggered; most of them yelled.

And so they came to Benson's house, a substantial log dwelling of two rooms, larger by half than most of the cabins of the settlement. They yelled, and then listened, and the house was as silent as a tomb. Then Mike took the lantern and walked closer to the house.

"Taggart! Benson!" he roared. "Show yourselves. Taggart! To git married is a manly act, and you should be proud of it, not skulk in the bridal chamber like a coward. We've come, as is customary, to drink your health in good whiskey. Show yourselves!"

But again the house was silent, and again the men

jeered. Mike stepped onto the rough porch running along the front of the house. His hand reached for the latch-string. A spurt of fire shot from an upper window, Mike's hand touched his burning neck and came away wet with blood. He staggered back from the porch. A woman screamed in the house.

Mike's companions shouted: "That shot came from Taggart!" "Kill him!" "Burn the house!" "Kill the Deacon!" And some ran to the wood-pile, then came back with pitch splinters. Mike, pushing aside two friends who had held him on his feet as he stood stunned, shouted:

"A scoundrel like that, boys, can't carry off Mary Benson! Take her from him, and give him the Injun run for it!"

The orange of the sputtering pitch splinters wavered against the brown of the log walls, and cracking brush was thrown into the open passage-way. The men dashed from the building to the black shelter of the woods, while two shots bit into trees. And now the dry logs of the house were licked by flame, and sparks flew above the tree-tops.

Piercingly a woman screamed, and Mike and Knuckles battered through crashing glass into the room. Choked with smoke, they peered at the floor. Mary lay there in her nightdress, bleeding, very still. A man brushed against Jabe as he staggered toward the window.

"Taggart! The window!" cried Knuckles. Mike's pistol spat, and Taggart fell to the ground as if mortally wounded. But outside, voices shouted, "Tag-gart!" And, "Get him!" There were shots as he leaped over a fence and disappeared in the darkness beyond the rim of the light of the fire.

Carrying Mary as if she were a child, Mike came from the window out of the choking smoke into the fresh night air. Tenderly he laid her upon the grass. And when he saw that blood trickled from her fore-head, where she had been struck, he frowned and said: "By God, Taggart will pay for this!"

Benson came towards Fink, his greasy face, shining in the firelight, as calm as if he were in the meeting house on a quiet Sunday. His words, however, were vibrant with anger:

"You have ruined me, Mr. Fink."

"You damned snake," said Mike, "I'll see you hanged yet, if watchin' your ways will secure justice to you."

Three days later Benson and his daughter disap-peared from the settlement. But even before their departure, Mike had shipped on a keelboat and was journeying down the river on his first trip to New Orleans.

III

Some years later, Mike and his crew were drinking one evening in the "grocery" of 'Siah Hodgkiss at the mouth of Bear Grass Creek, Louisville. One of the crew was Jabe Knuckles. Others of the crew, Kentuckians, Ohioans, two French Canadians, red-shirted, tanned, drank and, amused, listened to their captain as he told Mira, their host's daughter, of his "early and tender youth."

"You see, Miss Miry, I was born 'way off in eastern Pennsylvany, where there warn't a hill big enough to cool off on, or a river big enough for a good swallow. Well, my old folks hadn't more than a three-foot streak of land, and one cow. Which cow," and Mike drank solemnly, "which cow finally settled my fortune—"

"Cattle," murmured Jabe, far gone with drink, his eyes closed, "has got more to do with luck than some knows of. A bull is one of the signs."

"Yes," said Mike, "and a sleepy old calf, with a whiskey tit in his mouth, is another of 'em." The crowd laughed.

"Shut up, Jabe!" shouted a boatman.

"Yes, Miss Miry," continued Fink. "That cussed old cow drove me over the mountains; for it had the awfullest holler behind its shoulders you ever did see, and the old folks being particular careful about the critter, they just insisted that I should follow it around in wet weather, and bale its back out, so I quit."

The boatmen roared, and Mira, standing very close to Mike, who leaned back in his chair, his feet on a table, smiled into his eyes. Old Hodgkiss watched the pair anxiously as he drew another pitcher of whiskey from the barrel. He knew Mike's reputation.

Mike took Mira's little hand in his great fist and began to sing, only slightly off key, a crude love-song of
his own composition:

> Oh, my love she are handsome; she's not ver-ry tall,
> But her modest demeanyor does far surpass all.
> She's slim 'round the middle, her hair it hangs down;
> She's a bright morning star, O, she lives in this town.

As he sang, his arm slid around the girl's waist, and he
held her tightly as he finished.

Hodgkiss, bustling with his pitcher of whiskey, broke
in at the end of the verse. "Now, Capting Fink," he
whined. "You do sing your songs right straight
through and through one, and I always did say to
Mira—and Mira, there's that pesky bear's cub, now,
huggin' that shoat to death, and— Why don't you
go, Mira?"

But Mike held her close as she made a half-hearted
attempt to break away. He looked at a flaxen-headed
little boy who, dressed in a miniature boatman's costume, was at his feet, whittling out a tiny keelboat.
"Chase him, son," he said. And the boy sent the cub
running with a few blows of his keelboat, then rested
at Mike's feet while Mike continued:

> Pretty Polly, pretty Polly, your daddy are rich,
> But I ain't no fortune what troubles me much—

Here Mike slipped a gold piece into her bosom—

> Would you leave your old daddy and mammy also,
> And all through the wide world with your darlin' boy go?

Hodgkiss, uneasily watching, expostulated. "Cap-ting Fink, there ain't a family man on the river that don't jest make you one of themselves, and you know how much I care about you sky-larkin' with Mira, but what on airth is the use of troublin' yourself to amuse her, when you see she ain't enjoyin' of it?"

"Why, Lordy massy, father," said Mira, smiling contentedly, "if I love a thing on airth, it is good singin'. Don't interrupt the captin now, really!"

Mike laughed loudly, impudently, and pulled Mira down on his knee. He sang again:

> O, some call me rakish, and some call me wild,
> And some say that I pretty maids have beguiled.
> But they are all liars by the powers er-bove,
> For I'm guilty of nothing but inno-cent love!

Mike demonstrated the truth of his claims of inno-cence by bending over Mira as she lay back in his arms and kissing her in a leisurely and thorough fashion. Mira sat up, her face pink, her eyes languorous, con-fusedly straightening her cap.

Again Hodgkiss pleaded. " 'Tain't that you don't sing right sweet and handsome, Capting Fink—and 'tain't that you ain't the most popular man on the river, either; but gals is gals, and whiskey's whiskey, and when they both get into the head at the same time, they're a leetle dust too hot for one another, that's all. And there's Mira, now, all red and ashamed about what you been a-doin' to her."

But Mira protested: "How you do go on about noth-

ing.   Jest as if Captin Fink isn't a gentleman!   And
jest 'cause Captin Fink always will sing and do things
when he comes along."

Mike ordered a fresh supply of brandy and tossed a
handful of silver into the whining publican's face.
And now, during a lull in the talk, Jabe Knuckles
steered unsteadily for the door, his weather eye cloudy,
muttering:

"Virgo, that's another sign!   Yes, and twins—twins
is another!"

"What's that you say?" cried Miss Mira.

"A prediction," said Jabe, leering.   Laughing, the
other boatmen followed him as he lurched through the
door.   Mike picked up the little boy, who had fallen
asleep on the floor, and carried him to a bunk in the
back of the grocery.

"Bedtime," said 'Siah significantly to Mira.

"Now, father," said Mira.   "Don't you worry on
my account.   Captain Fink is going to talk with me
awhile."

"And you needn't trouble yourself about sittin' up,"
said Mike.   But 'Siah planted himself firmly in a chair
and lit his pipe.   Mike looked at him frowningly.
Mira pouted.   At last Mike emptied his glass, looked
at 'Siah again, shrugged his shoulders, and began:

"I don't know exactly how to begin.   I'm on the far
side of thirty now, and I'm not such a good hand at
telling love stories as I was once.   But you're not
twenty yet, and a female, and that'll help you understand.   And at the end of this yarn I've something to

say to you, and that's what I'm after." He drummed the table with his fingers, and his eyes were dreamy.

"I was disappointed a good many years ago, Mira. Poor Mary Benson was a downright beautiful female, and as pure as an angel—" And he told her, in a monotonous tone, his eyes still staring into space, of that night when he had returned to find his love affair had been ended.

"Well," he continued, "then I went out on the river, thinkin' perhaps that I might find Taggart, or that I might forget. And I didn't find Taggart or Mary for a long time. I'd made a good many trips down to New Orleans and back on other men's keels, and at last I'd gotten me a keel of my own—Mary Benson, I called her.

"And I was going down to New Orleans when one of my hands, Injun Pete, who used to hunt with me in the old Allegheny country, got scent of pirates 'long Arkansaw, and 'twasn't long 'fore it was play snake, play 'possum, I tell you.

"You see, the half-breed was a mighty sour lookin' varmint, far as face went, and some of these Arkansaw spekylators got to feelin' his heart towards me, and he let on that he loved me 'bout as well as they did honesty, and they bit like young catties. Cuttin' my throat wasn't good enough for Injun Pete, he pretendin' to have all sorts of spite agin me. So soon he come to see the head devils in the business, and who should they be but Old Benson and Taggart, that he'd given his daughter to?

"The whole hell's work of that matter was plain enough now. Benson had been in the pirate business before he came up to the Monongahela to whip the devil around the meeting-house, and when Taggart made a call upon him for Mary he had to give her up or do worse.

"They were now spekylatin' together again, and expected to get me cheap, for certain. A big pile of money and a small chunk of revenge was their bargain, and this was the way they fixed it: Injun Pete was to keep dark 'til on our way up from New Orleans next time, after the cargo was sold. He was to know all about the money, and on our return to the Arkansaw shore, he was to give the word, when arrangements would be made to catch us foul in the right place. He was to secure our arms during the watch at night, let the varmints on board and then kingdom come to us! All was settled among 'em and we put out jest as innercent as could be.

"We didn't work very hard that day. That trip would a-suited Jabe Knuckles, and no mistake, but he hadn't took to boating then. Dark come, and we tied up only a few miles from Benson and his gang. And now, old 'Siah, a little more peach and sweetnin', sense you will set up, and I'll tell you somethin' to keep you wide awake."

While Hodgkiss mixed the grog, Mike walked over to the boy's bed, and covered him. Mira sat down by his side when he returned. Mike drank and continued:

"Without having learned their den exactly, Pete

had the hang of their tracks, enough to get along with, and leavin' only one man aboard the keel, nine on us set out to trap those river rats.

"We kept along the bank awhile to a bayou we had to go up. Then, as we got near the place, Pete, scoutin' ahead, saw two men pushing out into the Massassip', one of them Taggart, and they was watchin' us. I stepped out in the starlight, hailed the skiff, and commanded the men ashore, but they fired a signal shot and only pulled out faster.

"The thing was out. I cracked away at Taggart—and he tumbled for the bottom—I drew a bead on his eyes. At the same minute the skiff took a whirl against a sawyer and over she went, leavin' the live rascal hanging onto the branches. All we had to do was to make a rush up the bayou and lose no time about it.

"And up we went, and across two clearings, and through a belt of timber, and on to a lake, but here we was stopped. Pete was ahead, and just as he made a sign that all was right, there come a shower of balls, wounding two on us and killing Pete outright.

"We made another rush, and we were over a ditch and levee, and down upon a right smart log fort. We heard the sound of horses dashing off through the woods. No more fight was made. In we marched.

"There was an old nigger woman and two or three little snowballs in the first room, but we could get nothing out of them. I went into the second room."

Mike drank and paused a moment. His voice was

monotonous, his eyes were expressionless, as he continued.

"I found Mary there," he said. "She was right sick. I knew her though, spite of sickness and sufferin', and she knew me. She died in my arms that night. Taggart was dead, her father was a cut-throat, and her child—that boy—she gave him to me to bring up to ways of honesty. His first name was Carpenter. We managed to forget his last name.

"Damn you, Hodgkiss, can't you see my cup is empty?"

Mike drank, then, "Mira," he said, "you're young and foolish, and it may be that I'm wild and wicked. I've told you about this so you'd know I meant it when I say I never mean to marry. If I've trifled with you, it's been because you're foolish, and I stop it now, you see, 'cause I think it would be to my shame, and the worse for you."

Mira smiled as she rose and left the room. "Nobody wants to marry you," she said. "Good night."

And the next day, a little after dawn, Mike looked from his boat to the shore a few miles below the grocery and saw Mira standing there.

"I want to go with you," she shouted. And the boat twisted in to the shore.

IV

The story tells of another encounter Mike had with Benson a few years later, this time in New Orleans.

He had cleared three French ballrooms, had had two levee fights with *gens d'armes*, and had broken a bank in a gambling house. Hence he had been rather tired and heavy with drink when Benson tried to rob him. But the boatman saw through the trick, and Mike and his crew tarred and feathered Benson, and poured knock-out drops intended for Mike down his throat.

And the tale reveals that unknown to Mike, Benson had been aided in his scheme by a member of Mike's crew, Talbott. Talbott, Mike had met on the levee in New Orleans, and he had taken to him because he was, said Mike, "the ugliest white man yet." Disfigured by some terrible accident, he looked like a figure in a horrible dream. The flesh under both of Talbott's eyes had been cut away, leaving the white eyeballs exposed, and the upper part of the nose was gone, leaving a gap which was only partially covered by a black patch. Always his eyes seemed to glare; his face was as changeless as that of a hideous gargoyle. Talbott amused Fink awhile; later the keeler was repulsed by his ugliness.

The tale tells, furthermore, how Talbott went to Mira with news of an affair which the boatman had with another woman, and how, spitefully, knowing of Mike's hatred for him, Mira married Talbott and went away with him. Mike met Talbott at the battle of New Orleans, where Fink and his crew "did gallant service, their rifles pouring death into the ranks of the enemy. Pursuing the British, too, on their retreat, at the head of a new scouting party, Fink met Talbott,

OHIO RIVER BOATMEN—1827

and in such a questionable situation as led to a belief
that he had been and still was employed against the
American interest. They had a bloody personal encounter; Talbott was nearly killed, and so they lost
sight of each other."

Carpenter grew to manhood, learning, under Mike's
direction, to shoot, to fight, and to drink—and to do all
very well. Mike changed little with the years; Morgan Neville saw him in 1820 when he was about fifty,
"his proportions perfectly symmetrical . . . exhibiting the evidences of Herculean powers. To a stranger,
he would have seemed a complete mulatto. Long ex-
posure to the sun and weather on the lower Ohio and
Mississippi had changed his skin; and, but for the fine
European cast of his countenance, he might have passed
for the principal warrior of some powerful tribe. Although at least fifty . . . his hair was as black as the
wing of the raven. Next to his skin he wore a red
flannel shirt, covered by a blue capote, ornamented
with white fringe. On his feet were moccasins, and a
broad leather belt, from which hung, suspended on a
sheath, a large knife, encircled his waist." Settlers
continued to pour down the rivers into the new country, and cabins were closer along the banks; the land
along the rivers was becoming settled, and soon it
would no longer be a frontier.

There were changes, too, on the river. Keelboats,
flatboats, and barges were soon to become outmoded.
In 1811, *The Navigator* had heralded a change:

There is now on foot a new mode of navigating our western waters, particularly the Ohio and Mississippi rivers. This is with boats propelled by the power of steam. This plan has been carried into successful operation on the Hudson river at New York, and on the Delaware between New Castle and Burlington. . . . From these successful experiments there can be little doubt of the plan succeeding on our western waters, and proving of immense advantage to the commerce of our country. A Mr. Rosewalt, a gentleman of enterprise, and who is acting it is said in conjunction with Messrs. Fulton and Livingston of New York, has a boat of this kind now on the stocks at Pittsburgh, of 138 feet keel, calculated for 300 or 400 tons burden. And there is one building at Frankfort, Kentucky, by citizens who no doubt will push the enterprise. It will be a novel sight, and as pleasing as novel to see a huge boat working her way up the windings of the Ohio, without the appearance of sail, oar, pole, or any manual labor about her—moving within the secrets of her own wonderful mechanism, and propelled by power undiscoverable!

And so steamboats, at first awkward, ungainly, uncertain, later flamboyant and cocky, had steamed up and down the rivers navigated at the time by straining, swearing rivermen. At first the rivermen looked at the boats with amusement; they were freaks, these monsters, and they soon would pass. "Mike Fink, on seeing the first steamboat on the Mississippi river," records an almanac, "said that he thought that Noah's ark was passing by, and that the breath of all the creatures in creation was smoken through the stove pipe."

Later, when flatboatmen, bargemen, keelboatmen, were to see the steamboats taking over their trade, they

were to come to hate the smoking monsters. Always
there were fights on the western trails before the old
order yielded to the new: the packhorse men had
swooped down on wagons, battering them to pieces,
mobbing their drivers; the "waggoners" and teamsters
had battled against canalmen and rivermen. Now, in
the river towns, where steamboats and keels and flats
anchored side by side, the older rivermen were to fight
in the taverns and on boat decks with the newer.

In the fall of 1821, ten years after the first river
steamer, built by Nicholas Roosevelt, had astonished
the rivermen by journeying from Pittsburgh to New
Orleans in fourteen days, Mike's keelboat was descend-
ing the Mississippi, a few miles below St. Louis, bound
for New Orleans. It was an Indian Summer day, the
heat of the golden sunlight tinged with the first cool-
ness of autumn, and below the blue skies the trees
stretched crimson, brown and green branches above the
yellow stream.

The keelboat was gliding down the smooth current
of an open reach of river. At the steering oar lounged
Carpenter, tall, handsome, as brown as an Indian, his
cheek bulged with a chaw of tobacco. Sprawled over
cargo box and the shaded running-board the men
rested. A knot of them was gathered immediately beneath the steersman, and Mike Fink was the center of
the group as he pointed his finger at old Jabe Knuckles.

"That's a fact!" he said. "Old Jabe's gettin' pious!
He wants to quit bumpin' a keelboat into sandbars—
wants to settle down in St. Louie. And it's all been

sense he played too much lotto with old Madame Tisan there. But no man with as much sense as an alligator would want to live in St. Louie—

Adieu to St. Louie, I bid you er-dieu;
Likewise to the French and the mers-qui-ters, too,
For of all other nations I do you disdain,
I'll go back to Ken-tuck-y and try her er-gain!

"Shucks," said Jabe, "you're jest wrathy against St. Louie because you was arrested there for trimmin' off the nigger's heel with your rifle. But I'm tellin' you that St. Louie is the fur-tradin' center of the West, an' fur-traders in future is a-goin' to live off the fat o' the land. That's why I think o' settlin' there."

"Fat o' the land?" said Mike. "What do you keer about the fat o' the land? A man that likes some of the stuff you've et! God help us! Did you boys ever hear about Madame Tisan and Jabe's pup slickin's?"

"That's all a damned no such thing, Mike Fink," said Jabe, sitting up, his eyes blazing. "I didn't swaller the first mouthful, and you know it."

"Why you old snappin' turkle," said Mike, "I seen you pullin' har out of your teeth for a week, anyhow."

"Give us the yarn, daddy," said Carpenter, and some of the men clamored for the story.

"Well—keep her out more in the stream, boy—first time I come to St. Louie, about six, seven years ago— Jabe was along, of course—it was cold weather, and jest before fast time, or jest after it, one or other; greasy Tuesday, or something—they call it mardygraw in New Orleans—and a raft on us went down, night-time, to a dance doin's at Madame Tisan's—that Jabe's sweet on, now.

"Well, there was some awful pollyvooin' and French fashions, you know, but the gals was mighty peart lookin', as French gals always is, and it was, 'Wooly voo dance, Miss?' and 'Wee, Munsheer!' and dosey-do, and shassey, and toe-nail, and break-down, I tell you, jest as if we'd been all acquainted all along. Only there was somethin' underfoot."

Mike stooped, hoisted aloft with one hand a jug of whiskey, slowly and gracefully curved his arm and drank with relish.

"There was a hull lot of French pups about under-foot, and they kept puttin' their ki-yi-yi into the rest of the lingo, every now and then, when some alligator-hoss put his foot on 'em. And then Madame Tisan would go on jest as if she'd pupped 'em herself, and felt a nat'ral affection for 'em. Some cake doin's was to wind up the ball—a sorter slapjack party, and right over the fire was an almighty big open kittle, full of molasses slickin's and grease, to pour over the slap-jacks; and it was a-bilin' and creaming up beautiful, I tell you, when just about then I broke one of the cussed puppy's legs, and Madame Tisan mounted me in the most unairthly kind of loud French. The he polly-voos took it up too, and was mighty sassy and fighty—to one another, I reckon, for I didn't take the trouble to ask them what they said, and they knew bet-ter than to cuss me in the vernac'lar, I predicate.

"Well, before they calmed down some, jest to prevent mischief in future, I picked up a couple of the pups—they was all over curly, I tell you—and, in the row, I popped 'em keerful into the kittle!"

"By God!" roared a poleman, slapping his thigh. "Dog candy!"

"Don't squirm, old Jabe!" said Carpenter. The auditors were enjoying the story hugely—all except Knuckles.

"Well," continued Fink, "down they went and liked the sweetnin', I reckon, for they didn't come up again, and the kittle went on bilin', and bimeby, boys, it was cake time!

"It was cake time, old Jabe! Do you hear?" cried Mike. "And the way the slapjacks come in all smokin' in French, and the way the plates rattled and the munsheers jabbered was a caution. And every pollyvoo as he got his allowance shasseyed up to the fireplace, and old Aunty Tisan jest ladled out a reg'lar rise of sweetnin' over his plate and then he went to work swallerin'.

"Well, it all looked mighty temptin', and went mighty fast too, and bimeby old Jabe takes his chaw out'n his mouth, shasseys up with a plate, just like the rest, and then I begin to wink to the boys and they lay low for laughin' time. Aunty Tisan was getting tolerable down in the kittle, 'bout now, and first thing Jabe did was to begin pickin' his teeth and spittin', but it was right good for all that, and he took another turn at it. The pollyvoos likewise began feeling their teeth, and the old woman was stirrin' up faster and faster, and then there was all kinds of nasty faces and next all kinds of sackray damnations and monkey doin's. And last of all old Aunty Tisan ladled up one of the pups, safe and sound, all but the har!

"Oh, jehu mariar, wa'n't there a squeal! 'Sackray Americane!' was the first thing sung out, and I just give old aunty an idee that Jabe was the man, and Lord Almighty, didn't she comb him! He ain't got the creases out of his face yet. The ball broke helliniferous, I tell you.

"Well, old Jabe has been ever since playin' lotto with the widow to make up, but it ain't no use, boys. For the pup slickin's sticks in his teeth and no mistake!"

Jabe did not join in the roar of laughter that followed the story, and when the men had ceased, he said angrily:

"I reckon, Mike Fink, Aunty Tisan don't stick in my teeth half as much as Mira Hodgkiss does in yourn."

Fink's face was red with anger as he answered: "You damned sarpint! Man and woman, child and parent—years and years gone by, too—and you only waitin' for a chance to sting me! The devil in hell will be better for it!" His hand clenched Jabe's throat, his arm seized a leg. Then his muscles bulged as he lifted the struggling man in the air and staggered toward the edge of the cargo box. The crew, bustling to life, intervened as Mike, cooling somewhat, let Jabe tumble, sprawling. "Keep off, all on you!" he shouted, fingering his knife, which hung on his worsted belt.

His eyes fell on Carpenter, who had left his oar. "You too, you cussed imp of a black hearted—never mind; there's a streak of angel in you yet, or ought to be!" He lifted the jug to his lips, and drank long.

"Take your rifle," he said to Carpenter, more calmly. "Go forward! If your heart is true to me, I'll know it by your shot. If not, the devil is near, an' God forgive you!"

As if from a habit of mechanical obedience, the young man took up his shooting piece, went forward to the very bow of the dancing keelboat, and stood waiting. Fink filled a tin cup to the brim with whiskey, placed it on his head, stood with feet planted wide apart on the unsteady boat-planks. He laughed savagely, recklessly.

"Fire!" he shouted.

Carpenter's rifle came slowly to his shoulder, and there was a silence of lapping waters as he took aim. The rifle cracked, and whiskey spurted from the hole through the cup onto Mike's head and shoulders. The crew shouted as Mike flung the rest of the liquor down his throat. He strode forward, met Carpenter half way, and flung his arms around the boy. He splashed liquor into the cup, and Carpenter drank, while Mike lifted the jug to his lips. And now Mike, more genial, started towards Jabe.

"Maybe, Jabe," he said, "you'd better drink with me, and we'll forget about it."

But Jabe was silent, and Mike's eyes narrowed. Then a number of men shouted together:

"Steamboat ahead!"

And Mike, still scowling, whirled to look at a side-wheeler crawling upstream, deeply laden. From the black keelboat with its weathered gray sail Mike looked out at a white ship resplendent in the sunshine. The sun flashed upon her gilded fretwork, upon the glass of the pilot's house, upon the brass on her decks and cabins. Smoke from the laboring engine carried sparks from the smokestacks, and the paddles threw out shining drops of water. Her body was the body of a keelboat, for early builders had learned that only such boats could toil upstream, but she was moved not by the power of men but by the puffing machinery which churned on her deck.

"Shall we give her the channel?" Carpenter, who had returned to the steersman's post, asked Mike. Mike walked away from Jabe, his jaw set, his face still black with a scowl.

"Give me that sweep," he commanded. Grasping the heavy oar, he stood erect, his eyes fixed on the chugging steamer. "Man the oars!" he roared. And while the men found their way to their seats, his muscles moved beneath his browned skin, hardening. "Straight ahead!" he shouted. The keelboat had just moved around a bend in the river where the water was quite low, and where a bar from the Illinois shore threw the current over against the sandy bank on the Missouri side. The steady beat of the oars accelerated the speed of the boat.

Carpenter looked anxiously at the gleaming steamer. "Going to take the bank, ain't she?" he asked.

"If she does," said Mike, "by God, I'll sink her!"

And Mike steadily held his course; the boat did not swerve in either direction. "There's no river law that makes me give her the channel! I'm going to sink that God damned top-heavy tub!"

Then, as the two boats sped toward one another, Mike shouted a drunken challenge:

"I'm Mike Fink, king of the keelboatmen! I'm a Salt River Roarer, a ring-tailed screamer! I can out-jump, out-run, and out-fight ary man on the Massassip'! I got the best crew and the fastest boat on ary river, and if ary man says no, I'll be in his hair quicker than hell can scorch a feather!"

The steamboat whistle shrieked. Too late, the pilot tried to put out into the stream. There were shouts, the janglings of bells. Horrified faces peered over the rails of the steamer. Keelboatmen rushed to Mike's side to wrest the oar from him. Then the boats collided, almost head on, and one keeler splashed into the waters while others toppled. A crash that hurled the steamer's chimneys overboard, that tore the boat's starboard guard and bow to pieces, that smashed a side of the keelboat and sent the water pouring through a hundred gaping seams told the weight of the collision.

"She's sinking, Mike!" shouted the boatmen. "The keel's sinking!"

Mike tried to twist the bow to the bank. But she

was going down too fast, dragged bottomward by her cargo of lead.

"Ashore, all!" he cried at last, and boatmen splashed away from the sinking ship.

There were cries from the steamer as she lurched in the deepest part of the channel, and the boatmen, looking back, saw her slanting decks fling passengers into the water.

And the tale records that Jabe drowned, and that Mira, who was on the steamer, drowned also. But Talbott and his and Mira's daughter, also on the boat, were saved.

V

Mike and Carpenter found their way back to St. Louis, and there, through the winter, they haunted the taverns, spending the last of their money before springtime.

St. Louis was a colorful town in those days, the starting-point for a frontier just beginning to lure the adventurers who broke trails for settlers. Always in old America as new lands were filled in by settlements, some daring souls moved farther westward—hunters and trappers, wilderness lovers who felt cramped if neighbors raised cabins within a mile. Such were the men who set out from St. Louis to open trails into the next El Dorado for restless pioneers.

St. Louis had grown rich as a market for the precious furs which had been brought in by traders and trappers who had straggled back from rugged lands, some of

them after penetrating even into uncharted forests beyond the Rockies. A motley city it was, with its little
stone houses perched on a hillside aslant which a path
moved from the river to the city. There yellow-clay
streets, lined with wild-flowers, meandered between
gray limestone mansions or whitewashed homes. The
houses stood in yards surrounded by high fences on
which honeysuckle vines hung. And on the streets of
the city moved a varied crowd, sullen and dirty blan-
keted Indians who lounged against posts of doorways,
barefooted negroes and negresses, the charming French
aristocrats, "hectoring, bragging boatmen of the Mississippi" and "gay, grimacing, singing, good humored
voyageurs." "Now and then a stark Kentucky hunter,
in leathern hunting-dress, with rifle on shoulder and
knife in belt, strode along." The city was still tinged
somewhat by French influence; the *Gazette* still printed
some of the notices in French. "Here and there were
new brick houses and shops, just set up by bustling,
driving and eager men of traffic from the Atlantic
States; while, on the other hand, were the old French
mansions, with open casements, still retaining the easy,
indolent air of the original colonists; and now and then
the scraping of a fiddle, a strain of an ancient French
song, or the sound of billiard balls, showed that the
happy Gallic turn for gayety still lingered about the
place."

From that romantic city, since 1764, entrepreneurs
had sent traders to barter with Indians along the Missouri River, and since 1794, fur companies had op-

erated. The year after Lewis and Clark had penetrated the wilderness of America to the mouth of the
Columbia, fur-trading from St. Louis had received a
new impetus under the Spaniard Manuel Lisa, and as
the years passed, operations extended, companies battling for the treasury of furs which came out of the
forest lands each year.

March 20, 1822, the St. Louis *Missouri Republican*
published the following advertisement:

> To enterprising young men. The subscriber wishes to
> engage one hundred young men to ascend the Missouri river
> to its source, there to be employed for one, two, or three
> years. For particulars enquire of Major Andrew Henry,
> near the lead mines in the county of Washington, who will
> ascend with, and command, the party; or of the subscriber
> near St. Louis. (Signed) William H. Ashley.

This advertisement proclaimed the founding of one
of the most illustrious companies active in the boom
years of the fur-trade. The names of the two formers
of the company were well known in St. Louis: Ashley,
born in Virginia, who in St. Louis had become General
of the Missouri militia and later Lieutenant Governor
of the youthful state; and Henry, bred in Pennsylvania, an experienced fur-trader who had deserted the
expeditions of fur hunters to mine lead near St. Louis.
These were men worthy of a following. And to them
flocked the enterprising young men for whom they had
advertised.

In less than a month, the city of St. Louis and the
surrounding country had yielded up the required num-

ber, a roystering adventure-hungry crew of voyageurs, boatmen, trappers, and some less seasoned youths who "had relinquished the most respectable employments and circles of society." Among them was Jim Bridger, one day to be celebrated as a hunter and trapper of melodramatic splendor by Ned Buntline in dime novels and, later, by Emerson Hough in his fine story, *The Covered Wagon*. Among them, too, were figures later to be famed in the Indian fights and in the courageous journeys to unknown lands of which writers of sagas and histories of the fur-trade told—Thomas Fitzpatrick, one of the Sublettes, and perhaps Etienne Provot. They were to be joined later by Hugh Glass, whose great fight with a grizzly and whose struggling journey, despite a mangled body, through miles of forest while he lived on roots and berries or the prey of wolves from which he frightened the pack, were to become almost as famed by Western campfires as stories of Mike. A fine strong band of adventurers were these who set out, some never to return to the fair city of St. Louis.

And among them were Carpenter and the king of the keelboatmen. Legend says that Mike left the river because steamboats had replaced keels. But this is not so: the steamboat did not until 1826 come into such general use that it displaced the keelboat and the flat to any appreciable degree. It is more probable that Mike Fink, who loved the river best when it was least settled, who thrived on the thrill of adventures on new frontiers, was spurred on by the love of the typical

pioneering figure for the joy of the danger of unin-
habited wildernesses.

The wide valley through which the Missouri made
its curving way and the streams which joined it, the
main routes of most fur-expeditions, were to be the
chief paths of travel for the Ashley-Henry expedition.
Beaver and otter swam in the streams, and yellow elk,
buffalo, deer and bear were on the plains and in the forests through which they flowed. Up these waters keelboats and canoes could make their way, carrying merchandise and trinkets to barter for pelts; down those
streams they could carry their precious cargoes of furs.
"The plan was to ascend to the Three Forks of the
Missouri, a region which was believed to abound in a
'wealth of furs not surpassed by the mines of Peru.'
The party would be absent for three years, trapping on
all 'the streams on both sides of the mountains in that
region, and would very likely penetrate to the mouth
of the Columbia.'

In due time, the heads of the party were licensed to
travel into the Indian country, and on April 15, 1822,
the expedition set out in two big keelboats, boats one
hundred feet long, each with two apartments for the
crew and the passengers in the seventy-five-foot cargo
box. About one-third of the length of the boat from
the bow was a mast, braced rigidly for the cordelle,
rigged with a square sail. Forward of this was the
cook's caboose. Twelve oars projected from the fore
part of the cargo box, but the oars were to be used
chiefly to descend; going up the stubborn current of

the Missouri River was too heavy a task for oarsmen.

There were wild brawls in the saloons and dance halls the night before the expedition started, and many of the men nursed aching heads as they made their way down blurred streets in the morning. At the levee a huge crowd was gathered to bid the expedition good-by. Men shouted, women and children screamed, all waved as the boats were poled out into the grip of the muddy river and the boatmen bent to the running-board to shove the vessels upstream. Muskets rattled a farewell salute. Then the sounds of the shouting died away, and the smoke from the chimneys of St. Louis faded in the distance as the keelboats pointed their prows toward the wild forests and plains of the frontier.

Mike Fink, patroon of one of the boats, studied the river with interest. A thick muddy river it was, with a strong current which cut through the loose sand of the valley as water might twine through sawdust. Obviously, it was a shifty stream. There is a poem about the Missouri which scarcely exaggerates when it says:

> She glides along by western plains
> And changes her bed each time it rains.

He saw scores of huge trees which the water had undermined; they stretched out into the stream, waving green branches, holding to the insecure bank with claw-like roots. And he knew that many such trees had broken away to form planters or sawyers which were hidden by the turbid waters of the river. But the task of navigating this stream was much like the task of driving a boat up the Mississippi, and Mike, despite the newness of the scenery, which combined hills and bluffs like those on the Ohio with broad flat lands similar to those on the Mississippi, felt at home.

The boats anchored at noon, and the men devoured their noonday meal, a slice of fat pork and biscuits for each and the usual fillee of whiskey. Then again the boats moved into the channel. Most of the time, the men tugged the keels upstream with the cordelle, and often they had to leap into the cold water, for the banks rose high on one side of the river while the marshy lands on the other side offered no secure foothold. Night came at last, and Mike and Carpenter made wry faces as they dined on a pot of mush with a pound of tallow in it.

"God Almighty!" said Fink. "I never thought I'd see the day when I'd eat a mess of gruel and candles!" But his huge bowl was emptied in a very short time.

The western skies were red as the sun went down, and the river flowed like a stream of blood through the brown clay. Then the moon came out, mellowing the harsh river into silver, penciling the leaves and branches and trees against the sky. The woods seemed silent lands of mystery. And when the stars twinkled the river was dotted with shiny flowers, and a white path stretched to the moon. Wrapped in blankets and buffalo skins, the men slept under the stars.

Dawn came, and the men devoured their breakfast of hominy, then pushed on. This day, a fine breeze came up at eight o'clock, and the crew rested while the creaking sail carried the boat upstream. Redbuds blossomed on the shore, and the cottonwoods waved their leafy branches as the boat glided past. Now and then the boat passed one of the scattered plantations along the shore; here and there a scaffolding on a sandbar marked a hunting ground where settlers waited for deer to come down to the shallows to drink.

Mike and Carpenter talked with a seasoned trapper, who told them of the life of the trapping fraternity. A tall gaunt man, his hair stringing down over his shoulders, he was like Mike only in having a weathered face as brown as leather. He wore a coonskin cap, a hunting shirt, the sleeves of which reached to his knees, breeches with long deerskin leggings. And all his clothing was decorated with feathers, fringes and beadwork which usually adorned the clothing of Indians.

"Three nations," he said, "not including the Indians, is bringin' in furs—Americans, Spanish and French. An' they are so damn' many Frenchmen in the business that you can't get around from place to place without you can pollyvoo. We use lots of French words in these parts."

"I've been noticing that," said Mike. "T'other day a mannee called Andrew Henry a boorjaw, and I figgered that was French."

"Bourgeois? Oh, yes, that means he's the patroon —the head of the company. You're a boatman on the Mississippi; here in these parts they call a boatman a voyageur. They're French mostly on the Missouri.

They sing lots and they can push a pole or pull a cordelle like all hell."

"Good fighters?" asked Mike, as he looked with interest at a wiry French boatman who had spread his buckskin clad body on the deck.

"Can't fight worth a damn," said the trapper, and he spat accurately and neatly at a knothole ten feet away. Mike negligently squirted another splash of tobacco juice on the knothole. "Then there's the mangeurs de lard—"

"What're them?" asked Carpenter.

"That means pork eaters, and we call 'em that because pork's all they're likely to get to eat. They're the green hands, and they do all the dirtiest work and get paid the least."

"Do they have a French name for you trappers?"

"It's likely. But we manage mostly to get called just trappers. We're mostly Americans anyhow."

"Good," said Mike. "The boy and me signed on this voyage for trappers."

"Well," said the trapper, "I've allus wanted to see what a boatman'd do if he got a man's job trappin'."

"Hell and damn, don't talk to me about a man's job. I've wrestled keelboats up rivers so fast that they scraped the tar off the bottom of a boat. I've landed cargoes o' lead in New Orleans when the weather was so all-fired hot that the lead stuck together. And I've fought my way through cyclones on the Ohio and barrooms in Natchez. Don't talk to me about a man's job trappin'."

"Well, anyhow, you'll find it interestin'," said the trapper. "We wrestle keelboats and canoes up right lively streams, too, God knows. And we fight redskins and the varmints of the forests and mountains and plains as well. By God, any trapper worth his salt can lick his weight in wildcats."

"I've fought Indians," said Mike, "when I was an infant, and I've taken my share of b'ar, moose, and wildcat."

The trapper chuckled. "Maybe you'll do," he said. "I still think you'll find trappin' tolerable interestin'. On this very river, we'll go through six tribes that may either puff the pipe with us or fill our hides with arrows, or they may do both, the treacherous sarpints!"

"Good," said Mike; "my trigger finger's itchin'. War, famine and bloodshed puts flesh on my bones, and hardship's my daily bread."

"You'll thrive then in the fur country, trompin' through hundreds of miles to watch the traps, settin' traps with one hand with your other curled around your gun when your breath turns to icicles. It's work for a man, God knows."

The boat fought onward up the river. The wind died at noon and the men pushed with their poles. They passed the Tavern rocks, scratched over with rude Indian drawings of birds and beasts, then went up through a long reach of quiet river, followed by a stretch wherein a swift current pushed hard against the boat. Then rain and a wind which beat the river into fury caused the boats to scramble for the shore, and that night the men slept piled thick in the cargo boxes or under hastily improvised dripping shelters on shore.

The third day, the keelboats passed Boone's settlement where old Daniel Boone had in his last years founded another of many colonies. Even after he had passed eighty, it was said, the old pioneer had gone twice a year on the hunt, accompanied by a negro who skinned the game and kept the camp. Daniel Boone had died in 1820, but the settlement still thrived: a number of plantations stood on the edge of the bottom land. Another day's journey carried the party through a river which crooked and curved past several plantations. They usually consisted of a few cleared acres on the borders of the river, a small log hut and some log stables. Pigs grunted in the meadows, and cows munched grass under trees. The current swept down on the boat toward evening around a huge wooden island, which a voyageur told Mike was an "embarras," a collection of thickly tangled trees extending thirty yards. Oars and grappling hooks were used in vain, and at last the boatmen splashed into the cold water and dragged the boat around. The jolly voyageurs chanted a gay song, new to Mike's ears, as they splashed in the icy river:

> A frigate went a-sailing
>   Mon joli cœur de rose,
> Far o'er the seas away
>   Joli cœur d'un rosier,
>   Joli cœur d'un rosier,
>   Mon joli cœur de rose.

And now the sun was down, and the shivering boat-men steamed themselves dry by the evening fire over which the hominy and pork were cooking.

Days passed, weeks passed, and they still struggled northward against a stubborn current. The twenty-third day out one of the boats hit a riffle which drove them back five times. After the fifth trial, when the men had been within a boat's length of making the water above the riffle, ten men leaped into the swift stream with the cordelle, twelve rowed, and others shoved with poles. Mike's crew managed to crawl through with poles alone, while Mike swore and taunted them into enthusiasm. And the rest of the day Mike and his crew told the men on the other boat that good boatmen never backed downstream.

Later they had still more ammunition for argu-ments, when, fifty miles below the mouth of the Kansas River, a snag which Mike had dodged buckled through the planks of the other keel with a crash. The boat and its ten thousand dollar cargo of merchandise and trapping supplies lurched below the muddy surface of the river while the swearing crew and trappers splashed to the shore. Nothing was salvaged. With the re-maining boat, the party pressed on.

Two days later the keel came in sight of Fort Osage at the end of a three-mile stretch of river, on a high bluff above a curve in the stream. The boat had now gone three hundred miles, and during the last hundred the men had met only traders or hunters who passed them in canoes. The men sang joyously, whiskey was

FUR TRADING FORT ON THE MISSOURI—1825

distributed, and shouts echoed from the shore. Near the fort, Osage Indians, squaws, braves, and papooses, walking along the shore, curiously followed the boat. Some were wrapped in buffalo robes, some of the men were clad only in loin cloths. All looked dirty and greasy, and all the men carried bows, war clubs or guns. The expedition's commanders paid the traders at the fort a social call.

The boat sailed past tepees of Pawnees, Otoes and Sioux, past stockaded trading posts scattered miles apart along the river. The waters of the river rose; one day fifty drowned buffalo drifted past the boat. Spring was followed by the scorching days of summer. Hunters left the party at intervals to bring back buffalo, venison, grouse or rabbits. And one day in August, northwest of the Mandan villages, a band of deceitful Assiniboine Indians who had pretended friendship "swooped down upon the impotent horse guards [on shore] at a time when the main body with the keelboat had crossed with the channel to the opposite shore. Fifty horses . . . were driven away, while nearly a hundred men, all armed but out of range, gazed across the waste of sand and water and raged to no purpose."

The party halted for the season, not at the Falls of the Missouri, as it had intended, but at the mouth of the Yellowstone. On the tongue of land between the two rivers, the Missouri and the Yellowstone, the men raised some cabins and a stockade which were to serve as the center of trapping operations. Ashley and some

of the men went back to St. Louis, with the expectation
of returning the next spring with another party.

VI

Now the real work of the expedition began. Little
parties of ten or twelve men went out from the fort
to trap and hunt in various assigned localities. Most
of the men by now had worn to tatters the clothes they
had worn when they started from St. Louis, and they
were glad—for it was fall—to don the Indian-like
garb which trappers and hunters wore in the colder
months—a hunting shirt of dressed deerskin, a heavy
hooded cloak (capote), furlined moccasins with long
folds which wrapped around their ankles. With packhorses which were to carry the furs, and with meager
equipment—a rifle, some ammunition, traps, knives,
axes, some pans, some food, a little whiskey, much tobacco—they rode into the forests.

Mike and Carpenter and ten more men went to the
Musselshell, the country of the Blood Indians. There
they trapped the streams and the forests, and there they
bartered with Indians and free trappers—independent
workers who brought their pelts to no one company.
The knowledge of woodcraft which Mike had learned
during his youth and later during hunting expeditions
served him in good stead.

The trapper had to know many secrets. He had to
be able to discover whether cottonwood had been
felled by beavers to dam a stream or merely to provide

food. He had to set his traps accordingly, suspending them just right in the water, carefully keeping away all odors except that of beaver castor. He had to read animal signs as quickly as a scholar reads a printed page, and then act skillfully and wisely. Mike spent several months in the forests, working hard, and reaping a reward of many fine furs. Then, when the district offered no more rich pelts, the party returned to the fort as winter sent its first snowstorm sweeping through the forests.

Almost the first man Mike met at the fort was Talbott. The man had been engaged as a gunsmith—he had been a gunsmith for a time before in Louisville. It was only the intervention of several trappers and hunters that kept Mike from leaping at his throat. After that encounter Talbott usually kept away from his old enemy.

But Talbott had a daughter whom he had brought with him into that womanless land of the fur-traders, and the young men of the fort flocked through the snow to her cabin of evenings. With them went Carpenter, in love for the first time, stuttering, blushing, in the light of the log fire, as Mike had done in his youth when he courted Mary Benson.

Mike became gloomy and then nasty. "His temper," says the writer of the tale, "grew to be unbearable; he was a terror to all in the fort. The commanding officer, in the loose state of discipline then customary, found him unmanageable; and for the quiet ones, generally, they wished him at the devil. . . . Finally Fink, in a fury, withdrew from the fort altogether, prepared a rude sort of cave in the neighborhood for his winter's den, and he took Carpenter with him." "All was not harmony, even between Mike and 'his boy,' as he called him. The former had intentionally avoided the sight of Jane—Mira's child, by the man whom, of all earth, he most abhorred; and, apart from this consideration, there was something in the idea of the offspring of Mary Benson and Mira Hodgkiss coming together, which made his blood creep! True, there was no bar of blood, but that of circumstances seemed to him equally forbidding."

Carpenter would go into the black night from Jane's cabin, would crunch through the snow which wound through black trees up to the cave on the hill. And as he walked, stooping, into the cave and lay down to rest, he would hear Mike's voice.

"If you love me, Carpenter," Fink would say, "you won't sting me by giving your heart to the flesh and blood of a domestic poisoner and a traitor to his country. I'd rather see you dead, boy, and then die on your grave, than see you take that gal."

Through hours of blackness the voice droned on. Carpenter said nothing. At last he fell asleep.

Jane in the end partly decided the quarrel between the two by accepting another suitor, but the ill feeling between the pair did not die, and now both Carpenter and Fink snarled at one another in their gloomy cave. They were jolly some times after drinking deep of the whiskey which Mike had smuggled to their lair, but more often they sat arguing or angrily silent in the flickering light of their candles. Often Carpenter stayed away from the cave for days at a time. The whiskey ran out, and Mike went to the fort carrying two big jugs.

In the storeroom of the fort, he asked the clerk for whiskey, looking thirstily at the farther end of the room where barrels were piled.

"No, Mike," said the clerk. "You'll get your ration with the rest."

"Ration, hell," said Mike. "I'm not the kind of a man that's satisfied with washing his mouth out. I want whiskey to drink!"

He lifted his rifle, sent a ball driving through the head of a keg. He put his jugs beneath the spurting stream of liquor, reloaded his piece, then calmly walked away with his jugs in one hand, his rifle in another. "That's more like it," said Mike.

The winter wore on, and Mike and Carpenter began to hear rumors about themselves circulating in the fort —"whispers of crime, insinuations of vice." And each suspected the other of starting the lies. Both sometimes suspected that Talbott, who had been no friend of Carpenter in his suit, and who hated Mike, had originated the tales "but they had grown to have nearly as little confidence in each other as they had in him." So hatred and misunderstanding flourished.

Spring came at last, and trappers who had been out

all winter came with their bundles of furs back to the fort. Indians and halfbreeds and the mountain men, who hunted alone, had drifted in. And one day a crowd of them decided to go down to Mike's cave and rouse the keelboatman from his torpor.

"That old b'ar's slept long enough. Let's tell him it's spring!" said one.

"We'll take along some whiskey," said another. "He'll wake up when he smells that!"

So bearing a keg, the mountain men, the trappers from the post, some Indians in their skins and blankets, went through the grass and wild-flowers to the cave. There they started shouting, and at last Mike came out, his hair long, his beard black, his clothes torn. He was truculent at first, but the whiskey warmed him, and he became jolly as he listened to the talk and the tall tales of his guests as they told of their adventures. Carpenter joined the group, and, like Mike, felt friendly after a few drinks, "and," says the story, "when he made the first advance towards a reconciliation with his old protector, by calling on him to sing 'Neal Hornback,' Mike's heart quite opened towards him. He gave him his hand, took a 'big drink' with him, and complied."

"You see, boys," said Mike, "Neal was boatin' up Salt River, and Tom Johnston and me stole three kegs of whiskey that he was mighty choice about, and he went about wailin', and tellin' me how it was Johnston and Macdannily, and I never let on nothin'. Well,

you see, it made all sorts of a laugh, and I just made
a song about it."

Solemnly, almost dolefully, Mike chanted his crude
composition.

My name it are Neal Hornback,
I sail-ed from Mudford shore,
And ventured up the Poll-ing fork,
Where Indians' rifles roar,
Oh, the matter it are conclu-di-ed,
It are hard for to unbind,
I waded the forks of Salt riviere,
And left my kegs behind.

An hour or two before day,
I pick-ed up my gun,
Returned to my periogue,
And saw the mischief done.
I laid it on Tom John-sti-on,
Who were innercent and clear,
But for to destroy my charac-ture,
It plainly did appear.

I call-ed my friends er-round me,
And thus to them did s-a-a-y,
Macdannily and Tom John-sti-on,
Have stored my kegs er-way.
Oh, if they are the lads what stoled your kegs,
They have done the verry thing,
And if your kegs are miss-ing,
You'll not see them er-gin.

Neal's body it were enorm-ous,
His legs were long and slim,
Good Lord, it would make you sor-ry,
Was you to look on him.

He were crook'd back'd, hump'd shoulder-ed
And with thick lips is blessed,
And for to make him ug-i-ly,
The Lord has done his best.

The motley crowd joined in a storm of applause, and Mike grinned cheerfully. He turned to Carpenter.

"Boy!" he shouted, seizing his hand, "swap shots with me and be my own son again!"

"All right," said Carpenter, carelessly. He stooped for his gun while Mike marched off a hundred paces, then stood ready, a whiskey cup on his head. Carpenter's face was flushed with drink.

"Look out, old Mike!" shouted one of the trappers from the fort, "he'll pay you now!" Mike frowned.

"Fire!" said he. The rifle cracked, and the cup leaped from Mike's head, splashing whiskey on the turf. Mike, puzzled, lifted his hand to his matted hair. Puzzled, he looked at it: it was wet with blood. He looked up and his eyes fell upon Talbott, standing in a clump of trees some distance behind Carpenter. He frowned, and his hands trembled as he slowly raised his gun. Treachery?

"Boy," he said, sternly, "I taught you to shoot better than that!"

There was silence as he slowly took aim; every eye was straining to see the cup on Carpenter's head. The moment the shot sped from the gun, Carpenter fell. The crowd dashed to his side, circled around him. The bullet had crashed through his forehead. Mike

brushed his hands over his eyes and walked up, unsteadily.

Talbott sauntered up. "That job was a pretty plain
one!" he said.

Mike, bending over Carpenter, holding him in his
arms, dazed, did not hear him.

VII

Mike, of course, was not tried for murder. The
trapper was beyond the jurisdiction of law. "No court
or jury," wrote Josiah Gregg, "is called to adjudicate
upon his disputes and abuses save his own conscience,
and no powers are invoked to redress them save those
with which the God of nature has endowed him." But
Mike went about the fort and into the woods with the
look of a man who was condemned to die. Sometimes
he lay for hours on the grave of Carpenter, his face
buried in his hands.

He heard one day that Talbott had been talking,
that Talbott had said that Mike was guilty of willful
murder. His rifle across his arm, he walked through
the gate of the stockade, crossed the area, and entered
the doorway which led to the armory.

Talbott was there, bending his ugly head above a
rifle. Looking up, he saw Fink entering, his face harrowed as if with pain, his rifle in his hand. The gunsmith snatched up a rifle and leveled it.

"If you come closer, you're a dead man, Fink!" he
called.

"I'm come to speak to you, Talbott," said Mike, "about old matters—about my boy."

"Don't come closer. Don't. I give you warning!"

"I must speak to you about Carpenter," repeated Mike, still advancing.

"Another step, and by—"

Mike took another step, his last. The room rumbled the echo of an explosion, and Mike fell to the ground, holding up his rifle, but making no attempt to use it. His lips twisted into a grim smile.

"Well," he said, "now you feel safe and can listen to me for a minute."

Talbott stood over him. "I've saved you from the gallows," he said, "and that's all that can be said. The king of the keelboatmen! Old scores will be paid at last."

"Yes, Talbott—"

"More scores than you think, Mike Fink. You remember Mary Benson's wedding night? Talbott has owed you something of a grudge for that; but there's another hasn't forgotten it—Taggart—and he stands before you now!"

"My God! You—Taggart?"

"Yes, Taggart! Your rifle did this to me, down on the banks of the Arkansaw. By God, I swore I'd pay you for that, and by God, I did! Taggart, I am, but you never knew me, but you hated and were hated, just the same, damn you!"

Sweat beaded on Mike's forehead; his face was very white. "A man ain't entirely lost when his soul whis-

THE DEATH OF MIKE FINK

pers him the devil's near," he said, and his great voice had died to a whisper. "Taggart, Carpenter, my boy, that I murdered, was Mary's boy, your own son! And you—you—" and now his voice rose, "with your lies and slanders, brought his death, for doubt of treachery unnerved me!"

Taggart stood over him silent. And now Mike's talk became incoherent, for he had lost much blood.

"I'll bring back your daughter, Hodgkiss," he murmured. "It was my fault—and Carpenter, no mother, no friends—laid in the earth, too, cold and bloody, and his face turned from me. I didn't mean to kill—my boy!"

And the story ends:

"Thus died Mike Fink, and, as if fate had but one end reserved for all those who through life had been woven in his checkered history, Talbott or Taggart— a few weeks afterwards, driven from the fort more by his guilty imagination than by fear of arrest, was drowned in an attempt to cross the Missouri."

VIII

It hardly seems necessary to pick this tale to pieces, to point out that it is too full of coincidences (and the original story contained more than does this version) to be true, that it has in it more melodrama than life unfortunately is likely to have. It remains the best of all stories about Mike Fink, though it is highly colored by its author's imagination.

How highly it is colored one may judge as he reads the author's factual story of Mike's death, in which he tells of the event as he heard of it from Major Keemle, a former fur-trader who took down the song of Neal Hornback as Mike sang it, and who visited the fort where Mike died shortly before or shortly after. This may not be the true story of the death of the king of the keelboatmen, but it seems the most plausible of all those told in the many years which have passed since Mike was killed:

"The Last of the Boatmen" has not become altogether a *mythic* personage. There be around us those who still remember him as one of flesh and blood, as well of proportions simply human, albeit he lacked not somewhat of the heroic in stature, as well as in being a "perfect terror" to people!

As regards Mike, it has not yet become that favourite question of doubt—"Did such a being really live?" Nor have we heard of the skeptic inquiry—"Did such a being really die?" But his death in half a dozen different ways and places has been asserted, and this, we take it, is the first gathering of the *mythic* haze—that shadowy and indistinct enlargement of outline, which, deepening through long ages, invests distinguished mortality with the sublimer attributes of the hero and the demi-god. Had Mike lived in "early Greece," his flat-boat feats would, doubtless, in poetry, have rivalled those of Jason, in his ship; while in Scandinavian legends, he would have been a river-god, to a certainty! The Sea-kings would have sacrificed to him every time they "crossed the bar," on their return; and as for Odin, himself, he would be duly advised, as far as any interference went, to "lay low and keep dark, or, *pre*-haps," &c.

The story of Mike Fink, including *a* death, has been beautifully told by the late Morgan Neville, of Cincinnati, a gen-

tleman of the highest literary taste, as well as of the most
amiable and polished manners. "The Last of the Boatmen,"
as his sketch is entitled, is unexceptionable in style, and, we
believe, in *fact*, with one exception, and that is, the statement
as to the manner and place of Fink's death. He did *not die*
on the Arkansas, but at Fort Henry, near the mouth of the
Yellow Stone. Our informant is Mr. Chas. Keemle of this
paper [the *St. Louis Reveille*], who held a command in the
neighbourhood, at the time, and to whom every circumstance
connected with the affair is most familiar. We give the
story as it is told by himself.

In the year 1822, steamboats having left the "keels" and
"broad-horns" entirely "out of sight," and Mike having, in
consequence, fallen from his high estate—that of being "a
little bit the almightiest man on the river, *any* how"—after
a term of idleness, frolic and desperate rowdyism, along the
different towns, he, at St. Louis, entered the service of the
Mountain Fur Company, raised by our late fellow-citizen
Gen. W. H. Ashley, as a trapper and hunter; and in that
capacity was he employed by Major Henry, in command of
the Fort at the mouth of Yellow Stone river, when the oc-
currence took place of which we write.

Mike, with many generous qualities, was always a reckless
dare-devil; but, at this time, advancing in years and decayed
in influence, above all become a victim of whiskey, he was
morose and desperate in the extreme. There was a government regulation which forbade the free use of alcohol at the
trading posts on the Missouri river, and this was a continual
source of quarrel between the men and the commandant,
Major Henry,—on the part of Fink, particularly. One of
his freaks was to march with his rifle into the fort, and demand a supply of spirits. Argument was fruitless, force not
to be thought of, and when, on being positively denied,
Mike drew up his rifle and sent a ball through the cask, de-
liberately walked up and filled his can, while his particular

"boys" followed his example, all that could be done was to look upon the matter as one of his "queer ways," and that was the end of it.

This state of things continued for some time; Mike's temper and exactions growing more unbearable every day, until, finally a "split" took place, not only between himself and the commandant, but many others in the fort, and the unruly boatman swore he would not live among them. Followed only by a youth named Carpenter, whom he had brought up, and for whom he felt a rude but strong attachment, he prepared a sort of cave in the river's bank, furnished it with a supply of whiskey, and, with his companion, *turned in* to pass the winter, which was then closing upon them. In this place he buried himself, sometimes unseen for weeks, his *protegé* providing what else was necessary beyond the whiskey. At length attempts were used, on the part of those in the fort, to withdraw Carpenter from Fink; foul insinuations were made as to the nature of their connection; the youth was twitted with being a mere slave, &c., all which (Fink heard of it in spite of his retirement) served to breed distrust between the two, and though they did not separate, much of their cordiality ceased.

The winter wore away in this sullen state of torpor; spring came with its reviving influences, and to celebrate the season, a supply of alcohol was procured; and a number of his acquaintances from the fort coming to "rouse out" Mike, a desperate "frolic," of course, ensued.

There were river yarns, and boatmen songs, and "nigger break-downs," interspersed with wrestling-matches, jumping, laugh, and yell, the can circulating freely, until Mike became somewhat mollified.

"I tell you what it is, boys," he cried, "the fort's a skunk-hole, and I rather live with the *bars* than stay in it. Some on ye's bin trying to part me and my boy, that I love like my own cub—but no matter. Maybe he's *pis*oned against me; but, Carpenter (striking the youth heavily on the shoulder), I took you by the hand when it had forgotten the touch of a father's or a mother's—you know me to be a man, and you ain't a going to turn out a dog!"

Whether it was that the youth fancied something insulting in the manner of the appeal, or not, we can't say; but it was not responded to very warmly, and a reproach followed from Mike. However, they drank together, and the frolic went on, until Mike, filling his can, walked off some forty yards, placed it upon his head, and called to Carpenter to take his rifle.

This wild feat of shooting cans off each other's head was a favorite one with Mike—himself and "boy" generally winding up a hard frolic with this savage, but deeply meaning proof of continued confidence;—as for risk, their eagle eyes and iron nerves defied the might of whiskey. After their recent alienation, a doubly generous impulse, without doubt, had induced Fink to propose and subject himself to the test.

Carpenter had been drinking wildly, and with a boisterous laugh snatched up his rifle. All present had seen the parties "shoot," and this desperate aim, instead of alarming, was merely made a matter of wild jest.

"Your grog is spilt, fer ever, Mike!"

"Kill the old varmint, young 'un!"

"What'll his skin bring in St. Louis?" &c., &c.

Amid a loud laugh, Carpenter raised his piece—even the jesters remarked that he was unsteady,—crack!—the can fell, —and a loud shout,—but, instead of a smile of pleasure, a dark frown settled upon the face of Fink! He made no motion except to clutch his rifle as though he would have crushed it, and there he stood, gazing at the youth strangely! Various shades of passion crossed his face—surprise, rage, suspicion—but at length they composed themselves into a sad expression; the ball had grazed the top of his head, cutting the scalp, and the thought of treachery had set his heart on fire.

There was a loud call on Mike to know what he was waiting for, in which Carpenter joined, pointing to the can upon his head and bidding him fire, if he knew how!

"Carpenter, my son," said the boatman, "I taught you to shoot differently from that *last* shot! You've *missed* once, but you won't again!"

He fired, and his ball, crashing through the forehead of the youth, laid him a corpse amid his, as suddenly hushed, companions!

Time wore on—many at the fort spoke darkly of the deed. Mike Fink had never been known to miss his aim—he had grown afraid of Carpenter—he had murdered him! While this feeling was gathering against him, the unhappy boatman lay in his cave, shunning both sympathy and sustenance. He spoke to none—when he did come forth, 'twas as a spectre, and only to haunt the grave of his "boy," or, if he did break silence, 'twas to burst into a paroxysm of rage against the enemies who had "turned his boy's heart from him!"

At the fort was a man by the name of Talbott, the gunsmith of the station: he was very loud and bitter in his denunciations of the "murderer," as he called Fink, which, finally reaching the ears of the latter, filled him with the most violent passion, and he swore that he would take the life of his defamer. This threat was almost forgotten, when one day, Talbott, who was at work in his shop, saw Fink enter the fort, his first visit since the death of Carpenter. Fink approached; he was careworn, sick, and wasted; there was no anger in his bearing, but he carried his rifle (had he ever gone without it?) and the gunsmith was not a coolly brave man; moreover, his life had been threatened.

"Fink," cried he, snatching up a pair of pistols from his bench, "don't approach me—if you do, you're a dead man!"

"Talbott," said the boatman, in a sad voice, "you needn't be afraid; you've done me wrong—I'm come to talk to you about—Carpenter—my boy!"

He continued to advance, and the gunsmith again called to him:

"Fink! I know you; if you come three steps nearer, I'll fire, by—!"

Mike carried his rifle across his arm, and made no hostile demonstration, except in gradually getting nearer—*if* hostile his aim was.

"Talbott, you've accused me of murdering—my boy—Carpenter—that I raised from a child—that I loved like a son—that I can't live without! I'm not mad with you *now*, but you must let me show you that I couldn't do it—that I'd rather died than done it—that you've wronged me—"

By this time he was within a few steps of the door, and Talbott's agitation became extreme. Both pistols were pointed at Fink's breast, in expectation of a spring from the latter.

"By the Almighty above us, Fink, I'll fire—I don't want to speak to you now—don't put your foot on that step—don't."

Fink did put his foot on the step, and the same moment fell heavily within it, receiving the contents of both barrels in his breast! His last and only words were, "I didn't mean to kill my boy!"

Poor Mike! we are satisfied with our senior's conviction that you did *not* mean to kill him. Suspicion of treachery, doubtless, entered his mind, but cowardice and murder never dwelt there.

A few weeks after this event, Talbott himself perished in an attempt to cross the Missouri river in a skiff.

EPILOGUE

EPILOGUE

HOW MIKE FINK BECAME A FOLK-HERO, AND HOW
MANY TALES WERE TOLD ABOUT HIM

I

Fort Henry basked in the sunshine of a spring day in 1823. Fort Henry, or Henry's Post, was a little cluster of log cabins surrounded by a high log stockade, no fort at all, according to modern standards, but a haven, at least, for hunters and trappers who had penetrated into the country of the Assiniboine and Crow Indians and who might at any moment be forced to seek refuge from arrows and bullets behind its barky stockade. On one side danced the buff Missouri River, more muddy and tempestuous than usual as the spring floods swept down with it towards the mouth of the Yellowstone River which joined it four miles below the fort. On the other sides stretched a wilderness, an almost unknown land of great green forests, vast plains, mighty snow-peaked mountains of which venturesome travelers told unbelievable tales.

Not long before, some of the men of the fort had heard the war-whoops of the Blackfeet while bullets whizzed about them in a battle with the Indians near Great Falls. Four of their comrades had been killed, and the party had hastily returned to the fort. Immediately Major Henry, the commander of the post, had

243

sent messengers to another party led by William Ashley on its way up the Missouri to join them. The Blackfeet were on the war-path, he said; he needed immediate help. But not long after his messengers had trotted out of sight, two haggard men had spurred their weary horses through the gates of the fort. They had come from Ashley.

They brought news of war and mutiny and a plea for immediate aid. Two hundred miles down the river, near the mouth of the Grand, the treacherous Ree Indians had swooped on Ashley's men, their rifles spurting fire in the black night. Some of the party had been shot; some had drowned as they tried to swim through the swirling stream to the expedition's boats. The boats bearing the expedition had drifted with the survivors down the river below the Ree towns. Ashley had asked the men to push out past the towns again, but they had refused, remembering too vividly the horror of the pitched battle. He wrote: "A resolution has been formed by most of them to desert. I called for volunteers to remain with me under any circumstances until I should receive the expected aid. Thirty only [of a hundred] volunteered . . . consequently I am compelled to send one boat back." He wanted Henry to send reënforcements at once.

Leaving twenty men to hold the post, Henry and the rest of the men of the fort started out to join the stricken party.

And soon after, the post being quiet, some forgotten trapper sat down, sweated profusely, chewed his pencil, and wrote a letter home to St. Louis. It is no longer possible to determine all of the things that letter said; the years have doubtless turned his paper to dust, and he, poor fellow, is dust also. No doubt he told of stirring brushes with painted savages, of battles with beasts, struggles with swift streams.

Certainly he told one story which was to live for years on the lips of pioneers, trappers, frontiersmen—the story of a man who had recently met violent death in that wilderness post. All of his life, that man, now asleep in his grave in the forest, had been in the midst of the rugged life which had swirled on the advancing frontier; Fort Henry, with the menacing Missouri on one side, the wilderness on the other, a center of dangerous adventure, had been an appropriate background for the death of that man, the blustering, hard-muscled, sharp-shooting Indian scout, keelboatman, and trapper —Mike Fink.

Somehow, the letter found its way down the winding river which squirmed through hundreds of dangerous miles to St. Louis. There a newspaper, the *Missouri Republican*, on July 10, 1823, printed the tale of Mike's death, drawing its facts from the trapper's letter. Such was the origin of the first printed story about Mike Fink.

But other stories about him, which had not waited for newspapers to spread them, were already in circulation up and down the river. In Pittsburgh from which, as a boy, Mike had darted with scouts into the land of hostile redskins, he had become, even before his death, a legendary hero.   After he had left Pittsburgh, in the days when the Ohio and Mississippi rivers were alive with boats of all kinds bearing brawny pioneers to new Western frontiers, Mike, as the roistering captain of a keelboat, had won fame because of his jokes, his marksmanship, his fights.   And all up and down the rivers, from Pittsburgh to New Orleans and back to St. Louis, yarns were told of the acknowledged king of the hardiest group of men on the frontier.   Now the tale of his death, with its elements of mystery, its elements of melodrama, was added to the growing group of tales about him, and it seemed that Mike had become a folk-hero whose deeds were to be treasured through generations.

It is still possible, more than a century after Mike Fink's death, to catch glimpses of men who told those tales or who listened to them—glimpses which help one see how those stories passed from lip to ear, moving from one section of the nation to another as restless Americans moved Westward.   For example—

A few years after the death of Mike Fink, a gangling young man of sixteen was working on the farm of James Taylor, at the mouth of Anderson Creek, on the Ohio River.   A tall young man he was, with long legs, long arms, a long skinny neck and a homely face. Dressed in his rough linsey clothes and his coonskin cap, he plowed the fields, and, in addition, like Fink, something of a boatman, he operated the ferryboat across the Ohio.   His name was Abraham Lincoln.

Says Lincoln's biographer, Carl Sandburg: "At Anderson Creek ferry, he saw and talked with settlers, land buyers and sellers, traders, hunters, peddlers, preachers, gamblers, politicians, teachers, and men shut-mouthed about their business. Occasionally came a customer who looked as if he might be one of the 'half-horse, half-alligator men' haunting the Ohio water course those years. There was river talk about Mike Fink . . . the toughest of the . . . crowd; he was a famous marksman . . ." and a famous fighter. It is not hard to picture Lincoln listening, his gray eyes sparkling, as tales of Mike's exploits were told by rivermen who had seen Fink pole upstream through swift currents, or, drunk and swaggering, shoot a whiskey-filled cup off the head of an unsteady comrade. Later, when lawyers swinging around the circuit regaled one another with stories by tavern firesides of evenings, Lincoln probably amused his fellows with his droll yarns about the boatman.

Another glimpse: One day in the late twenties Morgan Neville, part owner of the *Pittsburgh Gazette*, spick and span in his graceful top hat, his ruffled shirt, carrying a gold-headed cane and a valise, marched to the stageplank of a steamer moored at Louisville. A negro rushed to his side.

"Let me tote yo' gripsack, suh?"

Neville handed him his valise and followed him up the plank, then up a shiny staircase to the forward guards. Through a doorway he caught a glimpse of a long cabin, a thick flower-decorated carpet lying on its curved floor, above it, white glass chandeliers bathed in the colored light which filtered through the skylights. He walked on a mushy carpet to his stateroom. The negro placed the valise on the floor, Neville tossed him a dime, then wandered to the deck, looked over the side. The landing swarmed with colors, moving figures. Black roustabouts were "coonjining"—chanting an improvised song—as they heaved the cargo on the boat. The mate lazily watched them, ready if need be, with a spurring stream of eloquent profanity. Men, women and children chattered farewell messages to passengers. The resplendent captain, chatting with two lively belles, lifted his hat to Neville in a graceful curve, and Neville returned the salute.

A few minutes later, as the boat turned out into the stream with a blast of her whistle and the jangling of bells, Neville stood on the hurricane deck, near one of the two tall red-topped chimneys. He climbed past the texas deck to the gilded, glass enclosed pilot-house, and stood beside the bronzed tobacco-chewing pilot, who was twisting the boat through the Middle Chute passage of the Rapids of the Ohio.

"Hello, Dan," said Neville, putting his hand on the pilot's shoulder.

The pilot glanced up quickly, then turned back his gaze to the churning river. "Well," he exclaimed, "I'll be fly-blowed to a certainty if it ain't Morgan Neville."

"So you've gone over to the steamboats after all, Dan."

"Yes, my old keelboat kind o' fell to pieces, an' the

steamers tempted me with gold about that time, so I sold her for lumber an' started steering this here floatin' palace."

"I see quite a few old keelboatmen on the steamers these days."

"Yes, it looks as if these steamers 'd come to stay. There's a lot o' keelboat patroons standin' up in glass cages an' wishin' they had hold of an oar top a keel-boat cargo box. An' some of the keelers is mates or even captains on these vessels. Some on 'em is up the Missouri in the fur-tradin' country, and some is farmers, with families. The river ain't what it was in the days of Mike Fink—never will be, I reckon. No good fights any more, no sprees or pranks—no nothing."

"What has become of Mike? He was an old acquaintance of mine."

"He was killed in a scrimmage," said the pilot. "He'd refused some right good offers on the steamboats—said he couldn't bear the hissin' of steam, an' he wanted room to throw his pole. He went to the Missouri—" And as the steamer chugged downstream, the pilot told Neville the strange tale of Mike Fink's death.

Similarly the stories of Fink were told in many places and to many persons. Perhaps a pioneer family, sitting on old-fashioned three-legged stools before their fireplace, listened to tales told by a visitor; the light of the fire flickered on the log walls, the deer's antlers, the pewter plates, the twirling spinning wheel—as the visitor told of Mike's jokes, his great shots, his fights.

Perhaps the scene was the large room of one of the white taverns that stood, shaded by chestnuts, elms, and magnolias, beside the National Road, holding above its door a gilded sign which invited travelers to pause for the night before taking up their journey to Kentucky. The Pike boys and the travelers, warmed with whiskey, sat before the great fireplace and listened to tales of the King of the Keelboatmen.

Decades passed, and still the tales were circulated. In 1847 Lieutenant J. W. Abert led an expedition which studied New Mexico, recently acquired. He published, in due time, the story of his explorations in an executive document of the Thirtieth Congress, telling, on one of its pages, of a visit paid him by an old trapper one day when rain kept the expedition in its tents. His tongue loosened by liquor, the old trapper told pleasant tales of a man who (the story-teller said) had hunted in the Rocky Mountains—Mike Fink. In 1847 a writer checked off the names of cities in which he had, within the last fifteen years, heard yarns about Mike—Cincinnati, Louisville, New Orleans, Natchez, and St. Louis.

As the years passed, however, the oral tradition somehow died. No longer did the rivermen remember the deeds of Mike. The keelboats which had been of tremendous importance in early days had disappeared from the rivers, and even the steamboats which replaced them, in time lost their glamor. Mike belonged at last to a forgotten day, his escapades no longer celebrated by tale spinners. Just when he passed out of

oral legend, it is impossible to say; as late as 1895, a
new tale about him came to the surface. Mike sur-
vives to-day outside of books only as a dim bogey man
used to frighten children in homes along the rivers
which were scenes of his glory. Said Meigs O. Frost, a
New Orleans writer, in 1932: "Back in the sandy bottoms and the thick brush, there are barefooted children
in little cabins who kind of believe Mike is on the river
yet. Their Mammies scared them into good behavior,
when they were very little, by tales of Mike Fink."
"Mike Fink'll get you!" they were told—and still are
told, when too obstreperous. Eventually, however,
save in this vague homage, a folk-hero was forgotten by
the folk.

II

But in the meantime, writers had preserved on
printed pages some of the stories which had been orally
circulated. In the magazines, newspapers, almanacs,
and books of the 19th century one may still find these
tales—sources of this book—on pages yellow with
years. It is illuminating and interesting to trace their
development down through the last century.

Six years after Mike died, the first literary treatment
of his exploits was published in the most incongruous
publication imaginable—a ladies' annual.

The ladies' annuals have been called the ancestors
of the ladies' magazines, including the famous *Godey's;*
it seems it would have been more accurate to call them
the maiden aunts, for they were far too chaste to be-

come ancestors. Blessed with such titles as *The Opal*,
A Pure Gift for the Holy Days, *The Harebell*, *The
Lily*, *Friendship's Offering* and *The Gift of Sentiment*,
these genteel volumes, "embellished" with engravings,
with gilt-edged pages, and with "elegant" binding, appeared at Christmas time each year between 1826 and
1860, and were duly presented by the beaux to the
belles of the time. Pictures of young girls with turtle
doves, sweet love stories of Dresden china heroines,
many with garnishings of moral lessons, and poems
about death which made it possible for readers to have
a good cry, filled the books' pages.

Into this genteel and lacy company swaggered Mike
Fink, the cheek of his bulldog face stuffed with chew-
ing tobacco, his flannel shirt a vulgar scarlet. And before he departed, he shot a whiskey cup off a boatman's head, killed an unsuspecting Indian from am-
bush, and finally managed to be brutally murdered.
The annual in which he made his startling appearance
was *The Western Souvenir*, published in Cincinnati in
1829, daintily bound in satin cloth and boasting:

> So glossy in silk, and so neat in brevier,
> There never was book like our new Souvenir!

To be sure, the book was "written and published in the
western country, by western men, and chiefly confined"
to western subjects, but it contained pictures of "The
Peasant Girl" and "The Deserted Children," and tales
of a Greek revolution and a French village—and the
tanned boatman was the least bit incongruous.

Morgan Neville it was who lifted the story from the campfire and steamboat saloon tall tale sessions into the realm of polite—very polite—literature. Neville (1783-1840), son of an aide-de-camp of Lafayette, who was born in Pittsburgh, and who moved to Cincinnati about 1824, had a varied career typical of the West as lawyer, sheriff, newspaper editor, secretary of a life insurance company, practical politician, and receiver of public moneys in Cincinnati. A skilled violinist, faultless in his French, a friend of the Duke of Orleans (later Louis Philippe) and the elegant Blennerhassett, the possessor of an excellent library, he was a distinguished figure even in the Cincinnati of the thirties—a city which made European visitors exclaim delightedly that they had found an oasis of culture in the wilds of America. A dabbler in story-telling, "he wrote little and only for his own diversion, and he made no attempt to collect his work." A few of his meandering, easy-chair tales are preserved in dusty annuals and forgotten magazines, although most of his writings, published in newspapers, have vanished.

Yet in Neville's day, the story he told of Mike was so well appreciated that several authors spoke of it with enthusiasm, and it was soon picked up and copied in varied publications. It was reprinted in 1829, the year of its first appearance, in Samuel Cumings's *The Western Pilot*, a book primarily designed to aid boatmen, embellished with worm-like sections of the Ohio and Mississippi Rivers, accompanied by directions for avoiding sandbanks and sawyers. Later editions also carried the story. When Mary Russell Mitford, in 1832, culled from American publications tales for her English collection, *Lights and Shadows of American Life*, the yarn of Mike Fink was imported into quiet England. And when a panorama of the Mississippi River was carried in triumph through the United States and unrolled in various show houses before the eyes of the admiring Americans, a little pamphlet was published, *Banvard's Geographical Panorama of the Mississippi River, with the Story of Mike Fink, the Last of the Boatmen, A Tale of River Life*. The booklet described the three-mile canvas, which the *Boston Post* styled "a masterpiece" which was an honor to the artist and to America, and which *The Louisville Courier* called "the greatest and proudest work of art in the world." And on ten pages of this book, Morgan Neville told how the king of the keelboatmen banged down tincups and Indians. Perhaps Longfellow saw Banvard's panorama when he was collecting local color for *Evangeline*, and perhaps he bought a descriptive pamphlet; but if he read Neville's story he did not allow it to influence his work—though a tinge of influence would have done no harm.

Meanwhile, other writers had taken up the story of Mike. A St. Louis correspondent, who stoutly affirmed that he had learned of the hero "from an intelligent and respectable fur-trader," furnished some additional details to Neville's sketch and they were published in Timothy Flint's *Western Monthly Review* for July, 1829. The worthy fur-trader, before leaving for Santa Fé, gave some vivid details about Mike as an Indian fighter, as a wit, and as a boatman, and a remarkably detailed story about Mike's death, full of convincing information. Some quaint little booklets, *The Crockett Almanacs*, which contained stories of the hero, Davy Crockett, recently killed in the Alamo, and which were published for a time by Crockett's heirs and his friend, printed weird woodcuts of boatmen and several additional stories—of Mike's death (1838), of how Mike beat Davy at shooting (1840), tried to scare Mrs. Crockett (1851), treated the Indians, hunted a moose (1852), killed a wolf with his fists (1853), and made amusing remarks about a steamboat and a gymnastic school (1854). And the same publication elevated Mike's wife and his daughter to legendary heights.

The almanacs were published in Nashville at first and later in Philadelphia, New York, Boston and Baltimore. In New York, in 1842, William T. Porter, editor of *The Spirit of the Times*, a journal of "the turf, agriculture, literature and the stage" which first printed many famous Western and Southern humorous stories of the time, published a story of Mike's death which differed materially from previous accounts. And a week later, July 16, Porter printed a thrilling story of Mike and a vengeful Indian, sent in by a Louisiana correspondent. The author was T. B. Thorpe (1815-78), painter, newspaper editor, colonel in the Mexican war—still remembered for the imaginative tall tale he created, "The Big Bear of Arkansas." From St. Louis in 1844 came *The St. Louis Reveille*, bearing a new tale of Mike by J. M. Field, actor, newspaper-reporter, actor-manager, and editor. Before 1845, in New Orleans, James Rees, a prominent manager and playwright, had written a play called *Mike Fink, the Last Boatman of the Mississippi*, which, unfortunately, does not seem to have survived.

Thus the tide of treatments swelled in the '40's and '50's, and that they had spread far and wide was indicated by the fact that the authors sent them out from many cities. Before 1860, Mike had been celebrated, in addition, in *The Cincinnati Miscellany*, *The Paris* (Ind.) *Citizen*, a history of Louisville, *The Western Boatman*, *Harper's Magazine*, the reminiscences of a blind preacher published in New York, and *Lloyd's Steamboat Directory*, which disapproved of Mike's character, furnished a new version of his murder, and told graphically of many steamboat explosions. Then, though there are a few exceptions, original legends of Mike seem to have passed out of circulation in print for several decades, until in 1895 Frank Triplett discovered or invented the story which told of how Mike was defeated by the sturdy sheriff; and this was the last new story of Mike to be discovered.

But before the flood subsided, two authors had written extended stories of the boatman which have interesting features.

III

Emerson Bennett (1823-1905), one of these authors, in 1844 was in Cincinnati, selling linen mark-
ing stamps, soliciting magazine subscriptions, sleeping
in cheap lodgings, and living chiefly on free lunches and
beer. A few years later, he had become a great man,
banqueted everywhere, dashing through the park behind a pair of spirited trotters, his luxurious dwelling
complete with the splendors of a colored butler and a
wine cellar.

His rise to affluence had followed the discovery that
he could write thrilling stories of the West exploiting
such glamorous figures as the outlaws of the Osage,
Simon Kenton, Daniel Boone and Simon Girty. He
had been born on a Massachusetts farm, had knocked
about the world a bit, then had tried his literary skill,
with no great luck, in New York and Philadelphia,
whence, his heart broken after a quarrel with his sweetheart, he had started westward. One day, in a Cincinnati restaurant, he had heard some neighboring diners
talk of a story, *The Unknown Countess*, which he had
written in far-off Philadelphia, and had submitted,
with no evident success, to the *Dollar Newspaper* in
that city. It had been printed, and had been copied
in a Cincinnati newspaper. The sale of stories became
easy after the success of this tale. Published in newspapers, Bennett's romances boomed circulation lists
amazingly, and then in book form they sold in numbers which even in these days would be satisfactory to

authors and which in those days were dazzling. *The Prairie Flower* and *Leni Leoti* each sold about 100,000 copies. And there were other successes—*The Forest Rose; a Tale of the Frontier*, *The Outlaw's Daughter*, *The Forged Will; or Crime and Retribution*, and others, some fifty books in all.

The first stories took place on the early frontier. As the years passed, backgrounds moved farther and farther westward, following the shifting frontier. In his last days, living in an old gray house on an old gray street, the large stately old man found his novels as out-moded as his long black frock-coat, his black bow-tie, and his square-toed boots. He died in 1905 in the Masonic home in Philadelphia.

As the titles indicate, his were stories of romantic heroes and heroines, horrible Indians, bandits and outlaws, against backgrounds of forests and mountains, stuffed with sentiment, comedy, mystery and action. In other words, though they cost twenty-five cents, they were primordial dime novels, even being wrapped in characteristic bindings, for they bore "yaller kivers" of a hue later adopted for Beadle novels. To-day they have the quaintly pleasant flavor of old-fashioned melodrama. And one of them was *Mike Fink; a Legend of the Ohio*, the first edition of which appeared in 1848, the second in 1852, and the third in 1853.

The design of this book was not to give a veritable history of Mike, says Bennett in the preface, a bit guiltily, "as some might suppose from the title page." It was instead, it seems, "rather to use him as a character, in illustrating a certain portion of events which took place during the period that he was known as a boatman on the Ohio." Bennett, after this preliminary, sketched the historical background of his tale:

> At the period when my story opens—the beginning of the nineteenth century—there was a band of outlaws congregated at a place called Cave-in-Rock, on the Ohio, whose bloody and daring deeds have already been the theme of many a wild and romantic legend. For a considerable period, they were in the habit of attacking and murdering such crews of keel-boats and broad-horns as they could on any pretence decoy ashore at their rendezvous, and then manning the crafts with their own bands, running them down to New Orleans, and disposing of the cargoes for their own benefit. This daring and bloody practice was for a time carried on so secretly and effectually, on the principle that "dead men tell no tales," that the real cause of the loss of said boats and crews was not suspected by any—it generally being supposed that the former had been snagged and sunk and the latter drowned.
>
> On a legend of this kind I have founded the present tale, in which the romantic Mike Fink and others figure in opposition to the outlaws of the Ohio; and if my story is not strictly authentic in all its details, I trust it will at least be found in accord with the time, the scene, and the being set forth.

The outlaws of Cave-in-Rock of whom Bennett speaks were, indeed, historical figures. The famous cave, on the northern bank of the lower Ohio, in Hardin County, Illinois, about twenty miles below Shawneetown, was for some years the rendezvous of some of the most brutal outlaws, counterfeiters and river pirates, some of whom operated in the fashion described by Neville. "Any history of these outlaws," says a historian who has given exciting and authentic accounts of them, "would doubtless be looked upon as wild fiction unless the statements were carefully verified by court reports and contemporary newspaper notices, and the records of early writers . . . The adage that 'truth is stranger than fiction' is exemplified fully in their careers."

Of such picturesque and melodramatic figures as the outlaws and Mike Fink, who was, for all his faults, rather angelic beside them, few American novelists could have written so well as Emerson Bennett— Simms, perhaps, or Robert Montgomery Bird, or Ned Buntline, the old masters of blood and thunder. Only a novelist of the hair-raising school, however, could have done them justice. Bennett was exactly the man for the task, and as a historian has said, although Bennett's story is fanciful, "in many respects the atmosphere and manners of the time are portrayed . . . without undue exaggeration." Because of this, because of its honorable position as an ancestor of the dime novel, and because, despite its rather too sugary hero and heroine and their somewhat too elegant language, it still manages to thrill and to amuse any lover of mystery and adventure stories, *Mike Fink; a Legend of the Ohio*, deserves to be reprinted.

There never was, it is true, a robber chief named Camilla at the cave; but the Harpes and Mason, its true inhabitants, were at least as wicked, as desperate, and as picturesque. And though Mike Fink, so far as

is known, did not have the pleasure of routing the outlaws, the action was perfectly in character, and the rest
of the deeds of Mike here recorded ring true. By the
time the book was printed, Mike had risen to such
heroic stature that he could have done almost anything.

Furthermore, it was only fair that Mike, like a true
legendary hero, should take the deeds of some others
unto himself. He was destined to provide others with
deeds appropriate to him. Already, in 1832, a novelist
had given Mike Fink's best trick to Daniel Boone, of
whom a fictional boatman said: "I remember I stood
once a hundred yards off, and let him shoot a rifle ball
at a tin pint mug right on the top of my head, and I
wish that I may be utterly onswoggled if he didn't tip
it off as slick as bear's grease, anyhow." Years later,
Emerson Hough had Jim Bridger in *The Covered
Wagon*, with due credit to Fink, perform the same
feat, and the episode later added a high spot to a very
good moving picture. If Mike was credited with glories not his, it was only a fair exchange. Whether Bennett's story is based on a widespread legend or not (and
there are some indications that it was), it interestingly
demonstrates how legendary heroes accumulate great
deeds.

IV

The other extended tale about Mike, written by
J. M. Field (1810-56)—*Mike Fink, the Last of the
Boatmen* (1847)—represents other tendencies in the
literary growth of legendary personages. One such

tendency might be called rationalization. Frequently, after the outlines of a legend have persisted for a time, some writer comes along and, in telling the tale, attempts to motivate the extraordinary actions of the characters. Thus Shakespeare (if one may make a slightly blasphemous comparison), coming upon the crude tales or plays of the past which dealt with the strange actions of a Hamlet or a Lear, tried to conceive what had caused the characters in the old stories to act as they did, and to write plays which made their action plausible. Another tendency was to add details to the story which seemed simply on the grounds of logic to belong to it. Other additions to the original tale might be made in the interest of dramatic economy, in order that the actions might be dramatically appropriate.

Of the numerous tales which dealt with Mike's life and death, Field's went further than any other in providing motivation, logic, sentiment and drama. Forging together many of the links in Mike's colorful life, it stands out among the many narratives about the keelboatman.

Further, Joseph M. Field was able to offer excellent authority for his version. He had heard, he said, Morgan Neville, "a noble old gentleman," talk of Mike in 1832. He had, moreover, heard yarns about Mike in several cities along the Mississippi and Ohio rivers. And one of his informants was a man who may have seen Mike die or who may have heard the tale of his death soon after the event from eye-witnesses.

But despite these facts, one who reflects cannot accept Field's detailed story as a true one. Life seldom works out as dramatically as does Mike's story as told by Field; and it is only in melodramas and detective tales that stories fit together in such a perfect mosaic. One cannot help suspecting that Field, who had been an actor for several years, a theater manager for a time, and who had "signalized himself as a dramatist, in the production of several local dramas," including *The Tourist* and *Such as It Is*, must have carried to his task of a historian on this occasion too many of the traits of a playwright. Earlier he had written an account of Mike's death which is probably much nearer the truth than is his elaborate version.

But if Field's fine yarn is not history it is excellent fiction, and one cannot but pay tribute to the ingenuity of the folk who devised parts of the tale and the writer who made a neat mosaic of those parts.

V

Thus one may trace the development. of legends about Mike Fink in oral and in written tradition. From the many tales emerges a clearly defined character who takes his place alongside other great legendary figures of America—Daniel Boone, Davy Crockett, John Henry and Paul Bunyan. It is hard to understand why Mike Fink, unlike these folk heroes, was forgotten. It is not hard to see why, like these mighty

men, he won the affectionate admiration of 19th century Americans.

A rough, crude man they loved, for the coonskin pioneers themselves were rough and crude. Powerful men
who could take care of themselves, they could respect
a hero even stronger than they, a man who could roar
like a bull and fight like a wildcat. They loved his
burly jokes, for their primitive belly laughter rumbled
loudest when it was provoked by rough-and-tumble ca-
pers or homespun witticisms. Since the law, more often than not, had hindered their exploitation of the
lush frontiers, they even loved Mike's lawlessness.
Further, the king of the keelboatmen was as American
as a buckskin hunting shirt or a log cabin, and these
men loved America.

It is easy to see why, therefore, though he is no
longer a hero of spoken or written tales, Mike Fink is
still a figure in American histories. Historians for
many years have recognized the fact that he has a
place in the pages of their books. As early as 1847,
he had entered a history which retold one of the older
tales about him, and thereafter historians who wished
to recapture for their purposes the coloring of keelboat
times or the era of the trappers consistently used stories
about him.

For their purpose he was and is perfect—a hero
somehow untouched by the Victorian school of historians who would not allow that excellent swearer,
Washington, to use the inelegant expression "flea-
bite," and who, by some magic, took away the frontiers-

man's chawing tobacco and whiskey and turned him into a figure in an animated Rogers group.

Mike and the rowdies of the river who admired him were as typical of the frontier days as the folk who carried Bibles and preachers westward with them. And when Indians were to be killed, boats were to be wriggled between snags, or when new lands were to be opened by trappers, these roughnecks were perhaps even more important than their pious brethren.

The keelboatmen, for example, and their strange craft, played a significant part in western growth; they "heralded a new era in internal development," an era during which exchanges between the North and the South, vastly important in the economic and political history of the nation, had their beginnings. Further, as Professor Archer B. Hulbert has pointed out—

> The narrowness of the keelboat . . . permitted it to ply far up the larger tributaries of the Ohio and to a considerable way up its smaller tributaries—territory which the barge and the flatboat could never reach. It is probable, therefore, that the keelboat brought much territory into touch with the world that otherwise was never reached save by the heavy freighter and the pack-saddle. . . . In this connection it is proper to emphasize . . . that the inhabitants of the Central West, from the earliest times until to-day, have found the favorite sites of occupation to be in the interior of the country, beside the lesser tributaries of the Ohio. Thus as the pioneer settlements spread up on the Licking, Muskingum, Hockhocking, Scioto and Miami, a boat like the keelboat, which could ply in any season of the year and on the narrow creeks and "runs," was an inestimable boon.

Again, take for instance the salt industry, which in the day of the keelboat was one of the most important, if not the most important, in the Central West; as values were a century ago the best of men did well to "earn his salt." These salt springs and licks were found at some distance from the main artery of travel, the Ohio, and it was the keelboat . . . which did the greater part of the salt distribution, returning usually with loads of flour.

Fink represents a type which developed on each frontier and on each trail into developing sections— the skilled experts, as tough as shoe-leather, and as useful. Without these hardy entering wedges frontiers could not have developed. All of them were distinguished by their hardihood and their ability to do some of the important things the environment of the frontier demanded—fur-traders who could kill three buffalo, make a bull-boat from the skins and paddles with sticks and buffalo shoulder blades, and thus equipped navigate to their destination, men who could trade for furs with Indians and who could hunt; Indian fighters who could flatter, bluff or annihilate the redskins, as seemed most opportune; wagoners of the National Road who could train two days on whiskey, then drive two tons of merchandise four hundred miles over the rickety road in thirty days; hardy miners who, with cup, pan, pick, shovel, bread and whiskey on their packhorses, could wander off into the hills and later return loaded with paydirt; cowboys, grotesque in high-heeled boots and chaps, who rode so well they seemed parts of their horses, who knew cattle intimately, and who could make their Colt revolvers bark with remarkable efficiency.

Mark Twain objected to the expression "Westward the star of Empire takes its way" as a sentence describing the march of pioneers. If the author, said Mark, "had been conversant with facts, he would have said: Westward the Jug of Empire takes its way," for whiskey was ever "the van-leader" in the march of American civilization. The roughnecks who broke the trails, who carried the settlers to their wilderness homes, were the heaviest drinkers, the bloodiest brawlers, the wildest gamblers, the lustiest lovers. They were reckless and mighty, and because they were reckless and mighty, they were useful. This frontier type is well represented by Mike Fink.

Fink was representative of the older America in another way. America moved westward continuously in his day, and Mike's life was a series of incursions into new territory farther west. Three times the frontier shifted during his lifetime and three times he shifted the scene of his activities. A ranger in Pennsylvania in its early days, a keelboatman on rivers swarming with pioneers, toward the end of his days he became a trapper. Historically, in the great Westward movement, boatmen and trappers were definitely parts of the stirring days which created them.

The stories about him, then, have a certain historical value. Some of them—how many it is impossible to say—have foundations firmly planted in fact. Some of them, fantastic though they are, offer important hints about the thoughts and the dreams of the American folk who created them. To those who hold a romantic view of the frontier and to those who see the frontier as an extension of the realm of Puritan suppressions, stories of the rowdy Mike Fink created by worshipful frontiersmen will bring disconcerting refutation.

Though there are notable exceptions, most of them have literary value. They are amusing, puzzling or exciting, and many of them, compared with other tales of the period of their origin, are strikingly real. And it may be that the chief value of the stories of Mike Fink, in American literature, was that they battered with some effect at the strongholds of the overdelicate drawing-room literature of 19th century ladies' books and magazines. Among the swooning, sighing narratives of the time, they seem as incongrous and husky as Mike did when he wandered into the ladies' annual. Morgan Neville, as Professor Pattee says, "was the pioneer in what may be called the 'Mike Fink' school of fiction," and that school led towards realism.

We owe a debt of gratitude to the early celebrators of Mike Fink for their creation of a great American hero, for their services to realism, and also for tales which make it possible for us, even in these distant days, to visit the virile frontiers of a lusty young America.

BIBLIOGRAPHY

The chronicler Wace, in the Middle Ages, mournfully considering the task of telling the truth about King Arthur, characterized stories about him: "Nor all a lie, nor all true, nor all fable, nor all unknown, so much have the story-tellers told, and the fablers fabled, in order to embellish their tales, that they have made all seem fable." Shaking our heads, we repeat his words, applying them to the stories about Mike Fink which are the source of this volume.

To be on the safe side, librarians will perhaps do well to classify this work as fiction, though it is not only fiction but also biography, history, legend and, at rare intervals, poetry. The book's materials made this mixture necessary. Mike Fink was a real figure whose historical background was significant. Yet the scores of stories about him were sometimes folklore, sometimes fictional works of creative artists.

Our first hope was that we might collect all original stories about our hero and print them in their most authentic forms. Persuaded that the work we contemplated could not be published, at least at this time, we hit upon the expedient of writing a narrative which made use of the most important tales about him and which would, we hoped, aid the reader's understanding of the man by portraying in detail his background. Our sources fell, therefore, into two classes—original narratives about the King of the Keelboatmen, and writings which recaptured the atmosphere and the life of his times.

The stories which dealt with Fink directly were the chief sources of what we have written. We attempted to bring together all of the discoverable stories about the keeler which were told by his contemporaries or orally transmitted by his descendants and to tie them together as well as possible. If the collection listed in our bibliography is incomplete, it is only because the missing stories have eluded us after rather strenuous searches. In rewriting these tales we have tried to treat them with due reverence. We changed them only when details seemed so improbable or ridiculous that it was impossible for us either to believe them or retell them believably or entertainingly to 20th century readers. Sometimes we used their phraseology, and usually, when they contained dialogue, we reproduced it with few changes. Usually we accepted them or, if we had doubts, told them with a few remarks concerning their probability.

Sources which had to do with the days during which Mike lived were used for two purposes. Often they made possible vivid descriptions of the scenes or the deeds of our hero which original story-tellers merely sketched. Sometimes they made it possible for us to fill in gaps in the history of Fink by telling what probably happened to him. Large portions of the first two chapters of the book are based upon writings about others of Fink's day whose lives doubtless were similar to the life of the Indian scout and keelboatman. Other sections of the book are chiefly retellings of stories about the boatman, with the background filled in at various times. As the bibliography indicates, travel books, autobiographies, biographies, and histories have been useful as secondary sources. In addition, now and then, we have used fictional works as sources, since some of the novelists of the 19th century were occasionally more effective in catching the real flavor of the times than were other writers. Some of the material in the first section, for example, was taken from Bird's *Nick of the Woods* and Longstreet's *Georgia Scenes*, two fine fictional works which contain much realistic detail. We have tried to give the book historical accuracy throughout.

We have added little of our own original material. Sometimes we have invented dialogue when it was needed to characterize the figures of the narrative or to vivify their actions. Sometimes, too, we have particularized narrative material which was previously generalized. Here and there we have removed details which seemed improbable. As a rule, however, we have felt that changes or additions, no matter how much we were tempted to make them, would rob this work of its authenticity, even though they might add verisimilitude.

We are pleased to have an opportunity to acknowledge the assistance of several people who have been more than kind in answering queries and in helping us to secure information—Miss Stella M. Drum, Librarian of the Missouri Historical Society; the late William E. Connelly, Secretary of the Kansas Historical Society; Mr. John S. Worley, Curator of the Transportation Library of the University of Michigan; Mr. Leland D. Baldwin, of the University of Michigan; Miss C. S. Freret, of the Louisiana State Museum; Professors Archer Taylor, Percy Boynton, and John M. Manly of the University of Chicago; Mr. Clarence S. Brigham, Librarian of the American Antiquarian Society; Mr. John Wilsen Townsend of Lexington, Kentucky; Mr. J. Christian Bay, Librarian of the Crerar Library, Chicago; Mr. William C. Smith; Mr. Bernard DeVoto, of Harvard University; Dr. William J. Peterson, of the State University of Iowa; Professor Gilbert H. Barnes, of Ohio Wesleyan University; Mr. George W. Fuller, Librarian of the Spokane Public Library; Miss Constance M. Rourke; Mr. Otto Rothert, Secretary of the Filson Club of Louisville, Kentucky, and Mrs. Gertrude L. Woodward of the Newberry Library, Chicago. The bibliography indicates others to whom we are indebted for assistance.

PART I

Under each original article the reprints of that article are listed, lettered a, b, c, etc.

1. *St. Louis Republican*, July 16, 1823. Newspaper story of report of Fink's death.
2. MORGAN NEVILLE. The Last of the Boatmen, in the Western Souvenir, A Christmas and New Year's Gift for 1829. Edited by James Hall. Cincinnati: N. & G. Guilford (1829).

Reprinted in:

(a) SAMUEL CUMINGS. The Western Pilot, Containing Charts of the Ohio River and of the Mississippi. . . . Accompanied with Directions for Navigating the Same. Cincinnati: N. & G. Guilford, 1829. Also reprinted in editions of the same work in 1832 and 1834.

(b) MARY RUSSELL MITFORD. Lights and Shadows of American Life. London, 1832. Vol. II.

(c) BANVARD's Panorama of the Mississippi, Painted on Three Miles of Canvas, Exhibiting a View of a Country 1,200 Miles in Length, Extending from the North of the Missouri River to the City of New Orleans, Being by Far the Largest Picture Ever Executed by Man. Boston: John Putnam, Printer, 1847, pp. 33-43.

(d) HIRAM KAINE. Mike Fink, in *The Cincinnati Miscellany or Antiquities of the West*. Cincinnati: Robinson and Jones, 1846. Number for October, 1845, pp. 31-32.

(e) A. DE PUY VAN BUREN. Jottings of a Year's Sojourn in the South. Battle Creek, Michigan, 1859, pp. 305-312.

3. Mike Fink. The Last of the Boatmen, in the *Western Monthly Review*. Edited by Timothy Flint and pub-

lished in Cincinnati by E. H. Flint, July, 1829, pp. 15-19.

Reprinted in:

(a) *Missouri Intelligencer*, September 4, 1829.
(b) H. M. CHITTENDEN. The American Fur Trade in the Far West. New York: Francis P. Harper, 1902, IV, 707-712.

4. SMITH, JACKSON & SUBLETTE. Vol. 32. Record Book containing copies of letters from Indian Agents and others, to the Superintendent of Indian Affairs at St. Louis, from September 10, 1830, to April 1, 1832. Official Report of Mike Fink's Death.

5. *Crockett Almanac, 1838.* Vol. I, No. 4. Nashville: Published by the Heirs of Col. Crockett (n.d.). Contains story, "Mike, the Ohio Boatman," and a wood-cut showing Mike Fink with shot-gun laid over his arm, standing at tiller of keel-boat.

6. *Crockett Almanac, 1840.* Vol. II, No. 2. Nashville: Published by Ben Harding (n.d.). Crockett Beat at a Shooting Match, illustrated with wood-cut.

7. WILLIAM T. PORTER. Mike Fink's Death, in *The Spirit of the Times*, New York, July 9, 1842, p. 217.

8. T. B. THORPE. The Disgraced Scalp-lock, or Incidents on Western Waters. *The Spirit of the Times*, New York, July 16, 1842, p. 229.

Reprinted in:

(a) *Brother Jonathan*, 1842, II, 342-344.
(b) WILLIAM GILMORE SIMMS. Transatlantic Tales, Sketches and Legends. By Various American Authors. Collected and Arranged by Gilmore Simms. London: N. Bruce, 1842, pp. 60-65.
(c) *The Cincinnati Miscellany*, 1846, II, 332-334, as The Flatboatmen of the West.
(d) T. B. THORPE. The Mysteries of the Backwoods, Philadelphia, 1846, pp. 118 ff.
(e) T. B. THORPE. The Hive of the Bee-Hunter. New York: Appleton, 1854, pp. 163 ff., as "Mike Fink, the Keel-Boatman."
(f) JOSEPH DUNBAR SHIELDS. Natchez, Its Early His-

tory. Louisville: John P. Morton & Co., 1930, pp. 261-263.

9. J. M. FIELD. The Death of Mike Fink. *St. Louis Reveille*, October 21, 1844.

Reprinted in:

(a) *Louisville Journal*, December 25, 1844, as The Last of Mike Fink.
(b) J. M. FIELD. *Drama in Pokerville*. Philadelphia, 1847, pp. 177-183.
(c) *Paris* (Ky.) *Western Citizen*. Wisconsin Historical Society, Draper Mss. 29CC45-46.
(d) JAMES H. BRADLEY. Sketch of the Fur Trade of the Upper Missouri River. *Contributions to the Historical Society of Montana*. 1923, pp. 320-324.

10. CHARLES CIST. The Last of the Girtys, in *The Cincinnati Miscellany*, January, 1845. Cincinnati: Robinson & Jones, 1846, pp. 125-126.

Reprinted in:

(a) *Western Literary Journal*. (Date unknown.)
(b) *The Western Boatman: A Periodical Devoted to Navigation*. Cincinnati, June, 1848, p. 129.

11. "K." Correspondence. *The Cincinnati Miscellany*, February, 1845, pp. 156-157.

12. JOHN S. ROBB (SOLITAIRE). Trimming a Darky's Heel. *St. Louis Reveille*, January 25, 1847.

Reprinted in:

Spirit of the Times, February 13, 1847, p. 605.

13. J. M. FIELD. Mike Fink, The Last of the Boatmen, in the *St. Louis Reveille*, June 14 and June 21, 1847.

14. HENRY HOWE. Historical Collections of Ohio, 1847. Reprinted frequently up to 1902. I, 321-322, contains: A Talk with a Veteran Riverman—Captain John Fink, and Mike Fink.

15. EMERSON BENNETT. Mike Fink, A Story of the Ohio. *The Great West*, Cincinnati: Holland & Jones, 1847. (Exact date unknown.)

Reprinted in:

Mike Fink. Cincinnati: 1848; Revised Edition published by U. P. James, Cincinnati, 1852.

16. ANON. Lige Shattuck's Reminiscences of Mike Fink, in *St. Louis Reveille*, February 28, 1848.

Reprinted in:

Spirit of the Times, April 15, 1848, p. 89.

17. LIEUT. J. W. ABERT. Report of, on His Examination of New Mexico, in the Years 1846-'47. Executive Document, Thirtieth Congress—First Session, No. 41. Washington, 1848, p. 503.

18. "SCROGGINS." Deacon Smith's Bull, or Mike Fink in a Tight Place, in *Milton* (Pa.) *Miltonian*, 1851. (Date unknown.)

Reprinted in:

(a) *Spirit of the Times*, March 22, 1851, p. 52.
(b) *Mississippi Palladium* (Holly Springs, Miss.), June 6, 1851, p. 4.
(c) T. C. HALIBURTON (Editor). Traits of American Humor, by Native Authors. London: Coburn and Co., 1852, III, 79-87.

19. *Crockett Almanac, 1851*. Philadelphia, New York & Boston: Fisher & Brother (n.d.). Contains: Mike Fink Trying to Scare Mrs. Crockett; and an article on Hands of Celebrated Gougers, including Mike Wink.

20. *Crockett Almanac, 1852*. Philadelphia, New York, Boston & Baltimore: Fisher & Brother (n.d.). Contains: Mike Fink's Treat to the Indians; Mike Hunting a Moose; Bravery of Mike Fink's Wife.

21. BEN CASSEDY. History of Louisville. Louisville, 1852, pp. 75-79.

Reprinted in:

An Old Tale for the New Year, or Mike Fink . . . New York: J. A. Anderson, 1928.

22. *Crockett Almanac, 1853*. Philadelphia, New York, Boston & Baltimore: Fisher & Brother (n.d.). Contains: The Celebrated Mike Fink Attacked by a Wolf While Fishing in the Mississippi; Sal Fink's Victory Over an Old Bear and Cubs; Mike Fink Killing a Wolf with His Fists.

23. *Crockett Almanac, 1854*. New York: Philip J. Cozans (n.d.). Contains: Mike Fink's First View of a Steamboat; Sal Fink, the Mississippi Screamer; How to

Escape a Bear; Mike Fink's Idea of a Gymnastic School.

24. JAMES B. FINLEY. Autobiography of Rev. James B. Finley; or Pioneer Life in the West. Edited by W. P. Strickland. Cincinnati: Printed for the Methodist Book Concern, 1854, pp. 309, 327-329.

Reprinted in:

A. DE PUY VAN BUREN. Jottings of a Year's Sojourn in the South. Battle Creek, Michigan, 1859, pp. 312-314.

25. T. B. THORPE. Remembrances of the Mississippi, *Harper's Magazine*, December, 1855.

Reprinted in:

(a) W. H. MILBURN. Ten Years of Preacher Life. New York, 1859, pp. 216-222.
(b) JOHN C. VAN TRAMP. Prairie and Rocky Mountain Adventures, or Life in the New West. Columbus, Ohio, 1866, p. 95.

26. JAMES T. LLOYD. Lloyd's Steamboat Directory. Cincinnati: James T. Lloyd & Co., 1856, pp. 35-38.

27. W. P. STRICKLAND (Editor). Peter Cartwright; The Backwoods Preacher: An Autobiography of Peter Cartwright. London, 1858, p. 180.

28. RICHARD EDWARDS AND M. HOPEWELL. Edward's Great West and Her Commercial Metropolis, Embracing a General View of the West, and a Complete History of St. Louis. St. Louis: *Edward's Monthly*, 1860, p. 591.

29. MENRA HOPEWELL. Legends of the Missouri and Mississippi. London: Ward, Lock & Tyler [1874?], pp. 372-378.

30. JAMES KEYES. Pioneers of Scioto County. Being a Short Biographical Sketch of Some of the First Settlers of Scioto County, Ohio. Portsmouth, Ohio, 1880, pp. 3-4.

Reprinted in:

HENRY T. BANNON. Stories Old and Often Told, Being Chronicles of Scioto County, Ohio. Baltimore: Waverly Press, 1927, pp. 116-118.

31. FRANK TRIPPLETT. Conquering the Wilderness. Chicago and New York: The Werner Co., 1895.

32. WILLIAM EPLER. Some Personal Recollections of Peter Cartwright. *Illinois State Historical Society Journal*, XIII, 1920, 379.

PART II

Secondary Sources: Rewritten Material and References
In Chronological Order

1. James Hall. Statistics of the West, at the Close of the Year 1836. Cincinnati: J. A. James & Co., 1837, p. 220.
2. J. W. Monette. History of the Valley of the Mississippi. New York, 1846, Vol. II, Ch. I, Sec. 2.
3. Henry Howe. The Great West. New York & Cincinnati, 1847, II, 245-255.
4. "De Grachia." The Old Bear of Tironga Bayou, Arkansas. *Spirit of the Times*, 1847. Vol. XVI, February 13, 1847. Mentions Mike Fink as a great hunter.
5. James Hall. The West: Its Commerce and Navigation. Cincinnati, 1848, p. 112.
6. Charles McKnight. Our Western Border One Hundred Years Ago. Philadelphia: J. C. McCurdy & Co., 1875.
7. J. Thomas Sharf. History of St. Louis and County. Philadelphia: H. Evarts & Co., 1883, p. 1093.
8. W. H. Perrin, J. H. Battle and C. Kniffin. Kentucky, a History of the State. Louisville and Chicago: F. A. Battery & Co., 8th edition, 1888, pp. 234-235.
9. Emerson W. Gould. Fifty Years on the Mississippi: or Gould's History of River Navigation. St. Louis: Nixon-Jones Printing Co., 1889, pp. 4156-59-65.
10. Firman A. Rozier. Rozier's History of the Early Settlements of the Mississippi Valley. St. Louis: Pierrot & Son, 1890, p. 64.
11. William Henry Perrin. Western River Navigation a Century Ago, *Magazine of Western History*, August, 1890, XII, 340-345.
12. W. H. Venable. Beginnings of Literary Culture in the Ohio Valley. Cincinnati, 1891, p. 228.
13. John R. Musick. Stories of Missouri. New York: American Book Co., 1897, pp. 86-88.

14. ARCHER B. HULBERT. Waterways of Westward Expansion; The Ohio River and Its Tributaries, 1903.
15. ARCHER B. HULBERT. The Ohio River, New York, 1906, pp. 211-216.
16. ARCHER B. HULBERT. The Paths of Inland Commerce. New Haven: Yale University Press, 1921, pp. 63-64.
17. WALTER B. STEVENS. Missouri, The Center State, 1821-1915. Chicago: J. J. Clarke Publishing Co., 1915, pp. 707-8, 712-3.
18. T. J. DE LA HUNT. A Holiday Gift Book from out of the West in 1829. *Evansville* (Ind.) *Courier*, December 1, 1918.
19. JOHN G. NEIHARDT. The Three Friends. New York: Macmillan, 1919.
20. JOHN G. NEIHARDT. The Splendid Wayfaring. New York: Macmillan, 1920.
21. EMERSON HOUGH. The Covered Wagon. New York, 1922, p. 281.
22. OTTO A. ROTHERT. Outlaws of Cave-in-Rock. Cleveland: Arthur H. Clark, 1924, p. 327.
23. RALPH L. RUSK. Literature of the Middle Western Frontier. New York: Columbia University Press, 1925, I, 73, 275, 306.
24. CARL SANDBURG. Abraham Lincoln: The Prairie Years. New York, 1926, I, 78-79.
25. DOROTHY A. DONDORE. The Prairie and the Making of Middle America. Cedar Rapids: The Torch Press, 1926, pp. 234, 401, 447.
26. HERBERT AND EDWARD QUICK. Mississippi Steambotin', A History of Steamboating on the Mississippi and Its Tributaries. New York: Henry Holt & Co., 1926.
27. LUCY L. HAZARD. The Frontier in American Literature. Philadelphia: Crowell, 1927, pp. 127-133.
28. LYLE SAXON. Father Mississippi. New York: Century Co. (1927), pp. 137-138.
29. LEWIS R. FREEMAN. Waterways of Westward Wandering. New York: Dodd, Mead & Co., pp. 118-121, and 168-173.
30. *Popular Biography.* Vol. I, No. I, November, 1929.
31. EDWIN L. SABIN. Wild Men of the Wild West. New York: Thomas Y. Crowell Co., 1929, pp. 59-67.

32. ROBERT M. COATES. The Outlaw Years. New York: Macaulay, 1930, pp. 111-113.
33. ROBERT E. RIEGEL. America Moves West. New York: Henry Holt & Co., 1930, p. 165.
34. FREDERICK R. BECHDOLT. Giants of the Old West. New York: Century, 1930, pp. 32-34.
35. ETHEL C. LEAHY. Who's Who on the Ohio River and Tributaries. Cincinnati: E. C. Leahy Pub. Co., 1931, pp. 66-74.
36. CHARLES HENRY AMBLER. A History of Transportation in the Ohio Valley. Glendale, Cal.: Arthur H. Clark Co., 1931, pp. 53-58.
37. HELEN HARDIE GRANT. Peter Cartwright: Pioneer. New York: The Abingdon Press, 1931, pp. 115-116, 149-150.
38. HARRIS DICKSON. When New Orleans Was Young. *Collier's* for April 4, 1931, p. 25.
39. CONSTANCE ROURKE. American Humor: A Study of the National Character. New York: Harcourt, Brace & Co., n.d. [1931], pp. 53-55, 65, 152, 310.
40. BERNARD DEVOTO. Mark Twain's America. Boston: Little, Brown, and Company, 1932, pp. 60, 92, 241.

PART III

Background; Literature Relating to the Period

Arranged Alphabetically According to Authors

Alter, J. Cecil. James Bridger: Trapper, Frontiersman, Scout and Guide. Salt Lake City: Sheperd Book Co., 1925.

Ashe, Thomas. Travels in America Performed in 1806. London, 1808.

Audubon, John J. Delineations of American Scenery and Character. New York: G. D. Baker & Co., 1926, pp. 23-28, 56-63.

Baird, Robert. View of the Valley of the Mississippi; or The Emigrants' and Travellers' Guide to the West. Philadelphia: H. J. Tanner, 1834.

Bird, Robert Montgomery. Nick of the Woods, or The Jibbenainosay. Philadelphia, 1837.

Brackenridge, H. M. Journal of a Voyage up the River Missouri; Performed in Eighteen Hundred and Eleven. Baltimore, 1816, pp. 11-15.

Bradley. Description of the Keelboats and Mackinaw Boats Used in Early Days on the Upper Missouri. *Montana Historical Society*, 1923, IX, 140-141.

Branch, E. D. Westward. New York: Appleton, 1931.

Carson, W. Wallace. Early River Transportation. *The Mississippi Valley Historical Review*, June, 1920, VII, 26-38.

Chicago Literary Budget. Vol. II, No. 49, December 9, 1854. Biographical sketch of Emerson Bennett, pp. 385-6; also reveals first appearance of the novel, "Mike Fink."

Chittenden, H. M. History of Early Steamboat Navigation on the Missouri River. New York: Francis P. Harper, 1903.

Churchill, Winston. The Crossing.

Clemens, Samuel L. Life on the Mississippi. Boston: Osgood, 1883.

Craig, Neville B. History of Pittsburgh.

281

CROCKETT, DAVID. The Autobiography of David Crockett. Edited by Hamlin Garland. New York: Charles Scribner's Sons, 1923.

CUMING, FORTESQUE. Sketches of a Tour to the Western Country. Pittsburgh, 1810.

DAHLINGER, C. W. Pittsburgh, a Sketch of Its Early Social Life. New York: Putnam, 1916.

DALE, H. C. The Ashley-Smith Explorations. The Discovery of a Central Route to the Pacific, 1822-1829. Cleveland: Arthur H. Clark Co., 1918.

DICKSON, HARRIS. River Boom. *Collier's* for May 9, 1931, pp. 75-77.

DILLON, J. G. The Kentucky Rifle. National Rifle Association.

DUNBAR, SEYMOUR. A History of Travel in America. Indianapolis: Bobbs-Merrill, 1915, I, 288-92.

EVANS, ESTWICK. A Pedestrian's Tour of Four Thousand Miles. Concord, N. H., 1819.

FLINT, JAMES. Letters from America. Edinburgh, 1822, p. 86.

FLINT, TIMOTHY. Recollections of the Last Ten Years. Boston, 1826.

FLINT, TIMOTHY. The First White Man of the West. Cincinnati, 1856.

GABRIEL, RALPH HENRY. The Lure of the Frontier. New Haven: Yale University Press, 1929, p. 160.

GRISWOLD, RUFUS W. The Prose Writers of America. Philadelphia, 1846. On Morgan Neville.

GRUNBIE, SYDNEY. Frontiers and the Fur Trade. New York: John Day Co., 1929.

HALL, JAMES. Letters of the West. London, 1828, pp. 90-94.

HAZARD, LUCY. The American Picaresque, in The Trans-Mississippi West. Boulder: University of Colorado, 1930, pp. 195-217.

HULBERT, ARCHER B. The Ohio River, A Course of Empire. New York: Putnam, 1906.

LONGSTREET, AUGUSTUS B. Georgia Scenes, Augusta, 1835; New York: Harper, 1840.

M'CLUNG, JOHN. Sketches of Western Adventure. Louisville, 1879.

OGG, FREDERICK AUSTIN. The Old Northwest. New Haven: Yale University Press, 1919, p. 114.

RICHARDSON, ALBERT D. Beyond the Mississippi. Hartford: American Pub. Co., 1867.

ROTHERT, OTTO A. The Outlaws of Cave-in-Rock. Cleveland: Arthur H. Clark Co., 1924.

SCHARF, THOMAS. History of St. Louis and County. Philadelphia: H. Everts & Co., 1883.

SPENCER, THOMAS EDWIN. The Story of Old St. Louis. St. Louis Pageant Assn., 1914.

STRICKLAND, W. P. The Pioneers of the West. New York, 1856, p. 197.

TURNER, FREDERICK JACKSON. The Frontier in American History. New York, 1924.

VESTAL, STANLEY. Kit Carson, the Happy Warrior of the Old West. Boston: Houghton Mifflin, 1928.

WINSOR, JUSTIN. The Westward Movement. Boston: Houghton Mifflin, 1899.